Praise for
A Year of Biblical Womanhood

"Funny and fearless, Rachel Held Evans is twice the woman I'll ever be."

— Daniel Radosh, writer
for *The Daily Show with
Jon Stewart* and author of
Rapture Ready!

"A bittersweet cocktail of wisdom and absurdity that will charm you, entertain you, seduce you and, finally, instruct you! *A Year of Biblical Womanhood* is funny, droll, charming, and deadly serious, all in one set of covers."

— Phyllis Tickle, author and
lecturer

"Because I first heard Rachel's voice in reaction to public tomfoolery about women's roles in the church and society, I half-expected *A Year of Biblical Womanhood* to be sort of . . . reactionary. After all, how could a liberated woman covering her head and bowing in reverence to her liberated husband be anything else? Yet with her signature wit, Rachel Held Evans' *A Year of Biblical Womanhood* offers a disarming treatment—aka 'fair and balanced'!—of biblical womanhood. Specifically, readers will be equipped to read the texts more faithfully and to discern what faithfulness looks like for women and men today. Modestly cloaked in starched apron garb, Rachel Held Evans serves a feast to thoughtful men and women who are hungry for insight."

— Margot Starbuck, author
and speaker

"*A Year of Biblical Womanhood* will instruct as it delights, and delight as it instructs. Of course it's about womanhood, an incredibly important subject for 100% of the population. But it's about a lot more too—how we read and interpret the Bible, for starters, and how we—both men and women—grapple with issues like justice, charity, silence, and grace in today's frenetic world. On top of that, Rachel is such a gifted writer . . . you'll be warmed by her good sense, good humor, and keen eye for beauty and insight on every page."

— Brian D. McLaren,
author, speaker, activist,
brianmclaren.net

"A triumph! Rachel Held Evans has written a comprehensive, impeccably researched, heartfelt, whimsical, scripture honoring book about the role and experience of women in Christian society. This magnificent achievement should be required reading in every church, home, student ministry, college, and seminary in the world. *Eshet Chayil!*"

— Ian Morgan Cron, author,
*Jesus, My Father, the CIA,
and Me: A Memoir of
Sorts* and *Chasing Francis:
A Pilgrim's Tale*

"Rachel Held Evans is my kind of woman, Christian, and writer. She cares too much about the Bible to read what it says without wrestling with what it *means*. Rachel's new book is full of humor, humility, and truth."

— Glennon Doyle Melton,
author of Momastery.com
and *Carry On, Warrior*

"*A Year of Biblical Womanhood* will challenge, amuse, inspire and entertain you. I applaud Rachel's sharp sense of humor as she attempted the near impossible. I also appreciate her gut-honesty, willingness to try crazy things, and ability to admit when she didn't have all the answers. A compelling story told brilliantly."

> — Mary DeMuth, author
> of *Everything: What You
> Gain and What You Give
> to Become like Jesus*

"With curiosity, honesty, and humor, Rachel Held Evans takes readers along on her year-long adventure in Biblical womanhood that manages to be both hilarious and thought-provoking."

> — Gretchen Rubin, author
> of *The Happiness Project*

"An unexpected, laugh-out-loud then turn the page and tear up, enjoyable and poignant read. By following Evan's journey, you'll see yourself and the women of the Bible in deeper and nuanced ways."

> — Shayne Moore, author
> and activist

"Rachel's disarming and inviting sense of storytelling coupled with her sharp wit makes for delightful retellings of biblical stories. This peek into her courageous venture into a year of "biblical womanhood" ought to be required reading for all thoughtful evangelicals—male or female—whose response to Scripture is usually an unqualified nod of approval."

> — Jennifer Bird, associate
> professor of religion,
> Greensboro College

"When Christians allude to "biblical womanhood," they seem to mean someone safely feminine and clad in floral prints. In her project, Rachel Held Evans uncovers something far more mysterious, a picture by turns glorious and disturbing. Blending laugh-out-loud moments with serious cultural critique, Evans discovers that living the actual teachings of the Bible means surrendering idealized role-playing in favor of becoming an *eshet chayil*—a woman of strength and wisdom."

— Jana Riess, author of
*Flunking Sainthood:
A Year of Breaking the
Sabbath, Forgetting to
Pray, and Still Loving My
Neighbor*

"Rachel Held Evans is smart and funny and gutsy, willing to tackle the most sacred cows, willing to ask the trickiest questions. For all of us who have found the term "biblical womanhood" somewhere between confusing and crazy-making, her voice is one of intelligence and courage."

— Shauna Niequist, author
of *Cold Tangerines*
and *Bittersweet*,
www.shaunaniequist.com

"*A Year of Biblical Womanhood* is thoughtful, witty, and eye-opening, one of the most important books I've read in a long time. In detailing her "Old Testament" adventure, the always earnest Rachel Held Evans flexes her writing muscle by painting vivid scenes, inspiring prose, and offering well-played opinions doused with persuasive theology. *A Year of Biblical Womanhood* is a brave book, proving Evans' knack for packing a powerful punch while still managing to remain devout, humble, full of grace."

— Matthew Paul Turner,
author of *Churched*

A YEAR OF
BIBLICAL
WOMANHOOD

A YEAR OF BIBLICAL WOMANHOOD

How a Liberated Woman Found Herself
Sitting on Her Roof, Covering Her Head, and
Calling Her Husband "Master"

RACHEL HELD EVANS

COVER PHOTO BY MAKI GARCIA EVANS
MAKIMAKEUP.COM

THOMAS NELSON
Since 1798

NASHVILLE   DALLAS   MEXICO CITY   RIO DE JANEIRO

Published in Nashville, Tennessee, by Thomas Nelson. Thomas Nelson is a registered trademark of Thomas Nelson, Inc.

Thomas Nelson, Inc., titles may be purchased in bulk for educational, business, fund-raising, or sales promotional use. For information, please e-mail SpecialMarkets@ThomasNelson.com.

Published in association with the literary agency of WordServe Literary Group, Ltd., 10152 S. Knoll Circle, Highlands Ranch, Colorado 80130.

Library of Congress Cataloging-in-Publication Data

Evans, Rachel Held, 1981–
    A year of Biblical womanhood : how a liberated woman found herself sitting on her roof, covering her head, and calling her husband "master"? / Rachel Held Evans.
        p. cm.
    Includes bibliographical references and index.
    ISBN 978-1-59555-367-6
    1. Women—Religious aspects—Christianity. 2. Women—Biblical teaching. 3. Christian women—Religious life. 4. Sex role—Religious aspects—Christianity. 5. Sex role—Biblical teaching. 6. Evans, Rachel Held, 1981– I. Title.
    BT704.E925 2012
    277.3'083092—dc23
    [B]   2012014499

Printed in the United States of America

17 RRD 10 9 8

To Dan, for making every year an adventure, and to all the women of valor whose stories have yet to be told.

Contents

Consider the lilies—is the only commandment I ever obeyed.

—EMILY DICKINSON

Introduction

*Does not the very nature of things teach you that
if a man has long hair, it is a disgrace to him, but
that if a woman has long hair, it is her glory?*

1 CORINTHIANS 11:14–15

I STARED BACK AT MYSELF IN THE SALON MIRROR, WONDER-
ing whatever happened to the woman who sat in this same hydraulic
chair just a year ago.

After 368 days without a haircut, I looked like a character from
Willow, or more precisely, a character from *Willow* in the process of
getting eaten by a character from *Spinal Tap.*

Before   **After**

I'd also gained thirteen pounds, developed a mild addiction to unleavened bread, turned thirty, and settled far too comfortably into a dress code of oversized T-shirts and peasant skirts.

A pretty, blond stylist stood over me, running her fingers through my monster hair, her nails catching in its mousy-brown tangles. "And what can I do for you today?" she asked with a sweet, East Tennessee twang that I could only assume masked her abject horror at the scene.

"Well, it's been a year since my last haircut," I said. "And as you can see, my hair's a little too thick to grow out without some . . . consequences. So, I guess I just want you to, you know, fix it. Maybe take five or six inches off?"

"Now, why in the world would you go a year without cutting your hair?" the stylist asked with a playful laugh, totally unfazed.

"Why?"

It was the question people asked each time I pulled a scarf over my head to pray or addressed my husband as "master," the question they asked after I spent an afternoon perched on my rooftop, adopted a computer-baby, camped out in my front yard during my period, and left eight pounds of dough to rise in my bathroom. It was the question they asked when they wondered what brought me to an Amish schoolhouse in Gap, Pennsylvania; a pig farm in Cochabamba, Bolivia; and a Benedictine monastery in Cullman, Alabama; or what inspired a thoroughly liberated and domestically challenged woman like me to suddenly take up baking and knitting and needlework.

I wasn't sure how to explain to my unsuspecting hairstylist that the reason I hadn't cut my hair in a year was because two thousand years ago, a Jewish tentmaker wrote a letter to his friends in the city of Corinth in which he mentioned that "if a woman has long hair, it is her glory" (1 Corinthians 11:15).

But because small-town hair salons represent the last remaining vestiges of a storytelling culture, and because you can't exactly make a run for it once someone's wrapped you in a plastic cape and clamped a dozen butterfly clips in your hair, I figured I might as well start from the beginning.

So, over the roar of hair dryers and the prattle of gossip, as little clumps of my "glory" fell to the floor, I told her about my year of biblical womanhood . . .

My husband, Dan, and I had a long-standing agreement that we would start a family as soon as we became independently wealthy or I turned thirty, whichever happened first. This arrangement suited me just fine until my twenty-ninth birthday, which happened on June 8, 2010, four months before this experiment of mine began.

It was a few days after my birthday that I sat on a living room floor crowded with toddlers, wrapping paper, inflated balloons, and deflated moms, wondering to myself if this was it—my last year of freedom. A teary young mom had just recounted in excruciating detail the suspicious contents of her two-year-old's diaper, when, as always seems to happen after a group of moms exchanges horror stories about parenting, someone asked in that familiar, cajoling voice, "So when can we expect a baby from you, Rachel?"

I've come to welcome this question as a compliment, an invitation of sorts. But pushing thirty left me with fewer acceptable responses, and the truth—that I'm absolutely, inexplicably terrified of motherhood—was too embarrassing to speak aloud. It crossed my mind that I could get away with a lie. You know: shrug my shoulders, conjure up some tears, and say something about God's perfect timing to imply that we were trying, because, really, who's going to conduct a thorough investigation into that? But instead I found myself saying, "I think I'd like to write another book first," which came across a lot more smugly than I intended.

Dan certainly wasn't pushing parenthood. He's the kind of guy who values efficiency above all else, and after seven years of marriage, our two-person family unit moved through the world like a

SWAT team. We communicated mostly in code and with hand motions, tackling everything from chores to road trips to our two home businesses as a highly organized team. Tasks were silently assigned to whoever could finish them first, so we wasted little time talking about division of labor or "roles." When it was time for dinner, someone made it. When the money dried up, someone took on another client. When the sponge next to the kitchen sink started to smell like death, Dan threw it out.

We'd seen what a few diaper bags and car seats could do to this situation, so whenever I brought up the issue of children, Dan shrugged his shoulders and said, "We're in no hurry." I'd quickly agree and then change the subject, pretending that the rhythmic gonging reverberating throughout my entire body was something other than my biological clock going ballistic on me.

But it wasn't just my friends pushing procreation; it was my church.

I was raised evangelical, which means I spent a good part of my life feeling sorry for the rest of humanity on account of its certain destiny in hell. This was not something my parents taught me directly, just something I picked up from preachers, Sunday school teachers, and Christian playmates along the way. After hearing time and again that "wide is the path that leads to destruction," I just assumed that Buddhists went to hell for worshipping Buddha, Catholics went to hell for worshipping Mary, and Al Gore went to hell for worshipping nature. I didn't even think to have a faith crisis about it until college.

The first time I saw Joyce Meyer preaching on TV, I figured she was going to hell too. I was about nine years old at the time, and I remember she wore a fuchsia suit, a short haircut, and massive gold earrings. Pacing back and forth on the stage, with a microphone in one hand and a Bible in the other, Joyce spoke with a conviction and urgency I'd never witnessed before. Her confidence frightened me. I wondered how she could be so brazen in the midst of her sin, how she could go on speaking about "the favor of our Lord," when everyone knows ladies aren't supposed to preach from the Word of God. According to my Sunday school teacher, that was a job the Bible reserved for men.

By that time, I'd received a lot of mixed messages about the appropriate roles of women in the home, the church, and society, each punctuated with the claim that it was God's perfect will that all women everywhere do this or that. In my world, women like Joyce Meyer were considered heretics for preaching from the pulpit in violation of the apostle Paul's restriction in 1 Timothy 2:12 ("I do not permit a woman to teach or to have authority over a man; she must be silent"), while conservative Mennonites were considered legalistic for covering their heads in compliance with his instructions in 1 Corinthians 11:5 ("Every woman who prays or prophesies with her head uncovered dishonors her head"). Pastors told wives to submit to their husbands as the apostle Peter instructed in 1 Peter 3:1, but rarely told them to refer to their husbands as "master" as he instructed just three sentences later in 1 Peter 3:6. By the time I was twelve, I learned I could single-handedly ruin a boy's relationship with God by the length of my skirt or the cut of my blouse (Matthew 5:27–28), but that good looks and pretty clothes weren't all bad, because that's how Queen Esther saved the Jews.

According to James Dobson, women weren't inferior to men, just created for different roles. Our ultimate calling, he said, is in the home, where we can serve God and our husbands by keeping things clean, having supper on the table at six, and, most important, making babies.

In my own home, little was said about gender roles or hierarchy. Submission was something my mom did once in 1976, not something she did every day. (More about that later.) A freethinker in a stridently traditional religious culture, Mom often came home from church overwhelmed with yet another casserole to make, nursery to keep, or wedding shower to plan. "The only people who enjoy potlucks are men," she used to say. "The women do all the work."

Despite her aversion to covered dishes, Mom never complained about her roles as a wife and mother, though she took a hiatus from her career as a schoolteacher to stay home with us when we were little. Smart, compassionate, and funny, she protected my sister and me from the pockets of legalism that surrounded us and told us we could be anything we wanted to be when we grew up, no matter what anyone said. She and my father both loved the Bible, but they seemed to know instinctively that rules that left people guilt-ridden, exhausted, and confused were not really from God. I think this is one of the reasons why, despite the fact that I vote for Democrats, believe in evolution, and am no longer convinced that everyone different from me goes to hell, I don't mind being identified as an evangelical Christian. Evangelicalism is like my religious mother tongue. I revert to it whenever I'm angry or excited or surrounded by other people who understand what I'm saying. And it's the language in which I most often hear God's voice on the rare occasion that it rises above the noise.

My first encounter with "biblical womanhood" happened in college, when there were whispers around the dormitory about whether God wanted young ladies at a Christian university to run for student body president. Apparently, there were rules about such things, rules that the apostle Paul wrote down in a letter to Timothy approximately two millennia ago. Rumor had it that biblical womanhood required stepping aside to allow godly men to take the lead. This sparked a few late-night dorm room debates, as some of my classmates argued that those instructions applied only in a church setting while others noted that there weren't a lot of godly men beating down the doors to plan our banquets and pep rallies that year. If I remember correctly, the point became moot when a woman ran uncontested.

Over the next few years, I found myself drawn into more and more of these conversations, especially as my girlfriends and I began getting married and starting families of our own. Many were influenced by evangelical complementarianism, a movement that began as a reaction to second-wave feminism and found some of its first expressions in the writings of Edith Schaeffer (*The Hidden Art of Homemaking*, 1971) and Elisabeth Elliot (*Let Me Be a Woman*, 1976). Hailed as model wives and homemakers, these women are highly esteemed in the Reformed tradition, where the oft-repeated saying is "As many people were brought to the Lord through Mrs. Schaeffer's cinnamon buns as through Dr. Schaeffer's sermons." But behind the winsome prose lies an uncompromising conviction: the virtuous woman serves primarily from the home as a submissive wife, diligent homemaker, and loving mother.

"This is a woman's place," says Elliot, "and all of us need to know what our place is and to be put in it. The command of God puts us there where we belong."[1]

The theological bulwark of the movement can be found in the Council for Biblical Manhood and Womanhood. Led by conservative pastor John Piper and theologian Wayne Grudem, the CBMW produced two pivotal documents that extended the influence of the movement beyond the confines of the Reformed tradition: "The Danvers Statement" (published in 1988) and *Recovering Biblical Manhood and Womanhood* (published first in 1991 and again in 2006). The CBMW enjoyed a resounding victory when, influenced by the Danvers Statement, representatives from the sixteen-million-member Southern Baptist Convention voted to amend their statement of belief to include a declaration on family life, noting that a woman should "submit herself graciously" to her husband's leadership.[2]

According to the Danvers Statement, the acceptance of feminist ideology among Christians has led to a "threat to Biblical authority as the clarity of Scripture is jeopardized and the accessibility of its meaning to ordinary people is withdrawn into the restricted realm of technical ingenuity." The statement says that rather than following the prevailing culture, women of God should pursue "biblical womanhood."[3]

Now, we evangelicals have a nasty habit of throwing the word *biblical* around like it's Martin Luther's middle name. We especially like to stick it in front of other loaded words, like *economics, sexuality, politics,* and *marriage* to create the impression that God has definitive opinions about such things, opinions that just so happen to correspond with our own. Despite insistent claims that we don't "pick and choose" what parts of the Bible we take seriously, using the word *biblical* prescriptively like this almost always involves selectivity.

After all, technically speaking, it is *biblical* for a woman to be sold by her father (Exodus 21:7), *biblical* for her to be forced to marry her rapist (Deuteronomy 22:28–29), *biblical* for her to remain silent in church (1 Corinthians 14:34–35), *biblical* for her to cover her head (1 Corinthians 11:6), and *biblical* for her to be one of multiple wives (Exodus 21:10).

This is why the notion of "biblical womanhood" so intrigued me. Could an ancient collection of sacred texts, spanning multiple genres and assembled over thousands of years in cultures very different from our own, really offer a single cohesive formula for how to be a woman? And do all the women of Scripture fit into this same mold? Must I?

I'm the sort of person who likes to identify the things that most terrify and intrigue me in this world and plunge headlong into them like Alice down the rabbit hole. This is the reason I have trouble making small talk and sitting still, and it's the reason I woke up one morning with a crazy idea lighting up every corner of my brain.

What if I tried it all? What if I took "biblical womanhood" literally?

As it turns out, there are publishers out there who will actually pay for you to jump down rabbit holes, so long as they believe said rabbit holes are marketable to the general public. So on October 1, 2010, with the support of Dan and a brave team of publishing professionals, I vowed to spend one year of my life in pursuit of *true* biblical womanhood.

This quest of mine required that I study every passage of Scripture that relates to women and learn how women around the world interpret and apply these passages to their lives. In addition, I would attempt to follow as many of the Bible's teachings regarding women as possible in my day-to-day life, sometimes taking them to their literal extreme.

From the Old Testament to the New Testament, from Genesis to Revelation, from the Levitical code to the letters of Paul, there would be no picking and choosing. A year of biblical womanhood would mean, among other things, rising before dawn (Proverbs 31:15), submitting to my husband (Colossians 3:18), growing out my hair (1 Corinthians 11:15), making my own clothes (Proverbs 31:21–22), learning how to cook (Proverbs 31:15), covering my head in prayer (1 Corinthians 11:5), calling Dan "master" (1 Peter 3:5–6), caring for the poor (Proverbs 31:20), nurturing a gentle and quiet spirit (1 Peter 3:4), and remaining ceremonially impure for the duration of my period (Leviticus 15:19–33).

Some practices I would observe just once. Others I would try to observe all year. Each month I would focus on a different virtue—gentleness, domesticity, obedience, valor, beauty, modesty, purity, fertility, submission, justice, silence, and grace.

Throughout the year, my "Biblical Woman's Ten Commandments" would serve as a guide for daily living:

1. Thou shalt submit to thy husband's will in all things. (Genesis 3:16; Titus 2:5; 1 Peter 3:1; Ephesians 5:22; 1 Corinthians 11:3; Colossians 3:18)
2. Thou shalt devote thyself to the duties of the home. (Proverbs 14:1; 31:10–31; 1 Timothy 5:14; Titus 2:4–5)
3. Thou shalt mother. (Genesis 1:28; Psalm 128:3; 1 Timothy 5:14)
4. Thou shalt nurture a gentle and quiet spirit. (1 Peter 3:3–4; Titus 2:3–5; 1 Timothy 3:11)
5. Thou shalt dress modestly. (Genesis 24:65; Deuteronomy 22:5; 1 Timothy 2:8–10; 1 Peter 3:3)

6. Thou shalt cover thy head when in prayer. (1 Corinthians 11:3–16)
7. Thou shalt not cut thy hair. (1 Corinthians 11:15)
8. Thou shalt not teach in church. (1 Corinthians 14:33–35; 1 Timothy 2:12)
9. Thou shalt not gossip. (Numbers 12:1–10; Proverbs 26:20; 1 Timothy 5:13–14)
10. Thou shalt not have authority over a man. (1 Timothy 2:12)

I took my research way too seriously, combing through feminist, conservative, and liberal commentaries, and seeking out Jewish, Catholic, and Protestant perspectives on each issue. I spoke with modern-day women practicing ancient biblical mandates in their own lives—a polygamist, a pastor, a Quiverfull daughter, an Orthodox Jew, an Amish grandmother. I scoured the Bible, cover to cover, isolating and examining every verse I could find about mothers, daughters, widows, wives, concubines, queens, prophetesses, and prostitutes.

Within a couple of weeks of starting the experiment, I was annoying my friends with random facts about biblical womanhood.

Take Proverbs 31, for example. As it turns out, we have a woman to thank for the ancient acrostic poem that outlines in excruciating detail the daily activities of an excellent wife, perpetuating a three-thousand-year-old inferiority complex among just about every woman in the Judeo-Christian tradition. The poem is recorded in the Bible by King Lemuel as "an oracle his mother taught him" (v. 1), a fact that totally upset my plan to cast the Proverbs 31 woman as an unrealistic archetype of the misogynistic imagination.

The Proverbs 31 woman rises before the sun each day, plans every meal, strengthens her arms, goes to the market, brings home exotic foods, runs a profitable business, dresses her husband and children, invests in real estate, cares for the poor, compliments her husband, spends hours at the loom, and burns the midnight oil, before starting it all over again the next day.

This, according to the oracle, is what a man should look for in a wife, which of course leads me to believe that King Lemuel's mom was the kind who didn't actually want a daughter-in-law. (Add a shrug of the shoulders and the accent of a Jewish grandmother to "A wife of noble character who can find?" and you get what I mean.)

However, as the leaves began to turn and day 1 of the year of biblical womanhood loomed before me, I found myself inexplicably drawn to Proverbs 31:25: "She is clothed with strength and dignity; she can laugh at the days to come."

I was pretty sure I couldn't find "strength" or "dignity" in the women's section at Kohl's, but when I considered the sheer absurdity of someone like me doing something like this, the best I could do was laugh at the days to come. And there was something strangely liberating about that.

EVE, THE FALLEN

For the first fifty-three verses of the Bible, God does all the talking. "Let there be light," God says. "Let the land produce living creatures," God says. "Be fruitful and multiply (NASB)," God says.

It isn't until the final verses of Genesis 2 that we encounter the first human words of the biblical narrative:

> *"This is now bone of my bones*
> *and flesh of my flesh;*
> *she shall be called 'woman,'*
> *for she was taken out of man."*
>
> (v. 23)

The story of man begins with a love poem about a woman.

The poem appears in the second creation account of Genesis, in which God forms man from the dust of the earth, fills him with the breath of life, and places him in the garden of Eden with the task of naming the animals. Adam's assignment reveals the congruous nature of the animal kingdom, and for the first time, the Creator observes a part of creation that is not good.

"It is not good for the man to be alone," God says. "I will make a helper suitable for him" (Genesis 2:18).

The Hebrew term *ezer*, or "helper," is employed elsewhere in Scripture to describe God as an intervener—the helper of the fatherless (Psalm 10:14), King David's helper and deliverer (Psalm 70:5), Israel's shield and help (Deuteronomy 33:29). In Genesis 2, it is modified by the word *kenegdo* to mean "a helper like himself," or a corresponding character. So, like most good stories, this one begins with both a hero and a heroine.

It is unclear how long our heroic pair revels in this state of divine symmetry, naked and unashamed, before everything falls apart. But at some point a villain appears, promising a better life should they defy the Creator's single stipulation and eat from the mysterious tree of the knowledge of good and evil. The fruit, described as "pleasing to the eye, and also desirable for gaining wisdom" (Genesis 3:6), proves too tempting for our heroine. She takes a bite and then gives some to her husband, who also eats. Immediately their eyes are opened, and the first pangs of shame enter human consciousness.

The man blames the woman, the woman blames the serpent, but God holds all three accountable for the act. As punishment, the serpent must slink through life on its belly in the dirt, and man must toil against stubborn, inhospitable land until his death. To woman belongs pain in childbirth and the grief of being dominated by men.

"Your desire will be for your husband," God tells the woman, "and he will rule over you" (v. 16).

It is within this somber context that man finally assigns woman a name. He calls her Eve, which means "life," for she is to be "the mother of all living."

For centuries, the figure of Eve has been a subject of great interest in Western art, literature, and philosophy. Upon her naked body man has projected his most visceral fears and desires concerning woman, so she is presented as both seductress and mother, noble savage and domesticator, deceiver and the deceived. The Portal of the Virgin at Notre Dame Cathedral includes a stone temptation scene in which the crafty serpent bears the breasts and face of a woman, nearly a mirror image of Eve. This motif repeats itself in medieval iconography, betraying the commonly held view that woman alone was the source of original sin, Eve a sort of biblical Pandora who cracked open the box and brought perpetual shame upon her sex.

"You are the devil's gateway," the theologian Tertullian told Christian women. "Do you not know that you are each an Eve? The sentence of God on your sex lives on in this age; the guilt, necessarily, lives on too."[4]

What we read into the Creation narrative often says as much about us as it says about the text. And for women emerging from the Judeo-Christian tradition, the vilification of Eve has been disastrous. A passage that might challenge readers to aspire to the love and mutuality of Paradise has instead been used for centuries to justify the perpetuation of the curse by forcing women into subordination, with theologians from the apostle Paul to Martin Luther noting somewhat begrudgingly that women are nonetheless necessary for procreation.

And so, at least symbolically, the blood of Eve courses through each one of her daughters' veins. We are each associated with life; each subject to the impossible expectations and cruel projections of men; each fallen, blamed, and misunderstood; and each stubbornly vital to the process of bringing something new—perhaps something better—into this world.

In a sense, Tertullian was right. We are each an Eve.

October: Gentleness

Girl Gone Mild

*Your beauty should not come from outward adornment,
such as braided hair and the wearing of gold jewelry
and fine clothes. Instead, it should be that of your
inner self, the unfading beauty of a gentle and quiet
spirit, which is of great worth in God's sight.*

—1 PETER 3:3–4

TO DO THIS MONTH:

- ☐ Cultivate a gentle and quiet spirit, even during football games (1 Peter 3:3–4)
- ☐ Kick the gossip habit (1 Timothy 5:12–13)
- ☐ Take an etiquette lesson (Proverbs 11:22)
- ☐ Practice contemplative prayer (Psalm 131)
- ☐ Make a "swearing jar" for behaviors that mimic the "contentious woman" of Proverbs (Proverbs 21:19; 19:13; 27:15 NKJV)
- ☐ Do penance on the rooftop for acts of contention (Proverbs 21:9)

My first mistake was to start the experiment in the middle of football season. First Peter 3:4 describes a godly woman as having a "gentle and quiet spirit," but if you've spent more than five minutes south of the Mason-Dixon during the month of October, you know that there's nothing gentle or quiet about the way a Southern woman watches college football.

I grew up in the great state of Alabama, which journalist Warren St. John deems "the worst place on earth to acquire a healthy perspective on the importance of spectator sports."[1] In Alabama, the third most important question after "What is your name?" and "Where do you go to church?" is "Alabama or Auburn?" So soon after I learned to identify myself as a nondenominational, Bible-believing Christian named Rachel, I learned to identify myself as an Alabama fan. My little sister and I knew what intentional grounding was before we'd acquired the dexterity to play with Barbie dolls, and as kids we liked to imitate my mother, who had the habit of willing an Alabama running back down the field by moving closer and closer to the TV set the longer he stayed on his feet. By the time he danced into the end zone, the whole family—Mom, Dad, Amanda, and I—would be huddled together around the TV, screaming our heads off, nervously looking for any yellow flags on the field.

Now exiled together in Tennessee, where Volunteer Orange looks good on no one, we gather every Saturday afternoon at my parents' house down the street to wear our colors, yell at the TV, and consume inordinate amounts of meat. It's a tradition that my husband, Dan, married into a bit unwittingly, but has come to love, primarily on account of Mom's pulled pork roast.

I think Dan may have been a little caught off guard the first time he realized that something about the autumnal equinox transformed his wife into a raving lunatic for three and a half hours each week and that eleven guys running around on a football field in Tuscaloosa, Alabama, could directly affect his sex life. But he's grown into the role, and now every autumn we both look forward to Saturday afternoons at the Held house—windows opened to the crisp, cool air, the scent of dry leaves mingling with wafts of slow roasted pork, the dull roar of crowd noise humming from the TV. And this particular October was especially significant because Alabama was defending its national title on Mom and Dad's brand-new, high-definition, 42-inch TV.

"This is going to suck," I said as we approached their front door on game day, leaves crackling under our feet.

"Yup. It's going to be awesome," Dan responded without really hearing me.

"Well, maybe for you, but screaming at the TV doesn't exactly constitute a gentle and quiet spirit," I said. "I'm going to have to bottle all my fandom up inside. No yelling at the refs. No snarky remarks about the cheerleaders. No cheering or booing. It's so stifling."

"Yeah, you're really suffering for Jesus on this one, Rach," Dan teased.

I managed to get through the first few games of the season in relative calm, with a few exceptions the day Bama lost to the South Carolina Gamecocks (and *Steve Spurrier*, of all people) in a 35-21 upset.

That particular game we happened to watch at my sister's house in Nashville and afterwards went to Rotier's downtown to sulk over burgers, sweet potato fries, and country music.

I remembered to cover my head before the blessing, in keeping with my sixth commandment ("Thou shalt cover thy head when in prayer"). It seems the upside to starting a project like this in October is that hoodies serve as nice, inconspicuous head coverings. You can observe 1 Corinthians 11 at every meal and church service and folks just think you're cold, not a religious freak. Same goes for scarves, knit hats, and head-warmers.

"But aren't you supposed to pray without ceasing?" Amanda asked, ever the Sunday school star, even at twenty-six.

"Yeah, maybe you should keep your head covered at all times," Dan piped in.

"Well, I might try doing that in March when I focus on modesty," I said, "or maybe when I visit Lancaster."

I had this thing planned out, I swear, but sometimes it seemed like nobody believed me.

"You should observe kosher," they said. "You ought to visit a convent," they said. "You need to have a baby," they said. "You gotta get yourself a rabbi," they said.

I was pretty sure that rabbis didn't operate on a work-for-hire basis, and the baby thing had been settled by Dan right away.

"We're not having a kid as part of an experiment," he said. "No way."

But the voices that seemed the loudest came from my blog, where readers responded in record numbers to my announcement about the project.

"This is going to be epic!"

"You're nuts."

"My stomach just knotted in anxiety for you."

"Way to make a mockery of God's Word."

"A. J. Jacobs already did this, you know."

"I think you're out of your mind, but then, most creative people are."

You would think that after three years of blogging, I'd have developed some kind of virtual superpower that involved freakishly thick skin, but scrolling through the comments sent my confidence lurching up and down so violently I felt seasick. The influx of praise and criticism made me doubt myself, and the next thing I knew I was under the covers at 10:30 a.m. on a Tuesday, crying about how hard it is to be a writer. (In addition to being "out of our minds," creative people can be a bit moody . . .)

I didn't have a lot of time for self-pity. The most immediate effect of my new "biblical" lifestyle came in the form of an adjusted routine that required that I make the bed before checking e-mail, cook Dan's breakfast before browsing Facebook, and finish the laundry before starting any new writing projects. This attempt to observe my second commandment ("Thou shalt devote thyself to the duties of the home") required a serious shift in priorities that proved a little disorienting for both of us.

The first morning Dan awoke to the smell of scrambled eggs, he assumed that pleased-but-cautious posture men get when they're not quite sure if they're supposed to be enjoying themselves or if the whole thing is a trap.

"Thanks, hon," he said after a second glass of orange juice. "I can do the dishes."

"No, you can't. That's my job now."

Dan looked doubtful.

"You sure?"

"Yeah. You think the Proverbs 31 woman let her husband do the dishes? Go relax. I'll clean up."

Dan leaped from his seat with the excitement of Ralphie Parker receiving his Red Ryder BB gun, and I found myself confronted with a stack of greasy plates that, compounded with those from the night before, would most certainly *not* fit in the dishwasher.

It occurred to me then that a year is a very long time.

Dan's Journal

October 15, 2010

I'm not used to reminding Rachel to make me lunch, but just now, we had a conversation that went something like this:

ME: Can you make me lunch?
RACHEL: Okay. Can you work on that picture for my blog?
ME: Wait. Are you telling me what to do?

RACHEL (SMILING): Well, you're telling me what
    to do.
ME (SMILING): Yeah, but isn't that what you signed
    up for?
We both pause.
RACHEL: Okay, I'll make you lunch, but would you
    mind if I dried my hair first? (It was up in a towel, as
    it had been for the last half hour.)
ME (IN A HALF-SERIOUS TONE): Well, I don't
    know; delayed obedience is disobedience.

Rachel got up to fix me lunch.

Wow. That conversation, or anything like it, would never have
happened before the project started. We both knew this whole
exchange was a bit tongue-in-cheek, but I still felt kinda bad. After all,
I didn't marry Rachel because I wanted someone to make me lunch.

She's told me in the past that if her hair stays up in the towel too
long, she'll end up with a bad hair day . . . I'm going to go tell her she
can dry her hair first.

When I told friends that my goal for October was to cultivate a
gentle and quiet spirit, a few of them laughed. Not in a mean way, but
in a sympathetic, knowing sort of way. This was partly because they
knew me, and partly because a lot of us church girls had the "gentle
and quiet spirit" thing rubbed in our faces at early ages. It seems the
apostle Peter's first epistle to the Christians of Asia Minor serves as a
handy deterrent for Christian girls whose pesky questions in Sunday
school or enthusiasm on the kickball field made their mamas worry.

"I'm intrigued to see if you succeed at the gentle and quiet spirit,"
one of my readers wrote in. "I've tried and failed miserably, but I
guess I'm just too loud and blunt and opinionated to fit the mold."

Another said, "It's sad that so many strong, gifted, 'feisty' women have been led to believe that they are to shelve that whole side of their personality because it is not 'gentle' or 'quiet' enough. I see women who could change their little piece of the world for the better, or perhaps an even bigger piece of the world for the better, sitting on their hands in this posture of 'gentleness.'"

A third added, "This verse has played over and over in my head as I continue to simply feel not good enough. Am I cut out for Christianity at all?"

I can relate. While Dan is patient and understated, I suspect I came out of the womb with an opinion about the delivery—and every intention of expressing it. Passionate, persuasive, and hyperbolically inclined, the Information Age has been good to me. I blog. I speak. I write books. I tweet. And every now and then, a reporter or representative from the Nielsen Company will actually *ask* my opinion about something.

In search of some direction, I looked to the book of Proverbs, a collection of wisdom sayings that gives us some of the most colorful quips, cracks, praises, and poetry about women found in Scripture. This preoccupation with the feminine should come as no surprise, considering the fact that King Solomon, the figure to whom the book is often attributed, had seven hundred wives and three hundred concubines.

Proverbs' cast of female characters includes the virtuous woman, the foolish woman, the excellent wife, the shaming wife, Lady Wisdom, and Lady Folly. Making multiple appearances is the so-called contentious woman, who seems to have the opposite of a gentle and quiet spirit[2]:

+ "It is better to live in a desert land than with a *contentious* and vexing woman." (Proverbs 21:19 NASB)
+ "A foolish son is destruction to his father, and the *contentions* of a wife are a constant dripping." (Proverbs 19:13 NASB)

+ "A constant dripping on a day of steady rain and a *conten-tious* woman are alike; he who would restrain her restrains the wind and grasps oil with his right hand." (Proverbs 27:15–16 NASB)
+ "It is better live in a corner of the roof than in a house shared with a *contentious* woman." (Proverbs 21:9 NASB)

The contentious woman gave me an idea for kicking some of my less-than-gentle habits.

I decided to make a swearing jar of sorts. Each time I caught myself in the act of contention, I'd put a penny (or nickel or dime, depending on the severity of the infraction) in the jar. Behaviors that qualified as contention included gossiping, nagging, complaining, exaggerating, and snark. The Bible includes no direct mention of snark, of course, but in a decision I would come to regret, I added this pervasive little vice of mine for good measure.

I labeled it "The Jar of Contention," and resolved that at the end of the month, each cent would represent one minute I'd have to spend doing penance on the rooftop of my house to simulate what it's like to share a house with a contentious woman, according to the book of Proverbs.

Within the first few days, The Jar of Contention held twenty-six cents and a crumpled note card upon which I'd scribbled a log of my transgressions:

10/6/10 — 1¢, *snarky comment about Dan letting Commandment #1 go to his head*

10/7/10 — 1¢, *snarky comment about the president of the Southern Baptist Convention using three forms of the word "serious" in a single sentence*

10/7/10 — 1¢, *complaining about the Jar of Contention*

10/7/10 — 1¢, *complaining about the experiment in general*

10/8/10 — 5¢, *ranting about negative comments on my blog (four of the five vices employed)*

10/8/10 — 1¢, *nagging Dan about taking out the garbage*

10/9/10 — 1¢, *snarky comment about Steve Spurrier during Alabama game*

10/9/10 — 1¢, *complaining about lack of defense during Alabama game*

10/9/10 — 1¢, *swearing during Alabama game*

10/9/10 — 1¢, *complaining about how Dan arbitrarily added swearing to the list of vices*

Apparently snark makes up a large percentage of my sense of humor, and I'm kind of a whiner. On the upside, I don't gossip a lot—a good thing, since abstaining from it was my ninth commandment.

Gossip is a surprisingly serious infraction in Scripture, and is listed along with wickedness, evil, greed, depravity, envy, God-hating, and murder as part of the apostle Paul's indictment against sinful humanity in Romans 1. Proverbs includes several warnings against gossip, and significant portions of Paul's letters to Timothy concern outbreaks of gossip among women in the early church at Ephesus. To qualify as leaders, Paul wrote, "women must likewise be dignified, not malicious gossips, but temperate, faithful in all things" (1 Timothy 3:11 NASB).

In fact, it was the sin of gossip, or *loshon hara* ("evil talk"), that took down one of the most powerful women in Israel. The prophetess

Miriam, sister to Moses and a worship leader among the people, was struck with a skin disease, something like psoriasis, after making some pointed remarks about her brother's wife, Zipporah, a Cushite (Numbers 12:1–16). As exemplified in the story, to be guilty of *loshon hara*, one need not tell a lie, for even true statements when told in spite are considered evil. Interestingly, Miriam's brother Aaron was not punished though he was complicit in the crime.

According to the Talmud, *loshon hara* kills three people: the one who speaks it, the one who hears it, and the one about whom it is told. "Kill" may strike the modern reader as a bit hyperbolic, but when you think of all the friendships lost, careers stunted, and opportunities thwarted as a result of gossip among women, violent language seems appropriate. We cause serious collateral damage to the advancement of our sex each time we perpetuate the stereotype that women can't get along.

As Tina Fey put it, "Girl-on-girl sabotage is the third worst kind of female behavior, right behind saying 'like' all the time and leaving your baby in a dumpster."[3]

I thought about this as I dropped a penny in the jar for gleefully passing along some not-so-flattering inside information about one of my female writing nemeses . . . and then another three for complaining about how hard it is to have a jar of contention. I was determined to keep my rooftop penance to under two hours, but as soon as November 1 appeared on the ten-day weather forecast, I checked to see if I'd need an umbrella.

> *As a ring of gold in a swine's snout, so is a*
> *beautiful woman who lacks discretion.*
> —PROVERBS 11:22 NASB

Of course I was late to my etiquette lesson.

By the time I pulled my sputtering little Plymouth Acclaim into

Mrs. Flora Mainord's upscale Knoxville neighborhood, it was nearly 5:00. My appointment was for 4:30, but I'd gotten stuck behind a school bus after exiting the interstate, so I had to watch a bunch of rich kids trot off to their lakeside homes and private tutors before taking a wrong turn and getting lost in a maze of water-themed street names: River Trail, River View, River Sound.

I really needed to pee.

Flora didn't seem to mind that I was late or that a veritable Liz Lemon had just stepped into her foyer for a crash course on refinement. A tall, middle-aged woman with dark hair and olive skin, she wore a black top, black slacks, and a cascade of glittering jewelry. Her home was decorated like a palace, with displays of crystal and china encased in antique cabinets and massive portraits of girls in white dresses framed in gold. On the right sat a formal dining room prepared for a five-course meal. On the left was a sitting room, from which I thought I heard Mariah Carey singing in the background. With all the fine furniture and silk pillows and bulky heirlooms, I wondered where Flora kept her husband.

"Would you like to visit the ladies' room to freshen up?" she asked with an accent more suited for Nashville than Knoxville.

I'd scoured the Internet for a local etiquette consultant, thinking that a class or two might help me file down some of my rough edges and get a little closer to achieving that gentle and quiet spirit Peter wrote about. But these days, certified etiquette consultants are about as hard to come by as personal rabbis, so I had to make the two-hour trek to Knoxville for a private class that covered formal dining, proper introductions, conversation skills, manners, thank-you notes, invitations, appearance, and business protocol. Flora came highly recommended and with an interesting story—beauty queen, weather personality, fashion consultant, entrepreneur, manners expert.

There was a fancy couch in the bathroom, which threw me off a bit, as did the series of delicate white hand towels placed on the sink. Not sure which one to use, I wiped my hands on my skirt.

Classy, Evans.

We began by browsing Flora's library of etiquette books, which included some charming first editions from Emily Post, as well as a few signed copies of Letitia Baldrige classics. I cracked a bunch of self-deprecating jokes about my scatterbrained ways because that's what my mom and I do when we're nervous, but Flora's plump cheeks remained frozen in a polite smile as she paused to let me finish and then returned to reading her favorite lines aloud: "Ideal conversation must be an exchange of thought, and not, as many of those who worry most about their shortcomings believe, an eloquent exhibition of wit or oratory." "The attributes of a great lady may still be found in the rule of the four S's: sincerity, simplicity, sympathy, and serenity."

We then moved into the dining room, where Flora had artfully arranged two table settings, one with my name on the place card and one with hers. I faced a total of five forks, four knives, three plates, two spoons, and an army of stemware, including a water goblet, champagne flute, white wine glass, red wine glass, and sherry glass. I had no idea rich people drank so much booze.

Flora serenely guided me through each item on the table, reminding me to be aware of my posture and bring my food to my face, not the other way around.

"Now, are you familiar with Continental-style dining?" she asked after bringing out an appetizer of crab cakes.

"I'm guessing you mean something other than the free breakfast we get at the Hampton Inn."

This time I was rewarded with an airy peal of laughter, and soon we settled into a natural, friendly dinner, which Flora had prepared herself.

What I loved about Flora's teaching style was how she wove into the conversation little anecdotes and tidbits from history. For example, once, at a state dinner, a guest of Eleanor Roosevelt mistook the finger bowl for a beverage, picked it up with his hands, and began to drink. Without blinking, Mrs. Roosevelt picked hers up and drank as well, a gesture Flora believed represented the essence of good manners.

"It's not about doing everything right," she explained. "It's about basic human decency, putting other people ahead of yourself."

After a second glass of champagne, I was having an easier time holding my knife and fork Continental-style without looking like a baby bird about to attempt flight. I'd also learned how to properly put a napkin in my lap (with the fold toward the table), write a thank-you note (within a week of receiving the gift), and accept a compliment (without dismissing it in feigned modesty). By the end of the night, I was sitting up straight, maintaining eye contact, and accepting compliments like a pro.

But had I achieved a gentle and quiet spirit?

The trucker who cut me off on the way home would probably have an opinion about that. He cost me five cents.

Deliver me from timidity of spirit and from storminess . . .
From all heedlessness in my behavior, deliver me O Lord.
—FROM GERTRUDE'S FOURTH
SPIRITUAL EXERCISE

As October drew to a close and the Tennessee hills lit up with one last blush of color, it became clear to me that the Jar of Contention wasn't really working.

Sure, I'd kicked some bad habits. I was complaining less, listening more, and getting pretty good at changing the subject whenever it turned to gossip. I'd even managed to go an entire day without putting a single penny in the jar. But my spirit remained restless.

Comments and e-mails about the project continued to pour in, and it soon became clear that the reaction-based culture of Facebook, Twitter, and twenty-four-hour news could easily turn someone like me into a one-stop freak show. Positive feedback sent my spirit soaring while negative comments made me defensive and angry. I hated that people I didn't even know had such a powerful effect on me and that a single comment from "Anon1" or "MilwaukeeDad" could keep me up at night.

Contemplatives have long taught that mastering the volatile human spirit is the key to serenity. "It is better to conquer yourself than to win a thousand battles," the Buddha taught. "He who is slow to anger is better than the mighty, and he who rules his spirit than he who captures a city," says Proverbs 16:32 NASB. In our increasingly fragmented, chatter-filled world, the quest to live and think deeply requires concerted acts of self-control. Staying grounded means growing some serious roots.

So in a last-ditch effort to master my not-so-gentle spirit, I decided to explore something I'd been meaning to try for a while: contemplative prayer.

Now, as a rule, evangelicals shy away from mysticism and meditation, as these practices can feel a bit too passive and introspective for our activist-driven, free-for-all religious sensibilities. But I'd been cheating on the low church for about a year now—observing the church calendar, reading the Book of Common Prayer, and sneaking off to St. Matthew's Episcopal Church to smudge ashes on my forehead—so trying out a little structured prayer suited me just fine. I'd done some research on Lectio Divina and centering prayer and decided to start there.

Lectio Divina, or "holy reading," isn't really about reading at all; it's about listening. It's about approaching the text as you would a sanctuary and inviting God to inhabit the words. Techniques vary, but one usually begins the Lectio Divina by slowly reading through a passage of Scripture, making note of any words or images that stir the soul. This is followed by a period of silent meditation. The same passage is read again, and the cycle can be repeated as many times as desired. Some liken this method to a meal, in which one feasts on the words of God, first by taking a bite (reading), then by chewing (meditation), then by savoring (prayer), and finally by digesting (contemplation). The idea is to pay attention, to isolate and enjoy each flavor of the text.

Similarly, centering prayer helps quiet the spirit so that it is calm and deep enough for truth to leave a wake. In centering prayer, one chooses a sacred word or phrase upon which to focus. This serves as a sort of starting point, an anchor to which to return should distractions upset mediation. The ultimate goal is to transcend all thoughts, feelings, images, and perceptions in order to simply rest in the Reality that is beyond words. The method has been practiced by Christians for centuries, particularly in the Eastern Orthodox Church.

I decided to practice contemplative prayer every morning for a week, using "peace" as my centering word and selections from the Psalms and Proverbs for Lectio Divina. I threw in some basic breathing exercises to help me concentrate and resolved to conclude each session with a meditation from St. Teresa of Avila, the legendary Spanish mystic and first woman to be named a Doctor of the Church:

> *Let nothing upset you,*
> *Let nothing startle you.*
> *All things pass;*
> *God does not change.*
> *Patience wins all it seeks.*
> *Whoever has God lacks nothing.*
> *God alone is enough.*

Teresa was said to experience such prolonged periods of ecstasy that she occasionally levitated during Mass. The challenge for me was to get through twenty minutes of prayer without falling asleep or giving up. When the whole family works from home, even the bedroom feels like an office. Just when I'd get started, the phone would ring, the dryer buzzer would sound, or Dan would knock gently on the door and say something about needing a five-pound bag of sugar for a video shoot. But on the few days that I managed to achieve coveted repose, something powerful, perhaps even mystical, happened.

I guess I'd always assumed that cultivating a gentle and quiet spirit would be counterintuitive for me, that meekness was a worthy goal for that other kind of woman—the kind who didn't care about theology or politics or changing the world. But the images and words that flooded my mind during prayer each morning were far from docile or weak. Instead, meditation filled me with a sense of security, strength, and unyielding resolve.

As I prayed, it felt as though my feet were extending through the ground, growing into long, winding roots, while my torso stretched like a trunk, my arms and fingers extending like branches. With every prayer and every silence the image of a great tree returned to me again and again until I found myself sitting up straighter, breathing in deeper, and looking up.

I don't know for sure, but I think maybe God was trying to tell me that gentleness begins with strength, quietness with security. A great tree is both moved and unmoved, for it changes with the seasons, but its roots keep it anchored in the ground. Mastering a gentle and quiet spirit didn't mean changing my personality, just regaining control of it, growing strong enough to hold back and secure enough to soften.

What they forgot to tell us in Sunday school is that the "gentle and quiet spirit" Peter wrote about is not, in fact, an exclusively feminine virtue, but is elevated throughout the New Testament as a trait expected of *all* Christians. Jesus used the same word—*praus*, in Greek—to describe himself as "gentle and humble in heart" (Matthew 11:29). Gentleness is one of the nine fruits of the spirit (Galatians 5:23), and Paul told the members of the Philippian church, "Let your gentleness be evident to all" (Philippians 4:5).

Far from connoting timidity or docility, gentleness is associated with integrity and self-control, particularly in the face of persecution.

The readers of Peter's epistle would have immediately recognized *praus* as the same word they used to describe a wild horse that had been tamed or a torrent of wind that had softened into a breeze.

"Blessed are the *praus*," Jesus said, "for they will inherit the earth" (Matthew 5:5).

What I tell you in the dark, speak in the daylight; what is whispered in your ear, proclaim from the roofs.
—MATTHEW 10:27

Overcast and sixty-three degrees. God couldn't have been too concerned about the eighty-nine cents in my jar of contention to let me get away with that sort of weather when he could have arranged a blizzard.

By this point I'd been reminded about a million times that the Bible didn't explicitly command contentious women to sit on their roofs, and that rooftops in the ancient Near East would have been flat and habitable anyway, but I was determined to engage in some kind of public display of contrition for my verbal misdeeds.

So after lunch on November 1, Dan pulled out the ladder and

the camera, and I spent an hour and twenty-nine minutes on the safest corner of our roof, reading over my list of transgressions, practicing a bit of centering prayer, and watching a small herd of cats mill about the neighborhood.

We live down a narrow street in a quiet part of town that was developed in the 1970s and includes a hodgepodge of little homes, ranging from split-levels to ranchers to Cape Cods. Only six cars passed during my lunch-hour vigil, and this included a mail truck from which a bored-looking employee of the United States Postal Service waved languidly back at me, unimpressed.

"It's okay," I assured her. "I'm a writer."

Either she didn't hear me or she sees things like this all the time.

It occurred to me in that moment that perhaps "gentleness" wasn't the worst virtue with which to start my year of biblical womanhood after all. It forced me to confront some of my uglier tendencies and reminded me that the next eleven months would require the strength of a great tree. I found myself reacting less and listening more. I held back, chose my words more carefully, and protected people's reputations by avoiding gossip. The change wasn't dramatic, but I started handling others with just a little more gentleness, a little more care, keeping in mind that we all have fragile days from time to time.

The criticism would continue. Storms of nasty comments and pointed critiques would blow through. But my roots were growing deeper.

This was a project I believed in. I may have been too broken and narcissistic and petulant to take it on . . . but then, most creative people are.

READ MORE AT RACHELHELDEVANS.COM:

"Strange Ways to Lose a Body Part in the Bible"— http://
    rachelheldevans.com/body-part
"The Ducking Chair"— http://rachelheldevans.com/
    ducking-chair

DEBORAH, THE WARRIOR

"Hear this, you kings! Listen, you rulers!
I, even I, will sing to the Lord . . ."
—JUDGES 5:3 UPDATED NIV

The book of Judges is one of the most violent and disturbing of Scripture, replete with gory accounts of war, plunder, child sacrifice, dismemberment, disembowelment, and rape. Set in the aftermath of Joshua's conquest of Canaan, the book recounts the tumultuous relationship between the Israelites and the Canaanites, as the two engaged in nearly constant skirmishes and raids against each other, but also in the exchange of culture as they intermarried and worshipped each other's gods.

Frustrated by Israel's lack of faithfulness, "the Lord raised up judges" to provide leadership for the kingless people (Judges 2:16).

One such leader was Deborah.

As both prophet and judge, Deborah exercised complete religious, political, judicial, and militaristic authority over the people of Israel. She was essentially Israel's commander in chief, said to issue her rulings from beneath a palm in the hills of Ephraim.

With tensions with the Canaanites rising, Deborah summons a warrior named Barak and orders him to organize a resistance among the tribes of Israel against Sisera, the commander of the Canaanite army.

Barak is doubtful.

"If you go with me, I will go; but if you don't go with me, I won't go," he says (Judges 4:8).

"Certainly I will go with you," Deborah responds with a hint of mockery. "But because of the course you are taking, the honor will not be yours, for the LORD will deliver Sisera into the hands of a woman" (v. 9 UPDATED NIV).

Sure enough, under Deborah's leadership the Israeli army defeats the Canaanites, nine hundred chariots strong, and the disgraced Sisera flees to the tent of a woman named Jael, whose husband had a trade alliance with the Canaanites. Loyal to Israel, Jael waited until Sisera had fallen asleep in her home and then promptly exhibited *her* gentle and quiet spirit—by driving a tent peg through the guy's skull.

Victory belonged to Israel, and it came at the hands of two women.

November: Domesticity

Martha, Martha

She watches over the affairs of her household.

—Proverbs 31:27

TO DO THIS MONTH:

- ☐ Cook through *Martha Stewart's Cooking School* (Proverbs 31:15; Titus 2:5)
- ☐ Clean through *Martha Stewart's Homekeeping Handbook* (Titus 2:5)
- ☐ Host a dinner party (1 Peter 4:9; Hebrews 13:2)
- ☐ Host Thanksgiving dinner (1 Peter 4:9)

I don't know if I've mentioned this yet, but you can't buy any sort of hard liquor in Rhea County, not even wine.

So when Martha Stewart's braised short ribs called for an entire bottle of Côtes du Rhône, to be reduced about a million times into a "rich and unctuous sauce," I was faced with the decision to either make the forty-five-minute drive to the nearest liquor store in Hamilton County or move on to the next recipe in *Martha Stewart's Cooking School*—orange braised rabbit.

Rabbit? Now, where on earth was I going to get a rabbit?

Fortunately, Martha's version of beef bourguignon, the French classic popularized in the States by the incomparable Julia Child, was Rhea County approved. Instead of burgundy, Martha's "beef and stout stew" called for 16 ounces of Guinness, which you can easily pick up at the local Wal-Mart because local legislators don't seem to mind if the county's citizens get drunk on beer, so long as it's not on Sunday.

The fact that Martha's beef stew recipe appeared complicated yet doable was just one reason I chose her as my guide through a month of domesticity. The elevation of homemaking as a woman's highest calling is such a critical centerpiece to the modern biblical womanhood movement, I figured no one less than the Domestic Diva herself would do. Besides, you have to admire a woman who can build an empire on crafts and apple pie, know enough about trading to commit securities fraud, go to jail for five months, and then come right back to cooking soufflés and decorating gourds on TV as if nothing had happened, casually mentioning that she learned this or that knitting pattern "at Alderson," like federal prison was just another Bedford or Skylands.

Furthermore, I loved poring over the pages of *Martha Stewart's Cooking School* and *Martha Stewart's Homekeeping Handbook* because they read like textbooks.

"This book has been designed and written as a course of study," Martha explains in the introduction to Cooking School, "very much like a college course in chemistry, which requires the student to master the basics before performing more advanced experiments."[1]

She takes the same approach in *Homekeeping*: "Consider the 'Throughout the House' section of the book as a master class on how to clean," she wrote. "Here you will find simple, clear instructions for the basic techniques needed to clean any household object or surface. The five fundamentals—dusting, wiping up, sweeping, vacuuming, and mopping—that constitute the core of any weekly household schedule are covered in 'Routine Cleaning,' with detailed descriptions of the best tools and equipment for each task."[2]

Martha didn't assume I knew what I was doing, but she didn't talk down to me either. A lot of women absorb their homemaking skills through osmosis, watching their mothers and grandmothers over the years, taking mental notes along the way. Not me. The perpetual student, I require a book and highlighter. Martha's array of charts and photographs, sidebars and endnotes felt familiar and calming to me. I could study detailed, step-by-step illustrations on how to bone a leg of lamb or polish silver, gaze at beautiful pictures of brightly colored soup garnishes and herbs set against pristine white backgrounds, and learn all about the science of bleach, the secret of poaching, and the history of bouillabaisse. Martha even includes "extra credit" sections at the end of each chapter for overachievers like me. All I'd have to do is whip up a little compound butter here and lemon curd there, and I'd be a regular Julie Powell in no time.

I just hoped my efforts would be domestic enough.

The importance of homemaking in the contemporary biblical womanhood movement cannot be overstated, and proponents tend to use strong, unequivocal language to argue that the only sphere in which a woman can truly bring glory to God is the home. This position is based primarily on an idealized elevation of the post–industrial revolution nuclear family rather than biblical culture, but proponents point to two passages of Scripture to make their case.

Proverbs 31:10–31, which, among other things, extols the domestic accomplishments of an upper-class Jewish wife, and Titus 2:4–5, in which the older women of Crete are encouraged by the apostle Paul to teach younger women to "love their husbands and children, to be self-controlled and pure, and *to be busy at home*" (emphasis added).[3]

Dorothy Patterson, in chapter 22 of *Recovering Biblical Manhood and Womanhood*, concludes from these two passages that "keeping the home is God's assignment to the wife—even down to changing the sheets, doing the laundry, and scrubbing the floors." Ambitions that might lead a woman to work outside the home, says Patterson, constitute the kind of "evil desires" that lead directly to sin.[4]

Debi Pearl, author of *Created to Be His Help Meet*, wrote, "A young mother's place is in the home, keeping it, guarding it, watching over those entrusted to her. To do otherwise will surely cause the Word of God to be blasphemed. Even if you could disobey God and it not produce visible ill consequences, it would only prove that God is long-suffering . . . but the judgment will assuredly come."[5]

"Quite simply, there is no such thing as 'Christian feminism,'" explains Stacy McDonald in a book titled *Passionate Housewives Desperate for God*. "We either embrace the biblical model . . . or we reject it and plummet over the cliff with the rest of the passengers on the railcar."[6]

All this talk of judgment and damnation and runaway railcars made me wonder how these ladies would feel knowing I'd chosen an ex-con for a teacher, was secretly squeezing a few business trips into my schedule, and had every intention of stocking up on liquor each time I crossed the county line . . . for the braised ribs, of course. Perhaps the real reason I'd chosen Martha Stewart to accompany me on this leg of the journey was the fact that her drive, intelligence, and unapologetic ambition allowed me to preserve some small part of myself as I ventured into a world that didn't yet feel my own.

Sure, Martha can be a real stickler for doing things her way, but you don't hear her saying that you'll go to hell if you don't.

The wise woman builds her house,
But the foolish tears it down with her own hands.
—Proverbs 14:1 nasb

Besides the fact that we were eating dinner at about nine thirty every night, the first week of cooking went well. I started with soups, because according to Martha, "the measure of a good cook is how well he or she makes soup. Not a complicated, multicourse meal or a delicate soufflé, but a simple soup."[7]

I'm not so sure I'd use the word *simple*, seeing as how Martha's basic chicken soup took me over three hours to make. This was mostly my fault, of course. Tearing a whole chicken into bite-size pieces requires that a girl get rather intimate with her meat, and I hate getting intimate with my meat. Wiggling those fleshy little legs until they separated from the joint made me feel like some kind of animal. Not even a pair of rubber gloves, two feet of distance, and closed eyes could convince me that I was doing anything but handling a carcass.

"How do you like the parsnips?" I asked as Dan took his first sip of soup that night.

"They're good."

"I've never cooked with them before. I didn't even know what they looked like until yesterday."

"Hmmm."

"They look kinda like seasick carrots, in case you're wondering. How do you like the chicken?"

"It's good."

"I used free range organic-fed chicken so we don't have to feel guilty. Do you think the pieces are too small?

"No. They're good."

"It tastes fresh, doesn't it? It smells fresh, too, like you can tell it's homemade."

"Yeah. It's good."

"Good grief, Dan. Could you please use a word besides *good*? How do you really feel about this soup? Tell me the truth."

Dan looked trapped.

"How do I *feel* about the soup?"

"It's watery and bland because I used water instead of stock. That's what you're thinking."

"Well, maybe a little, but overall it's . . . it's just good, okay? That's the best word I can come up with. I'm sorry I don't have a fancy vocabulary like you."

I let it go, mostly on account of the vocabulary compliment. Besides, it was nearly 10 p.m., and I hadn't started the dishes or decided whether to start the stock that night or the next morning. There's no time for arguing when you've just realized a mangled chicken carcass has been sitting out on your counter for an hour.

Fortunately, the rest of the week's meals conjured some better adjectives from the other side of the dining room table. Among our favorites were Martha's savory French toast BLT, Martha's roasted autumn harvest salad, and Martha's beef and stout stew.

The project had revealed its first truly surprising result: I enjoyed cooking. In the four hours it took me to prepare that beef and stout stew, I forgot about all the loose ends and screwups and unreturned e-mails in my life and instead concentrated all my scattered energy like a magnifying lens into one hot beam of unadulterated intention—chopping and mincing, browning and frying, grating and blanching, and stirring and boiling. Even when dinner didn't turn out perfectly, I found the process itself rewarding.

The first week of domestication would have gone down in the books as an indisputable success, were it not for all the housework.

My robust lexicon notwithstanding, I struggle to find the right words to describe just how much I despise, hate, abhor, revile, detest, and categorically abominate anything to do with home maintenance.

While cooking strikes me as an essentially creative act, cleaning seems little more than an exercise in decay management, enough to trigger an existential crisis each time the ring around the toilet bowl reappears.

Now, don't get me wrong; I like things to be clean. It's not as though Dan and I "live in squalor," as my mom likes to say. But each time the laundry basket starts to overflow or the fridge gets crowded with old leftovers, I put up a fight. And when I'm not in the mood for a fight, I just sit around and feel guilty about it.

In a matter of days, *The Martha Stewart Homekeeping Handbook* had turned this little complex of mine into full-blown neurosis. It started with the checklists—Martha's list of "to-dos" for every day, every week, every month, and every season. These would have been helpful guides had they not revealed what a complete and utter failure I am at everything I attempt. As it turns out, until I started this experiment, pretty much everything on Martha's "clean every day" list I did about once a week, pretty much everything on Martha's "clean every week" list I did about once a month, pretty much everything on Martha's "clean every month" list I did about once a year, and pretty much everything on Martha's "clean every season" list I'd never done in my life. That's right, folks; I'd never vacuumed our refrigerator grille and coil. We lived in squalor after all.

After trying and failing to cross every item off Martha's to-do lists, I decided to conduct a room-by-room deep-clean of the house, starting with the kitchen. According to Martha, "it's the room with more home concerns than any other."[8]

This was certainly true in our house. When we first purchased the house seven years ago, I made a big stink about replacing the old maple cabinets and mustard-yellow countertops, but I guess one can grow accustomed to cooking in a veritable cave when, by the grace of God, it includes a gas stove. Working with less than seven feet of counter space and no pantry, I'd assembled a motley crew of add-ons, including a wobbly folding table, a kid's writing desk, and a hideous microwave stand that a retired missionary was getting rid of, which really tells you something.

According to Martha, "it's not the amount of room you have that matters, but how you manage it." With most of my counter space cluttered with appliances and cereal boxes, and with cabinets so disheveled that finding the lid to the stockpot required spelunking experience, it was clear that I wasn't using my space as efficiently as possible, a problem I needed to solve before tackling something as involved as beef bourguignon.

So I took everything out—pots, pans, dishes, stemware, cutting boards, appliances canisters, pottery, platters, soup cans, cake stands, measuring cups, and muffin pans—piled it all in the dining room, and stood in my empty kitchen for two hours until I knew exactly where everything had to go.

Mom did this every now and then when we were kids. She'd put a Carole King tape in the stereo, empty all the drawers and cabinets in the kitchen, and clean the whole thing top to bottom while singing at the top of her lungs about the earth moving under her feet and the sky tumbling down, a-tumbling down. Amanda and I watched, bewildered, among the stockpots and frying pans. Shouting above the music, she told us, "It has to get messy before it gets clean"—a philosophy that pretty much sums up every meaningful experience of my life, from homemaking to friendships to faith. Sometimes you've just got to tear everything out, expose all the innards, and start over again.

Sure enough, cooking is a lot more fun when you're not at war with your kitchen. As much as I hate to admit it, the sixteen hours I spent deep-cleaning my kitchen turned out to be some of the most valuable hours of the project. The task required creativity, problem solving, innovation, and resourcefulness, and it forced me to confront the ugly air of condescension that permeated my attitude toward homemaking. It was out of ignorance and insecurity that I ever looked down my nose at women who make homemaking their full-time occupation.

I got so confident, in fact, I did something I'd have never dreamed of doing before: I called Mom and officially invited the whole family to our house for Thanksgiving dinner.

When Brother Lawrence sought sanctuary from the tumults of seventeenth-century France, he entered a Carmelite monastery in Paris, where his lack of education relegated him to kitchen duty. Charged with tending to the abbey's most mundane chores, Brother Lawrence nevertheless earned a reputation among his fellow monks for exuding a contagious sense of joy and peace as he went about his work—so much so that after his death, they compiled the few maxims and letters and interviews he left behind into a work that would become a classic Christian text: *The Practice of the Presence of God*.

"The time of business," explained Brother Lawrence, "does not with me differ from the time of prayer; and in the noise and clatter of my kitchen, while several persons are at the same time calling for different things, I possess God in as great tranquility as if I were upon my knees at the blessed sacrament."[9]

For Brother Lawrence, God's presence permeated everything—from the pots and pans in the kitchen sink to the water and soap that washed them. Every act of faithfulness in these small tasks communicated his love for God and desire to live in perpetual worship. "It is enough for me to pick up but a straw from the ground for the love of GOD," he said.[10]

After reading Brother Lawrence, I tried to go about my housework with a little more mindfulness—listening to each rhythmic swishing of the broom, feeling the warm water rush down my arm and off my fingers as I scrubbed potatoes, savoring the scent of clean laundry fresh out of the dryer, delighting in the sight of all the colorful herbs and vegetables and cheeses on my countertop. And sure enough, I found myself connecting to that same presence that I encountered during contemplative prayer, the presence that reminded me that the roots of my spirit extended deep into the ground. I got less done when I worked with mindfulness, but, somehow, I felt more in control.

I get the sense that many in the contemporary biblical woman-hood movement feel that the tasks associated with homemaking have been so marginalized in our culture that it's up to them to restore the sacredness of keeping the home. This is a noble goal indeed, and one around which all people of faith can rally. But in our efforts to celebrate and affirm God's presence in the home, we should be wary of elevating the vocation of homemaking above all others by insinuating that for women, God's presence is somehow restricted to that sphere.

If God is the God of all pots and pans, then He is also the God of all shovels and computers and paints and assembly lines and execu-tive offices and classrooms. Peace and joy belong not to the woman who finds the right vocation, but to the woman who finds God in *any* vocation, who looks for the divine around every corner.

As Elizabeth Barret Browning famously put it:

> *Earth's crammed with heaven,*
> *And every common bush afire with God,*
> *But only he who sees takes off his shoes;*
> *The rest sit round it and pluck blackberries.*

Faith's not about finding the right bush. It's about taking off your shoes.

Offer hospitality to one another without grumbling.
—1 PETER 4:9

It's a good thing I retired the Jar of Contention at the end of October or else it would have been fully restocked at the conclusion of November 8.

Up until this point, Dan had been the only witness to my culi-nary exploits. This seemed rather "unbiblical" to me, considering the fact that hospitality is such a celebrated virtue in Scripture. So on November 8, I invited the Falzone family (yep, rhymes with "calzone") over for a dinner of stuffed shells. Dayna had recently announced that Baby #3 was on his or her way, so it seemed as good a time as any to get together and celebrate.

I found the stuffed shells recipe in November's edition of *Martha Stewart Living*, and it looked easy enough: boxed jumbo shells stuffed with ricotta, radicchio, and prosciutto, baked in homemade or (gasp!) store-bought tomato sauce, and topped with butter, mozzarella, and parmesan—served with salad and bread. Arteries and blood pressure be darned, I could handle that.

It didn't occur to me until I was halfway to the grocery store that cooking stuffed shells for an Italian might not be the best idea. A Falzone probably has, you know, *standards* regarding his pasta. And if that weren't enough, I decided to go ahead and purchase all the ingredients for Martha's beef and stout stew that same day, which gave me a grocery list that came to three pages, typed and single-spaced, whose contents included unfamiliar items like cipollini onions, cremini mushrooms, slab bacon, and horseradish root, three of which proved wholly unavailable to residents of Rhea County.

Which brings me to a point I've been meaning to make for a while now—Martha Stewart hates rural America.

Well, that might not be entirely true, but I can say from experience that nothing makes a rural Tennessean feel precisely like a rural Tennessean than a list of ingredients that cannot be found within a thirty-mile radius of one's home. "Ask your butcher," says Martha. Or, "Talk with your fishmonger," says Martha. "Visit your Asian market," says Martha. "Try your local gourmet food purveyor," says Martha.

I'm tempted to remind Martha that not all of us have personal fishmongers, butchers, and stockbrokers to "tell us these things."

Of course, the upside to being strapped with an exotic grocery list is that I get to feel all superior whenever I walk into Wal-Mart or BI-LO with requests that make the produce guys scratch their heads. Around here, asking for arugula or chanterelles turns you into a regular foodie, as such delicacies must be specially ordered from Chattanooga or Atlanta. I admit to experiencing a touch of blithe satisfaction when the checkout clerk looked at my horseradish root and asked, "You mean to tell me you're gonna eat that?"

"Grate it, actually," I said, as if I knew what the heck I was doing.

That day it was the cipollini onions that threw everyone off. I started at Wal-Mart, where my friend Amber from frozen foods helped me find the produce guy, who helped me find the produce manager, who helped me find the store manager—none of whom had ever even heard of cipollini onions. Next thing I knew, a confluence of workers, managers, and fellow shoppers had assembled around me in the potato aisle, passing around my grocery list like it was an out-of-towner's bad directions.

"It's really not a big deal," I told the produce manager, a little embarrassed by all the attention I'd garnered. "It's a Martha Stewart recipe, so there's always some unattainable ingredient involved."

A forty-something with a wide girth, shoulder-length blond hair, and thick East Tennessee drawl, the produce manager seemed perfectly satisfied with that explanation.

"Yeah, I'd say she done put them in there just to throw you off," he concluded.

Just to throw me off. That sounded about right.

It was six o'clock when I finished cooking the prosciutto, radicchio, garlic, and onion and started stuffing the shells. We expected Tony and Dayna and the girls around six thirty. The bathroom hadn't been cleaned yet, so we may as well have been running around naked. I started rummaging through the cabinets, dramatically banging together pots and pans and releasing long, loud sighs in an attempt to coax Dan into the kitchen to see if he could help. Normally I would just ask, but we'd been trying to stick to traditional roles in deference to the project, which to the credit of the biblical womanhood advocates had resulted in a lot fewer arguments about division of labor. But as the clock ticked away and the jar of tomato sauce proved impossible to open, a fresh wave of resentment rolled over me.

"Can't you tell that I'm struggling in here?" I yelled.

After about a minute, Dan appeared around the corner.

"Yeah, but aren't you supposed to do this stuff by yourself? You know, for the project?"

I knew he wasn't taking advantage of the situation, just trying to preserve the integrity of the project, because Dan's big into integrity.

"You're just taking advantage of the situation," I wailed.

"Hon, you know that's not true. I'd be happy to help you."

"Well then, why don't you volunteer?"

"I didn't know that was allowed."

"OF COURSE it's allowed! No one said you can't initiate assistance to your wife when she's struggling."

"Okay. So what can I do?"

This felt wrong. As much as I wanted Dan's help and pity, bossing him around and turning him into the bad guy didn't honor the experiment or our relationship.

"Maybe you could just call Tony and Dayna and tell them to come at seven instead. I'll take care of everything else."

He let me bury my head in his chest and cry for a few minutes, leaving two distinct mascara marks on his white T-shirt. Sometimes, when I'm separating the laundry after a tough week, I find two or three similarly stained undershirts and I'm reminded of why I married this man.

Tony and Dayna arrived right at seven, just as the shells turned golden and the sauce bubbly. Dayna, who had been kind enough to bring a dessert of apple turnovers, innocently asked how the project had affected my workout routine, which, along with my aching feet, put me in a bit of a funk for the rest of the night, even though everyone seemed to enjoy the meal.

It wasn't until after dessert, as I faced a mountain of dishes alone in the kitchen, that I realized how much Addy and Aury, the little Falzones, were enjoying themselves. They'd asked me to turn up the music—Amy Winehouse, if you must know—and were dancing around and around the dining room table, giggling and waving their red paper napkins in the air like Bulgarian folk dancers. (Well, Aury was mostly lumbering and falling, as she was only two at the time.)

"Will you dance with us?" Addy asked, after the sound of a particularly raucous fall brought me around the corner to check on them.

"Well, okay."

So the three of us held hands and danced around the table to "Trouble," the scent of garlic and prosciutto still hanging in the air and the dishes still piled high in the kitchen.

Suddenly I remembered a mysterious verse from the book of Hebrews.

"Do not forget to entertain strangers, for by so doing some have unwittingly entertained angels" (13:2 nkjv).

Martha—not the one in my cookbook, but the one in the Bible—was one of Jesus' closest friends and disciples. According to the gospels of Luke and John, she opened her home to Him, shared meals with Him, and stood by His side as He raised her brother, Lazarus, from the dead. John reports that "Jesus loved Martha and her sister and Lazarus" (John 11:5). That Martha's name appears before her brother's suggests that this woman garnered considerable respect among the earliest followers of Jesus.

Despite her esteemed status, poor Martha is best known today for a less-than-flattering incident involving her sister, Mary. As the story goes, Jesus and some of His followers were traveling through the town of Bethany, where "Martha opened her home to [them]" (Luke 10:38), serving food and offering shelter for the night. Since sudden overnight company is the leading cause of insanity among women, Martha got a little stressed out with all the preparations that go into hosting a troupe of tired, hungry, first-century Jewish men for the weekend. Perhaps after attempting to grate some horseradish, she charged into the next room, where Mary sat at the feet of Jesus, listening to His teachings.

"Lord, don't you care that my sister has left me to do the work by myself?" Martha demands. "Tell her to help me!" (v. 40).

Folks were always asking Jesus to intervene in family disputes and other seemingly trivial matters. You would think this would have irritated Him, being God-in-flesh and all, but His response to Martha was gentle, almost tender.

"Martha, Martha," he said, "you are worried and upset about many things, but few things are needed—or indeed only one. Mary has chosen what is better, and it will not be taken away from her" (vv. 41–42 updated niv).

The Precious Moments New King James Version of the Bible that I toted around to Sunday school as a child included a cartoon illustration of this story that depicted Mary kneeling at the feet of Jesus, looking quite like the Virgin herself, with hands clasped together in prayer, body positioned at a perfect ninety-degree angle, eyes closed, and head covered, while Martha, looking rather like a Disney stepsister, with an enormous nose, angular jaw, and kooky hairdo, cast an exaggerated glare at her sister while balancing a platter of grapes in her hands—a sharp contrast between the servant and the student, considering the fact that good Christian girls are generally expected to be both.

Feminists like me love this story. Here we have Jesus gladly teaching a woman who was bold enough to study under a rabbi, which was patently condemned at the time. However, conservatives note that Martha served future meals to Jesus and His disciples, suggesting that Jesus called Martha out on her critical attitude, not her role as a homemaker. As tempting as it is to cast Mary and Martha as flat, lifeless foils of each other—cartoonish representations of our rival callings as women—I think that misses the point.

Martha certainly wasn't the first and she won't be the last to dismiss someone else's encounter with God because it didn't fit the mold. When an unnamed woman interrupted a meal to anoint Jesus' feet with an expensive perfume, some of those present complained that the money could have been donated to the poor (Matthew 26:6–13; Mark 14:3–9). When an invalid healed by Jesus ran through the streets, carrying the mat to which he had been confined for thirty-eight years, a group of religious leaders chastised him for lifting something heavy on the Sabbath (John 5). When my friend Jackie became the first woman to deliver a sermon from the pulpit of a megachurch in Dallas, she received hate mail from fellow Christians. When a new mom told me she felt closer to God since giving birth, I secretly dismissed her feelings as hormone-induced sentimentalism.

I guess we're all a little afraid that if God's presence is *there*, it cannot be *here*.

Caring for the poor, resting on the Sabbath, showing hospitality and keeping the home—these are important things that can lead us to God, but God is not contained in them. The gentle Rabbi reminds us that few things really matter and only one thing is necessary.

Mary found it outside the bounds of her expected duties as a woman, and no amount of criticism or questioning could take it away from her. Martha found it in the gentle reminder to slow down, let go, and be careful of challenging another woman's choices, for you never know when she may be sitting at the feet of God.

> *It's safe to say that every cook will be called upon to roast a turkey at some point in his or her life.*[11]
> —MARTHA STEWART

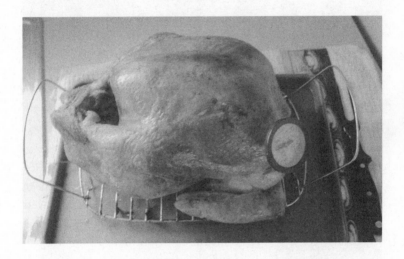

I suppose it's not a good sign when your copy of *Good Housekeeping* is stuck to the bathroom floor, covered in hair, toenail clippings, and dust bunnies, but by mid-November I'd gotten so good at cooking I figured God and Martha would cut me some slack on the cleaning front.

Since completing the beef stew, I'd moved on to desserts, popping chocolate chip cookies, cheesecake, and crème brûlée out of the oven like I was born with oven mitts on my hands.

Unfortunately, my dessert domination came to a fateful end the night before Thanksgiving when I attempted Martha Stewart's double-crusted apple pie. It had already been an intense week, what

with a twenty-four-pound turkey to thaw, groceries to buy, cen-
terpieces to assemble, and an apparently monumental decision to
make about whether or not to brine. (I'd reveal my final verdict,

but it appears this would turn 50 percent of
the population against me.) Now with less
than eight hours before my alarm was set
to go off the next morning, I found myself
on the kitchen floor, crying and cursing and
shaking flecks of pâte brisée (French for "pie
crust") out of my hair.

(Going into this project, I was determined
to avoid the whole crumple-to-the-kitchen-
floor-in-a-heap-of-sobs bit, as it's getting
a tad cliché, don't you think? So I feel it's
important to note that I didn't crumple to the kitchen floor in a
heap of sobs; I just happened to be sitting on the kitchen floor when
I started to cry.)

The evening had gone so well up to that point. My friend Carrie,
who would be joining us for Thanksgiving dinner, let me borrow

her apple peeler—an industrious little contraption that made me feel like Laura Ingalls Wilder as I cranked the iron lever to neatly core, cut, and peel ten Granny Smiths, their cool juices spraying all over my arms like sawdust from a circular. The peels came out in sweet-smelling coils that I munched on as I read Martha's instructions for preparing the pâte brisée.

"Perhaps because of the risk of overworking," says Martha, "and turning out something that tears in two or tastes more leaden than light, many home cooks shy away from homemade dough, opting instead for unfold-as-you-go boxed crusts."[12]

Losers.

"But making perfect pie dough from scratch should be part of any home cook's basic skills. And the best dough for homemade pies is pâte brisée . . . Getting the right proportion of butter to flour is crucial, as is using very cold ingredients and a light hand."

Bring it, Martha.

I confess that part of my motivation for tackling homemade apple pie the night before Thanksgiving dinner was the fact that my mother had advised against it.

"At least use a frozen pie crust," she said. "Why put all this extra stress on yourself?"

But I'd grown overconfident, so the fact that I'd never in my life used a pastry blender or a rolling pin didn't stop me from going right ahead and whisking together some flour, sugar, and salt, cutting in two sticks of butter, adding some water, and then kneading it all together to form two disks that looked exactly like the picture on page 438, thank you very much. Then I wrapped my pâte brisée in plastic and put it in the refrigerator while I combined my (slightly browning) apples with sugar, flour, lemon juice, cinnamon, ginger, and salt.

A taste test proved I was on the right track.

"Assemble the pie," commanded the directions.

No problem.

I dusted the counter with flour, placed the first pâte brisée on the surface, took out my rolling pin, and began my slow break from sanity.

To this day I am convinced that rendering that lump of dough into a crust that is precisely one-eighth of an inch thick and thirteen inches in diameter would require Douglas Adams–style rematerialization. I did everything the book told me to do. I rolled the dough from the center out to the edges. I turned it as I went along. I tried using parchment paper. But after thirty minutes of excruciating tedium, I decided that eleven inches in diameter would have to do. I unrolled the paper-thin dough into the pie pan, where it barely peeked over the edges, filled it with the apple mixture, wrestled again with the second round of pâte brisée, and then finally draped the "lid" over the filling.

"Use kitchen shears to trim overhang of both crusts to 1-inch," said Martha.

Well, I can safely skip that step.

"Press edges to seal."

Okay.

"Fold overhang under, and crimp edges: With thumb and index finger of one hand, gently press dough against index finger of other hand. Continue around pie."

This proved challenging given the amount of crust I had to work worth, but by the time I finished, it didn't look half-bad, almost like Martha's picture, in fact.

And then I realized I'd forgotten to add the butter to the filling.

Crap.

I immediately got on my phone to tweet about the predicament and solicit advice. Of the dozen or so friends who were online at 9 p.m. the night before Thanksgiving—most of them men—three suggested that I cut the butter into little slivers and stick it through the air slits, which turned out to be a good idea except that my air slits ended up looking more like giant gashes through which butter was bleeding out of my pie.

"Whisk egg yolk and cream in a bowl; brush over top crust," instructed Martha. "If desired, use cutters to cut chilled scraps into leaves or other shapes; adhere to top of crust with egg wash. This is a good way to hide imperfections."

Oh, Martha.

"Sprinkle with sanding sugar."

Sanding sugar, I could only assume, was powdered sugar finely sieved. So I decided to try out a little trick I saw in *Martha Stewart Living*—a "good thing" as she likes to call it. I took my half-gallon canister of powdered sugar, covered the opening with cheesecloth, held it over the pie, and shook.

Almost instantly the cheesecloth fell through, releasing an avalanche of powdered sugar onto my butter-bleeding pie.

This is when I decided to sit down for a while.

Dan had the good sense to be at a friend's house, playing *Halo* that night, so I wallowed alone in self-pity for a while before rousing myself to take a picture of the sugar-doused pie with my phone, tweet about the fiasco, and soak in the sympathy of my readers. Further inspection revealed that just one side of the pie caught the brunt of the disaster, so I began shoveling, first with a measuring cup, then with a spoon, and finally with a butter knife. When I finished, a thin layer of sugar remained, which promptly burned in the oven. Five hours before I was to put a twenty-four-pound turkey in, I pulled a charred, lacerated, butter-bleeding shadow of a pie out.

Icarus had flown too close to the sun.

That night I dreamed about giblets and gravy, and as often happens when I'm so rudely confronted with my inadequacies as a woman, babies. At some point Dan came home and asked if something was burning.

At 5:30 a.m. the alarm sounded, and I lumbered back into the dark kitchen to make some coffee and turn to page 149 of *Martha Stewart's Cooking School*, where the recipe for "Perfect Roast Turkey" slowly sharpened into focus.

I'd been warned about a million times to remember to take out the giblets, so I heaved the bird out of the refrigerator, placed it on top of a bed of paper towels to sop up all the nasty pink juices, pulled on some rubber gloves, and reluctantly began my day with my hand in a turkey's orifice. Talk about getting intimate with your meat.

Just as expected, I found the plastic bag of giblets nestled inside the chest cavity, but there was something else rattling around in there I wasn't so sure about, some kind of bone. The package instructions seem to suggest it was the poor gal's neck, but I called the Butterball Turkey Talk-Line just to be sure.

The Turkey Talk-Line was busy, probably because 6:00 a.m. on Thanksgiving morning is about the time most of us first-timers realize what we've gotten ourselves into. Fortunately, the menu included on option to listen to Betty or somebody talk about how to prepare a turkey, and I distinctly heard her say to remove the giblets and neck. So I pulled out the neck, ignored Martha's instructions to reserve the offal for gravy, and threw it with the giblets into the garbage. (We Southern girls make our gravy out of grease, not body parts.) I prepared my basting liquid, seasoned the cavity, lathered the bird in butter, and placed it in the roasting pan.

But something didn't look right. The poor thing appeared to be attempting flight.

I read back through Martha's instructions to see "fold wing tips under."

This proved to be the hardest part of the whole process because apparently I'm so weak I can't even arm wrestle a dead turkey, but also because the rest of the day went . . . well . . . perfectly.

My parents came over, along with our pastor, Brian; his wife,

Carrie; and their two young daughters, Avery and Adi. Carrie brought a pumpkin pie and banana pudding, so we didn't have to eat my butter-bleeding apple pie. The table looked beautiful, all the food came out on time, the turkey was tender and juicy, and the conversation was fantastic.

Everything went so perfectly I started to annoy myself.

How am I supposed to get any writing material out of this?

Or maybe it was my definition of "perfect" that had changed. Somewhere between the chicken soup and the butter-bleeding pie, I'd made peace with the God of pots and pans—not because God wanted to meet me in the kitchen, but because He wanted to meet me everywhere, in all things, big or small. Knowing that God both inhabits and transcends our daily vocations, no matter how glorious or mundane, should be enough to unite all women of faith and end that nasty cycle of judgment we get caught in these days.

Mom and Carrie helped me with the dishes. Brian volunteered to pick apart the carcass. Avery and Adi learned to play "Living on the Edge" on *Guitar Hero* with Dan and Dad.

Finally, after the company was gone, the dishes done, and the leftovers distributed, I sank into the living room couch with a glass of rosé and offered up a silent toast—to Mary, Martha, and me.

READ MORE:

"Is Voting 'Biblical'?"— http://rachelheldevans.com/voting-biblical

"Beef and Stout Stew"— http://rachelheldevans.com/beet-stew

TAMAR, THE TRICKSTER

"She is more righteous than I . . ."
—GENESIS 38:26

Tamar married into a family of wicked men.

Her father-in-law, Judah, was the son of Jacob and Leah, and a spiteful, troubled man, who sold his own brother into slavery. Judah had three sons—Er, Onan, and Shelah—and Tamar's father had arranged for her to marry the oldest, Er.

But Er was so wicked in the sight of God that God struck him dead, leaving Tamar a widow. According to the biblical law of the levirate marriage, if a man dies without children, his wife must be married to his brother, and the first son produced from that union counted as the heir of the deceased. So Judah gave Tamar to his second son, Onan. Knowing he would inherit a double portion of his father's possessions now that Er was dead, Onan did not want Tamar to birth an heir to Er's portion because he would go back to the smaller inheritance granted to the second son. So he "spilled his seed" during intercourse (v. 9 DRB), an act of disobedience that angered God so much that He struck Onan dead too.

Frightened by the fact that two of his sons had already died after marrying Tamar, Judah delayed her marriage to Shelah indefinitely.

"Remain a widow in your father's house until my son Shelah grows up," he told Tamar (v. 11 NASB). But he had no intention of allowing his only surviving son anywhere near her.

To be a widow and childless in Israel would mean social and economic catastrophe for Tamar. No longer a virgin, she held no value in her father's household, for she could not be sold to a suitor. But without a husband or son, she had no place in the clan of Judah. In a patriarchal culture where a woman's status depends upon her functional relationship to men, a woman like Tamar would be left with nothing—no family, no value, and no future.

Years passed, and Judah continued to refuse Tamar's rightful place in his family, so Tamar concocted a plan.

She learned that Judah's wife had recently died and that he planned to go to Timnah with some friends to shear his sheep. Tamar took off her widow's clothes, disguised herself with the veil of a prostitute, and waited inside the gate to Enaim where she knew Judah would come to do business.

When Judah arrived at Enaim on his way to Timnah, he assumed that Tamar was just another nameless prostitute selling her own "goods" in the market, and he shamelessly solicited her.

"And what will you give me to sleep with you?" Tamar asked, playing her role perfectly.

"I'll send you a young goat from my flock," Judah replied.

"Will you give me something as a pledge until you send it?"

"What pledge should I give you?"

"Your seal and its cord," Tamar answered, "and the staff in your hand" (vv. 16–18).

So Judah handed over his signet seal, the cord from which it hung, and his staff—all objects of identification, and all signs of his authority. Then he "lay with her," as the Bible likes to say, Judah never realizing that his mistress was his daughter-in-law.

After the tryst, Tamar sneaked away and put on her widow's clothing. Judah sent a friend to Enaim to exchange the baby goat for his things, but no prostitute could be found. The friend asked around, but was told there were no prostitutes that waited inside the gate of Enaim.

Embarrassed at having been swindled by a prostitute, Judah told his friend, "Let her keep what she has, or we will become a laughingstock" (Genesis 38:23).

Three months later, Tamar was boasting a baby bump. Neighbors accused her of "playing the whore" and alerted Judah to the situation. Suddenly, the man who wanted Tamar expunged from his household took full ownership of her and declared, "Bring her out and have her burned to death!" (v. 24). Under the patriarchal laws of the day, it would have been fully in his right to execute such an order. But Tamar was ready. She sent Judah his signet, cord, and staff with the message, "I am pregnant by the man who owns these. See if you recognize [them]" (v. 25).

Judah was embarrassed and humbled. "She is more righteous than I," he declared, "since I wouldn't give her to my son Shelah" (v. 26).

The author of Genesis was careful to note that, in keeping with Jewish law, Tamar and Judah never slept together again. Tamar gave birth to twin boys, the youngest of whom would become an ancestor to King David.

Tamar joins a storied troupe of crafty and courageous biblical women who used trickery, sexuality, and manipulation to work the patriarchal system to which they were born and survive to change the course of Israel's history. In fact, Tamar holds the rare distinction of being one of only four Old Testament women mentioned in the genealogy of Jesus. The others include Bathsheba, (a mistress), Ruth, (a foreigner), and Rahab (a prostitute).

God, it seems, prefers chutzpah to status.

December: Obedience

My Husband, My Master

She must neither begin nor complete anything without man: where he is, there she must be. She must be, and bend before him as before a master, whom she shall fear and to whom she shall be subject and obedient.

— MARTIN LUTHER

TO DO THIS MONTH:

- ☐ Call Dan "master" (1 Peter 3:1–6)
- ☐ Interview a polygamist (Genesis 30; Exodus 21:10)
- ☐ Hold a ceremony in honor of the victims of biblical misogyny (Judges 11:37–40)

If you ever decide to try a year of biblical living yourself, there are a few things you should know ahead of time:

First of all, translation matters. Where the New American Standard Version will have you singing, "My soul, my soul! I am in anguish! My heart is pounding in me; I cannot be silent," King James will make morning prayers significantly more embarrassing with "My bowels, my bowels! I am pained at my very heart; my heart maketh a noise in me; I cannot hold my peace" (Jeremiah 4:19).

Second, no matter how excited you are about your quest, you may want to keep it a secret for a while. Unless, of course, you really love getting ten e-mails a day from perfect strangers convinced they know exactly how you should be a "biblical woman" . . . then you should definitely announce it to the whole world right away.

And finally, if you're intent on trying to keep all the commands, you should know ahead of time that you're going to bump into at least three or four that you simply can't (or won't) keep. The Bible is a hundred times older than you are. Prepare to be humbled by it.

So far, the first two months of my "radical experiment" had been far from radical. Pulling homemade pies out of the oven, keeping the house tidy, practicing contemplative prayer, refraining from gossip—these are the sorts of things most people expect from a woman living biblically. Up until this point, I'd managed to avoid the fact that I'd planned a year of my life around a collection of ancient texts that routinely describe women as property.

It was time for a reality check.

Despite what some may claim, the Bible's not the best place to look for traditional family values as we understand them today. The text predates our Western construct of the nuclear family and presents us with a familial culture closer to that of a third-world country (or a TLC reality show) than that of Ward and June Cleaver. In ancient Israel, "biblical womanhood" looked different from woman to woman, depending on her status.

+ If you were a slave or concubine, you were expected to be sexually available to your master, ready to bear children on his wife's behalf should she not be able to conceive herself (Genesis 16:1–4; 30:3–4, 9–10; 35:22). The law permitted your master to beat you, but not to kill you (Exodus 21:20–21). Masters were encouraged to marry their female slaves and instructed to treat all of their wives equally, granting them comparable food, clothing, and conjugal rights (Exodus 21:7–11).

+ If you were a wife, you were still considered the property of your husband, but you enjoyed a higher status and more privileges than slaves (Exodus 20:17). Though your husband was not permitted to discriminate against you or your children because he favored one of his other wives, rivalry among you and the other wives would be common (Genesis 30:1–24, Exodus 21:10; Leviticus 18:18; Deuteronomy 21:15–17). Under normal circumstances, you could not inherit property, pursue divorce, or be trusted to make a vow (Deuteronomy 21:16–17; 24:1–4; Leviticus 27:1–8). Adultery was defined as sex with another man's wife, not mere infidelity, so your husband was permitted to venture outside of the marriage for sex. However, if you engaged in sexual relations with anyone besides your husband, you and your partner would be put to death (Deuteronomy 22:22). The mere suspicion of adultery could subject you to a strange ritual involving a drink concocted of holy water and dust that, if it made you sick, proved your guilt and sealed your fate (Numbers 5:11–31). Procreation was your most important duty as a wife, with infertility viewed exclusively as a female defect and often assumed to be a curse from God.

+ If you were widowed, you were to marry your husband's brother according to the Law of the Levirate Marriage found in Deuteronomy 25. The first son produced from this marriage would be considered the son of your late husband, "so that his name may not be blotted out from Israel" (v. 6). Since this situation could create a financial burden and would result in a reduced inheritance from their fathers, men often shirked the responsibility of taking a brother's wife. The law therefore permitted a woman to appeal to the elders of the land, who would summon the man and encourage him to fulfill his duty. If your brother-in-law still refused, you were instructed to strip his sandal from his foot, spit in his face, and publicly declare,

"This is what is done to the man who will not build up his brother's family line." According to the law, from that day forward, your brother-in-law's lineage would be spoken of in Israel as "The Family of the Unsandaled" (NIV).

+ If you were an unmarried daughter, you were considered the property of your father and could be either sold into slavery to pay off debt or married for a bride-price (Exodus 21:7; Nehemiah 5:5; Genesis 29:1–10). Marriages were typically arranged by the male members of the family before a girl reached puberty. While the virginity of your future husband was inconsequential, yours could mean the difference between life and death. If you failed to bleed on your wedding night, you were to be executed on the doorstep of your parents' home (Deuteronomy 22:21). However, if your new husband falsely accused you of premarital sex in order to get out of an unhappy marriage, your parents could save your life by producing evidence of your virginity in the form of bloodied sheets saved from the wedding night, thereby subjecting your husband to a heavy fine (Deuteronomy 22:13–19). If, before you were engaged, you slept with an Israelite man without your father's permission, the man would be required to pay your father the bride-price for virgins, regardless of whether he married you (Exodus 22:16–17). Daughters of priests who engaged in sexual relations outside of marriage were to be burned alive (Leviticus 21:9).[1]

+ If you were raped, your fate depended largely on where the event occurred. If it happened in the city, where presumably your cries for help should have been heard by passersby, you and your rapist were both stoned to death. If it happened in the country, out of earshot from the rest of the community, only your rapist was executed. If you were not already engaged when the rape occurred, you and your rapist were required to marry each other, without the possibility of divorce (Deuteronomy 22:28–29).

+ If you were a captive of war, you were considered plunder, along with any children, livestock, or treasure taken from the besieged city. You were permitted a brief time of mourning in which you shaved your head, trimmed your nails, and wept for those killed in battle. If you caught the eye of an Israelite soldier, he could marry you only after this time had passed and he could never treat you as a slave (Deuteronomy 21:10–14). However, if you were Hittite, Amorite, Canaanite, Perizzite, Hivite, or Jebusite, you were to be killed on the spot (Deuteronomy 20:10–16).

None of this information is easy to swallow. In light of passages like these, I have come to regard with some suspicion those who claim that the Bible never troubles them. I can only assume this means they haven't actually read it.

Clearly, I'd reached the limits of what I could authentically reproduce in my year of biblical womanhood. Most Jews and Christians have long abandoned the practices associated with hard patriarchy, so trying to conceive of how ancient Mesopotamian law would play out in the context of a modern Western society proved difficult. However, in my research, I did encounter a few groups committed to preserving as much of the patriarchal structure of Old Testament law as possible. They are part of what is known as the "biblical patriarchy movement," and perhaps the most influential of these groups is Vision Forum.

Founded by Doug Phillips, Vision Forum produces a prolific array of homeschool curricula, books, media, and even toys—all designed to bring "biblical patriarchy" back to modern-day culture. Calling for a return to "the eternal, unchanging truths found within the pages of Holy Scripture," Vision Forum released on its website a list of twenty-six principles that make up "The Tenets of Biblical Patriarchy."[2] Among these are admonitions that men serve as head of households, women work exclusively from the home, children are schooled at home, and young girls remain under the authority of their fathers until they are given in marriages that are overseen by their parents. Girls are typically discouraged from attending college and warned against the dangers of feminism, which Vision Forum describes as "an enemy of God and of biblical truth."

"While unmarried women may have more flexibility in applying the principle that women were created for a domestic calling," the document states, "it is not the ordinary and fitting role of women to work alongside men as their functional equals in public spheres of dominion (industry, commerce, civil government, the military, etc.)."

Sarah Schlissel of the Chalcedon Foundation fully accepts her role as a young woman in this patriarchal subculture. In an essay titled "Daddy's Girl: Courtship and a Father's Rights," she wrote, "I am owned by my father. If someone is interested in me, he should see him . . . No man can approach me as an independent agent because I am not my own, but belong, until marriage, to my father. At the time of my marriage, my father gives me away to my husband, and there is a lawful change in ownership. At that point, and at that point only, I am no longer bound to do my father's will. Instead, I must answer to my husband."[3]

The irony of course, is that while advocates of biblical patriarchy accuse everyone else of biblical selectivity, they themselves do not appear to be stoning adulterers, selling their daughters into slavery, taking multiple wives, or demanding that state laws be adjusted to include death sentences for rape victims . . . at least not yet. Those who decry the evils of selective literalism tend to be rather clumsy at spotting it in themselves.[4]

Still, like it or not, the Vision Forum's "Tenets of Biblical Patriarchy" bears a closer resemblance to what we actually find in the Bible than the 1950s throwback idealized by so many other groups in the "biblical womanhood" movement.

I've heard all kinds of explanations from Christian apologists for why the Bible includes such harsh laws about women: that the laws were progressive in comparison to the surrounding culture, that they were designed to protect women from exploitation, that they weren't strictly observed anyway. These are useful insights, I suppose, but sometimes I wish these apologists wouldn't be in such a hurry to explain these troubling texts away, that they would allow themselves to be bothered by them now and then.

As a Christian, I do take some comfort in the fact that Jesus got himself into quite a bit of trouble for his own selective literalism. Known for healing on the Sabbath, touching the untouchables, and fraternizing with prostitutes and tax collectors, Jesus liked to begin his sermons by quoting a passage of Scripture ("You have heard that it was said . . .") and then turning it on its head ("but I tell you . . ."). Perhaps the most famous example of this technique is captured in Matthew 5:43–45, where Jesus says, "You have heard that it was said, 'Love your neighbor and hate your enemy.' But I tell you, love your enemies and pray for those who persecute you, that you may be children of your Father in heaven" (UPDATED NIV).

This approach caused so much controversy in first-century Galilee that the religious leaders tried to test Jesus' commitment to the Scripture by bringing him a woman caught in the act of adultery. The man who shared her guilt makes no appearance in the story, but the Pharisees seemed intent upon executing the prescribed judgment upon the woman, right there in the temple courts.

"Teacher," they said to Jesus, "this woman was caught in the act of adultery. In the Law Moses commanded us to stone such women. Now what do you say?"

Jesus responded not with a sermon or a rebuke, but by stooping to the ground to write something in the sand with his finger. The text leaves the content of his message a mystery, though I'm sure you could find a handful of first-year seminarians happy to tell you exactly what it meant.

Frustrated, the Pharisees pressed Jesus again, to which he responded, "Let any of you who is without sin be the first to throw a stone at her."

He then went back to writing in the sand.

One by one the Pharisees left, starting with the oldest, until only the woman remained.

"Where are they?" Jesus asked her. "Has no one condemned you?"

"No one, sir," she said.

"Then neither do I condemn you. Go now and leave your life of sin" (John 8:3–11 UPDATED NIV).

Jesus once said that his mission was not to abolish the law, but to fulfill it. And in this instance, fulfilling the law meant letting it go. It may serve as little comfort to those who have suffered abuse at the hand of Bible-wielding literalists, but the disturbing laws of Leviticus and Deuteronomy lose just a bit of their potency when God himself breaks them.

> *Wives, in the same way, submit yourselves to*
> *your own husbands . . . For this is the way the*
> *holy women of the past who put their hope in*
> *God used to adorn themselves. They submitted*
> *themselves to their own husbands, like Sarah, who*
> *obeyed Abraham and called him her lord.*
> —1 PETER 3:1, 5–6 UPDATED NIV

"One week. That's as long as I can bring myself to do it."

"This translation says 'lord,'" Dan offered. "Should we use that instead?"

"Well, other translations say 'master,'" I responded, "which for some reason sounds less creepy to me . . . Or would you rather be called 'lord'?"

Dan looked as though he'd prefer a lobotomy to this conversation.

"I'd rather be called Dan, because both sound creepy, if you ask me. People are going to think I'm a jerk or that we're in a cult or something."

We sat at the dining room table, eating leftover Papa John's pizza for dinner and watching drops of frozen rain assail the sliding glass door. We were not really mad at each other, just stir-crazy and cold and a little on edge, as I expect any couple would be if they were stuck in the house, trying to figure out how to apply a two-thousand-year-old letter to their lives.

"I know!" I said. "We'll just play it like Larry Hagman and Barbara Eden."

I crossed my arms in front of me, and with a swift bob of my head, issued a cheery "Yes, Master!" then waited for a laugh.

Dan, who apparently managed to find his way through childhood without catching an *I Dream of Jeannie* marathon on Nick at Nite, looked at me like I'd cracked.

"This seems like it should be a turn-on, but it's not," he finally said.

The passage responsible for all this tension in the Evans home comes from a letter to the persecuted churches of Asia Minor attributed to Saint Peter. In it, Christian women are admonished to submit to their husbands and imitate Sarah, the wife of Abraham, who called her husband "master."

I wanted to try and take this passage as literally as possible, so we had some fun with it, working the *I Dream of Jeannie* bit whenever Dan asked me to pass the salt—"Yes, Master"—or beckoned me from another room—"I'll be right there, Master"—or requested help in locating his car keys—"Well, where the heck did you see them last, Master?"

We clipped along just fine until day 4, when suddenly, while exerting the extreme physical fortitude it takes to pull your pants down, I randomly threw my back out. The pain took my breath away and pulsed through my entire body after even the slightest movement. Somehow I managed to find my way to the living room recliner, where I perched like a hen on a nest of pillows for three days, watching *Cosmos* with Dan and complaining about all the Christmas shopping I wasn't doing.

Dan loves watching shows like *The Universe* and *Cosmos* because he says the vastness of space and time puts all the little stresses of life into perspective. These shows have the opposite effect on me, however, as I tend to experience a mini faith crisis each time Neil deGrasse Tyson cheerfully informs me that the earth's going to get burned up by the sun someday—if it's not smashed to bits by a meteor first. But what was I to do? This year, Dan was in charge of the remote control.

Obviously, this turn of events changed the routine a little. Dan remained master in name only, as my frail condition required some assistance: *Will you please get the heating pad for me, Master? Master, my water needs refilling. Oops, I dropped my pen, Master.*

At least he didn't have to worry about getting embarrassed in public any more.

I took some comfort in the fact that the woman hailed as my model for submission wasn't any good at it either. Saint Peter chose an unlikely candidate in Sarah, who in a pivotal moment in Israel's history usurped the wishes of Abraham, and apparently won the support of God in her defiance.

As the story goes, the aging Sarah urged Abraham to marry her slave Hagar so that she could bear him children on Sarah's behalf. Abraham obliged, and sure enough, Hagar became pregnant. This created considerable tension between Sarah and her slave, to the point that Sarah mistreated Hagar so badly, she fled. However God intervened, meeting Hagar at the famous well called Beer Lhai Roi to tell her that she would bear a son named Ishmael whose descends would be too numerous to count. Hagar returned and gave birth to Ishmael.

Not long after the birth of Ishmael, Sarah herself became pregnant and bore a son named Isaac. Concerned about the potential rivalry between the male offspring of the house, Sarah ordered Abraham to "get rid of that slave woman and her son, for that woman's son will never share in the inheritance with my son Isaac." Genesis 21 reports that "the matter distressed Abraham greatly," because he loved his son Ishmael and did not want to send him away. But God told Abraham, "Listen to whatever Sarah tells you," and so Abraham banished Hagar and her young son, who nearly died in the desert before God once again intervened to provide for them.

Frankly, the story makes Sarah look more like a potential cast member for *The Real Housewives of Canaan County* than a dutiful and submissive wife. But a survey of the Old Testament reveals that she was not alone, that, when it came to the futures of their families, the matriarchs often did whatever it took to get their way. Rebekah tricked her own blind husband into giving his blessing to her preferred son, Jacob. Rachel, despite being Jacob's second wife and barren throughout most of their marriage, ensured that her son Joseph won his father's favor over Leah's six older boys. What went down behind the flaps of the women's tents in Canaan influenced the fate of nations. Sarah's banishment of Hagar, for example, is hailed in both Jewish and Muslim traditions as the moment in which Islam was born.

"Master," it seems, is a relatively loose term.

Dan's Journal
December 13, 2010

Today marks the second day that Rachel has to call me "Master." I've specifically requested a few little things for her to do: put away some dishes, organize the mail, send our friend Quentin a bizarre instant message just for fun. Sure enough, she says, "Yes, Master," and does it! Though the words seem to depart from her lips with a bit of hesitation. The possibilities are quite tempting. Like maybe, "Clean out the garage." But it's pretty cold out there, and she's trying to finish writing the first few chapters of the book by the end of the month, so I don't think I'm going to have her do it.

Americans are obsessed with polygamy. My one-year stretch of biblical womanhood saw both the series premiere of TLC's *Sister*

Wives and the series finale of HBO's *Big Love*. Over the last decade, Warren Jeffs has become a household name, and Oprah's interview with the women of his polygamist ranch remains one of her most popular of all time. What was once a curious phenomenon at the fringes of fundamentalist Mormon culture has become a staple in the American entertainment diet.

Despite what some may think, the Bible never condemns polygamy. In fact, the reality of plural marriage in Ancient Near Eastern culture is implicit in many Old Testament laws concerning slaves, concubines, and levirate marriage. Some of the Bible's greatest heroes boasted multiple wives and handmaidens. Abraham had three. Jacob had four. David had eight wives and at least ten concubines, and according to 2 Samuel 12:8, these wives were given to him by God. Gideon had enough wives to produce seventy sons, and Solomon kept himself busy with a harem that included seven hundred princesses and three hundred concubines.

In many of these cases, the man's consequent procreative prowess is listed by the writers of Scripture as one of his most worthy virtues. While the New Testament speaks little of plural marriage, 1 Timothy 3:2 includes the apostle Paul's requirement that a church leader be "the husband of one wife" (NKJV) suggesting that, by that point in history, polygamy was not considered the ideal.

I wanted to track down a modern-day polygamist family to see what they had to say about the Bible and plural marriage. Given the nature of this lifestyle (illegal in all fifty states), I figured this would be a challenge, but as it turns out, the internet makes it pretty easy to find people. After a few days of searching, I happened upon BiblicalFamilies.org.

Run by a group of "Bible-believing Christians" who share "a deep burden for strengthening families who accept or practice plural marriage," BiblicalFamilies.org provides support and information to men and women engaged in or interested in pursuing polygamy.

But what surprised me the most about this Biblical Families

organization was that the people running it are not Mormon, but evangelical. The group identifies themselves as "Berean" in their approach, meaning they emphasize the primacy of Scripture, "taking at face value God's Word, and not depending so much on the traditions, and additions, of man . . . which of course is how we came to recognize the Biblical soundness of plural marriage."

I contacted Biblical Families about the possibility of an interview and immediately heard back from a man named Eric, who said his first wife, Lynn, felt comfortable sharing their story in more detail.[5] So for the next few months, Lynn and I corresponded via e-mail about her "biblical" lifestyle, which included a husband, a sister wife, and four children, ages ten to fifteen.

The daughter of a Baptist minister, Lynn grew up in Florida in the seventies. Her parents divorced when she was seven, a disruptive jolt in Lynn's childhood. While studying music at a community college in Florida, Lynn got involved in a nondenominational evangelical church, where she met Eric. "I decided about that time that what I really wanted to do was stay home and raise a family," says Lynn. "I love being a homemaker. I love being a mom. My family is my job, and I feel I do it well."

The two married, and about eight years later had a son together. Unbeknownst to Lynn, during her pregnancy, Eric developed feelings for a single woman at the church, named Rose—a new believer and herself a child of divorce. Still in love with Lynn and determined to avoid an affair, Eric turned to the Bible (and an internet search for "Christian polygamy") for guidance. After some research and prayer, Eric told Rose about his feelings and his newfound interest in plural marriage. Rose confessed that she cared for Eric, and told him she would consider his proposed solution to their quandary.

"Well, now Eric had some hard decisions to make," Lynn recalled. "He decided it was time to tell me about his new belief and about his growing feelings for Rose. It did not go over very well with me, as you might expect, but he was patient and tried his best to lovingly explain things. He gave me websites to look at and other material he had collected during his research. I knew I had to decide to either leave my marriage or learn what Christian plural marriage was all about. It took time, but God was with us, and eventually, about a year later, Rose joined our family."

Eric and Rose had three children together—a boy and twin girls. For the first seven years, the entire family lived in the same home (Lynn and Rose had separate bedrooms), but now they live in two houses within walking distance of one another. Eric, a computer programmer, usually spends three nights a week at Lynn's house and three nights at Rose's, with the seventh night flexible. Everyone gathers together for dinner at the end of each day.

"We never take the schedule too seriously," Lynn said. "We change it depending on what is going on in our lives. I usually cook Monday, Wednesday, and Friday. Rose cooks Tuesday, Thursday, and Saturday. Sunday is whoever feels like cooking, or whoever has food in the fridge!"

Rose's kids often spend the night at Lynn's, especially on weekends and during the summer.

"Rose and I are both involved in our children's schools," said Lynn. "When the kids were all in the same school for a year, we had a few funny moments of 'who is with whom?' but for the most part, people don't take the time to think much about it. The family in general has been so redefined in the last fifty years—divorce, single parents needing help from grandparents, gay unions—that people don't ask too many questions. We don't try to purposefully hide our family, but we don't share every detail with people who are just acquaintances . . . We just let people think what they think—that we are friends, we are step-parents who get along with each other well, etc."

I asked Lynn if she ever felt misunderstood.

"Most people think it's all about sex," she said. "That is like saying every man, and woman for that matter, only gets married for sex. Yes, sex is part of marriage, but it is by no means the sole reason for marriage or the most important factor. And then there's the idea that only weak, stupid, or brainwashed women would choose plural marriage. I find this opinion very offensive, as you might guess, and completely false."

While the polygamists featured in *Sister Wives* and Biblical Families say that their intentions are to try and normalize plural marriage, biblical accounts of polygamy provide the kind of dramatic reality-TV fodder that would make even The Donald drool. For a man to love one wife more than another was so common in biblical times that laws had to be made to protect the rights of the unloved wife's offspring (Deuteronomy 21:15–17). Jacob loved Rachel more than Leah (Genesis 30), and Elkanah loved Hannah more than Peninnah (1 Samuel 1). King Ahasuerus ditched Vashti before he made Esther queen. Competition between wives to produce sons for their husbands led to fights over mandrakes, the use of surrogates as pawns, provocation, banishment, and a few epic meltdowns that included outbursts like "Give me children, or I'll die!" (Genesis 30:1); "Get rid of [her!]" (Genesis 21:10); and "Don't I mean more to you than ten sons?" (1 Samuel 1:8). It seems that even the writers of the Torah found some entertainment value in polygamy. I suspect it is no accident that the Bible never uses the phrase "sister wife" when referring to a female members of a polygamous household. Instead, the author of 1 Samuel chose the word "rival" (1:6–7).

> *There is no agony like bearing an*
> *untold story inside of you.*
> —MAYA ANGELOU

I'm glad I have a biblical name. It's a name as old as the storied shepherdess of Paddan Aram—a woman so captivating her husband pledged seven years of service in exchange for her hand, a woman whose determination to bear children sent her digging for mandrakes and bargaining with God, a woman brazen enough to steal her father's idols and hide them in a camel saddle, a woman who took her last breath on the side of the road, giving birth, a woman whose tomb survived obscurity, conquest, earthquakes, and riots to become one of the most venerated and contested sites of the Holy Land.

Beautiful, impetuous, jealous Rachel. Rachel who fought to legitimize her existence the only way she knew how. Rachel who, though it killed her, won.

With Rachel, I notice the details. I absorb her stories as a child does, wide-eyed and attentive, the distance between long ago and yesterday as close as a memory. And like a child, I long for more, wishing at times that I could sit beneath Anita Diamant's fictionalized Red Tent, where Dinah learned the history of her family from four mothers—Leah, Rachel, Bilhah, and Zilpah—who Dinah says "held my face between their hands and made me swear to remember."

We recall with ease the narratives of Scripture that include a triumphant climax—a battle won, a giant slain, chariots swallowed by the sea. But for all of its glory and grandeur, the Bible contains a darkness you will only notice if you pay attention, for it is hidden in the details, whispered in the stories of women.

My quest for biblical womanhood led me to these stories late at night, long after Dan had gone to sleep, and I conducted my nightly research by his side in bed, stacks of Bibles and commentaries and legal pads threatening to swallow him should he roll over. The darkest of these stories mingled with my dreams, and I awoke the next morning startled as if I'd been told a terrible secret.

Perhaps the most troubling of the dark stories comes from the lawless period of Judges.

Jephthah was a mighty warrior of Gilead and the son of a prostitute. Banished from the city by Gilead's legitimate sons, he took up with a gang of outlaws in the land of Tob. Jephthah must have earned a reputation as a valiant fighter because, years later, when the Gileadites faced war with the Ammonites, the elders summoned Jephthah and asked him to command their forces.

When Jephthah reminded them that they had expelled him

from the city, they promised to make him their leader if he agreed. The opportunity to rule over those who once despised him proved too much for Jephthah to resist. As Jephthah charged into battle with his countrymen behind him, filled with "the Spirit of the LORD" (Judges 11:29), he made a promise to God: "If you give the Ammonites into my hands, whatever comes out of the door of my house to meet me when I return in triumph from the Ammonites will be the LORD's, and I will sacrifice it as a burnt offering" (v. 30).

The text reports that God indeed gave victory to Jephthah. He and his troops devastated twenty Ammonite towns, thus deterring the Ammonite king from further attacks. When Jephthah returned home, glowing with sweat and triumph, "who should come out to meet him but his daughter, dancing to the sound of tambourines" (v. 34). She was a virgin and his only child. The Bible never reveals her name.

When he saw her, Jephthah tore his clothes and wept. Surely he had expected an animal to come wandering out of the first floor of his home where they would have been stabled, not his daughter. He told his daughter of his vow and said he could not break it. The young girl resolutely accepted her fate. She asked only that she be granted two months to roam the hills and weep with her friends over a life cut short.

Unlike the familiar story of Isaac, this one ends without divine intervention. Jephthah fulfilled his promise and killed his daughter in God's name. No ram was heard bleating from the thicket. No protest was issued from the clouds. No tomb was erected to mark the place where she lay.

But the women of Israel remembered.

Wrote the narrator, "From this comes the Israelite tradition that each year the young women of Israel go out for four days to commemorate the daughter of Jephthah" (vv. 39–40).

They could not protect her life, but they could protect her dignity by retelling her story—year after year, for four days, in a mysterious and subversive ceremony that perhaps led the women of Israel back to the same hills in which Jephthah's daughter wandered before her death. It was a tradition that appears to have continued through the writing of the book of Judges. But it is a tradition lost to the waxing and waning of time, no longer marked by the daughters of the Abrahamic faiths.

I wanted to do something to bring this ceremony back, so I invited my friend Kristine over to help me honor the victims of the Bible's "texts of terror."

This may sound strange coming from a woman who calls her husband "Master" from time to time, but Kristine is something of an eccentric. Young, dreamy, and fiercely intelligent, she feels everything with such intensity that her laugh will startle you and her sadness frighten you. Having recently emerged from an uncommonly sheltered childhood, Kristine is only now learning how to interpret and respond to social cues, and so she navigates the idiomatic affectations of Southern culture with a sort of clumsy charm that disarms those of us who have grown too accustomed to them.

Once, when Kristine and I were at our friend Megan's apartment, wrapping Christmas presents for our church's angel tree, I complimented Megan on how tidy and inviting she keeps her home.

"Oh, you should see my bedroom closet," Megan said. "That's where I stuff everything before people come over."

"Can I?" Kristine asked.

A little caught off guard, Megan agreed.

Kristine went into the bedroom, opened the closet, laughed a little bit before returning to the living room to say, "Yeah, it's a total wreck in there, but I still want to be your friend."

That pretty much sums up Kristine.

We prepared for the ceremony for weeks—Kristine with wood and paint, I with poetry and prose. Finally, just before Christmas, while the tree was lit and paper snowflakes hung from the windows, Kristine came over with a heavy paper bag in her arms. We sat on the living room floor with the coffee table between us and began the ceremony.

We started with the daughter of Jephthah, whose legacy inspired me to honor her the way Israel's daughters once did. I read her story from Judges 11, followed by a short poem by Phyllis Trible recounting the young girl's tragic end. Kristine lit a tall, white taper candle on the coffee table, and together we said, "We remember the daughter of Jephthah."

Then Kristine read the story of the concubine from Judges 19 who was thrown to a mob by her husband, gang-raped, killed, and dismembered. I lit a tiny tea candle, and together we said, "We remember the unnamed concubine."

Next we honored Hagar, whose banishment from the house of Abraham nearly cost her life. I read her story from Genesis 21 and a poem by Tamam Kahn titled "No Less Than the Prophets, Hagar Speaks." For Hagar, we set aside a damask votive, which we lit before saying together, "We remember Hagar."

Finally, we remembered the Tamar of the Davidic narrative, whose rape in the king's house left her desolate and without a future. A heartbreaking poem from Nicola Slee pulled each of the stories together and connected them to the silent victims of misogyny from around the world. We resolved as Slee to "listen, however painful the hearing . . . until there is not one last woman remaining who is a victim of violence."[6] We lit a white pillar candle and said together, "We remember Tamar."

Then Kristine unveiled her diorama. Constructed of a small pinewood box turned on its side, the diorama featured five faceless wooden figures, huddled together beneath a ring of barbed wire. Nails jutted out from all sides, with bloodred paint splattered across the scene. Glued to the backboard was a perfect reflection of the five feminine silhouettes cut from the pages of a book. Around this Kristine had painted a red crown of thorns to correspond with the circle of barbed wire. Across the top were printed the words of Christ—"As you have done unto the least of these, so you have done to me." Kristine and I talked for a while after the ceremony was over—about our doubts, about our fears, and about how sometimes taking the Bible seriously means confronting the parts we don't like or understand and sitting with them for a while . . .

perhaps even a lifetime. Ours was a simple ceremony, but I think it honored these women well.

Those who seek to glorify biblical womanhood have forgotten the dark stories. They have forgotten that the concubine of Bethlehem, the raped princess of David's house, the daughter of Jephthah, and the countless unnamed women who lived and died between the lines of Scripture exploited, neglected, ravaged, and crushed at the hand of patriarchy are as much a part of our shared narrative as Deborah, Esther, Rebekah, and Ruth. We may not have a ceremony through which to grieve them, but it is our responsibility as women of faith to guard the dark stories for our own daughters, and when they are old enough, to hold their faces between our hands and make them promise to remember.

What, Sir, would the people of earth be without woman?
They would be scarce, sir, almighty scarce.
—MARK TWAIN

Okay, I'm just going to come right out and say it: A lot of women secretly hate Christmas.

Now, don't get me wrong. We love that picturesque moment in which the tree is lit, the fire is crackling, and children outfitted in matching candy-cane pajamas dance around the living room to Tchaikovsky, showing off armfuls of new toys while a twenty-pound ham bakes in the oven; we just hate the anxiety disorder we developed while attempting to produce it.

There seems to be some kind of universal agreement that the advances achieved through women's liberation need not apply during the holidays. It's as though the first trumpet peals of "It's the Most Wonderful Time of the Year" sent blasting over the PA at Bed Bath & Beyond are designed to trigger an internal short that shocks us all into Stepford mode, donning aprons and strained smiles and sweaters that have no business surviving another decade.

From the baking aisle to the post office line to the wrapping paper bin in the attic, women populate every forgotten corner of Christmas. Who got up at 4 a.m. to put the ham in the oven? A woman. Who elbowed you out of the last reindeer Pillow Pet left on the shelf? A woman. Who sent the Christmas card describing her eighteen-year-old son's incarceration as "a short break before college"? A woman. Who remembered to include batteries at the bottom of each stocking? A woman. And who gets the credit for pulling it all off?

Santa.

That's right. A man.

Oh, we would be a lot angrier about all of this if we weren't so tired. But by the time the 25th rolls around, we're all out of fight. Drained of our humanity, we have more important things to attend to—dishes, returns, disappointed in-laws, and a mild addiction to whatever holiday-themed Starbucks product we were pumping through our systems that year.

Christmas 2010 was no different for me, only this time I'd managed to add to my schedule a list of rabbis to contact, two more interviews to conduct, a writing deadline to meet, and a crisis of faith to worry about, thanks to Neil deGrasse Tyson and all those late-night sessions with the Bible's "texts of terror."

The year ended in a flurry of disjointed activities and fattening foods. Dayton saw its first white Christmas in twenty-one years. Under the tree was wrapped a present that said "To Master, from Rachel." We saw old friends and ate out a lot. Dan and I went to bed as soon as the ball dropped on New Year's Eve, like a couple of old fogies.

Somewhere in the midst of it all, I got an interesting e-mail:

Hello. I'm an Orthodox Jew who is interested in your "living biblical womanhood" project. For the record, in Bereshit (Genesis by you) where it talks about the "helpmeet," the Hebrew is not just Ezer, but Ezer k'gnedo, which means "the help that opposes." The Rabbis explain this term like two posts of equal weight leaned against one another. They stand because of equal force. My husband is a rabbi and he actually debated a complementarian evangelical once. The guy totally expected to have him on his side, but he was wrong! Anyway, thanks for taking on such an interesting project. I think Christians and Jews would get along a lot better if everyone paid more attention to what the Bible actually teaches. Let me know if you want to talk more! Blessings from Jerusalem.

—Ahava.

I'd finally found a Jewish source . . . and she was even better than a rabbi.

MARY, THE MOTHER OF GOD

There's a misconception among some Protestants that Catholic and Orthodox Christians worship the Virgin Mary. The icons, the rosary, the crowning, the Marian hymns—it's all a bit much, and so they dismiss out of hand any language of veneration that might elevate the mother of Jesus to a place of special esteem and call it idolatry.

It's a shame, really, because Mary has so much to teach us.

Like Eve, the mother of Jesus has been subjected to countless embellishments of the religious imagination— some of them fair, some of them more reflective of the prejudices and projections of the societies from which they came. Often she appears as a foil to Eve: the redemption of womankind and the standard of female virtue. Standing triumphantly atop the temptation scene on Notre Dame Cathedral's western facade is the statue of the crowned Mary, her royal robes grazing the top of the Eve's head. "What had been laid to waste in ruin by this sex," Tertullian wrote, "was by the same sex re-established in salvation. Eve had believed the serpent; Mary believed Gabriel. That which the one destroyed by believing, the other, by believing, set straight."

That a woman who managed to be both a virgin and a mother is often presented as God's standard for womanhood and can be frustrating for those of us who have to work within the constraints of physical law. Indeed, visions of Mary's virtue have been amplified though the centuries, far beyond what we find in the biblical text. The apocryphal Protoevangelium of James presents Mary as sinless, a perpetual virgin who spent the first three years of her life living in the temple and being fed by angels, and who somehow managed to give birth in a first-century Palestinian barn without feeling an ounce of pain. In 1854 the Catholic Church formally embraced as dogma the Immaculate Conception— the belief that Mary was born without the stain of original sin. It's as though, over time, Mary's feet have gotten farther and farther off the ground.

Much could be said in contrast about the "real Mary" of the biblical narrative: the teenage girl from Nazareth who gave birth on a dirty stable floor; the terrified mom who scurried frantically through the streets of Jerusalem, looking for her lost little boy; the woman who had enough influence over Jesus to convince him to liven up a wedding with his first miracle of turning water into wine; the grieved mother who wept in the shadow of the cross. But perhaps the most revealing glimpse into Mary's true character can be found in the Magnificat—a prayer beloved by saints and Southern Baptists alike.

According to Luke's gospel, when Mary was betrothed to Joseph, God sent the angel Gabriel to deliver an important message. His presence and his words frightened the young girl.

"Do not be afraid, Mary," said Gabriel. "You have found favor with God. You will conceive and give birth to a son, and you are to call him Jesus. He will be great and will be called the Son of the Most High. The Lord God will give him the throne of his father David, and he will reign over Jacob's descendants forever; his kingdom will never end."

"How will this be," Mary asked the angel, "since I am a virgin?"

Gabriel told Mary that the Holy Spirit would come over her: the "power of the Most High will overshadow you."

"I am the Lord's servant," Mary said resolutely. "May your word to me be fulfilled" (1:30–38 UPDATED NIV).

Fully yielded to the will of God, this young, peasant girl offered a bold and subversive prayer that reveals her own hopes for this special child and the future of Israel:

> My soul glorifies the Lord
> and my spirit rejoices in God my Savior,
> for he has been mindful
> of the humble state of his servant.
> From now on all generations will call me blessed,
> for the Mighty One has done great things for me—
> holy is his name.
> His mercy extends to those who fear him,
> from generation to generation.
> He has performed mighty deeds with his arm;
> he has scattered those who are proud in their inmost
>   thoughts.
> He has brought down rulers from their thrones
> but has lifted up the humble.
> He has filled the hungry with good things
> but has sent the rich away empty.
> He has helped his servant Israel,
> remembering to be merciful
> to Abraham and his descendants forever,
> just as he promised our ancestors.
>
> (VV. 46–55)

With this prayer, we encounter Mary as *Theotokos*—the Mother of God, a Greek term that sends many Protestants running for their commentaries, but which beautifully connects the humanity of Mary with her divine call. It comes from the Orthodox Church, and more accurately means "God-bearer" or, "the one who gives birth to God." *Theotokos* refers not to Mary as the mother of God from all eternity, but as the mother of God incarnate. She is what made Jesus both fully God and fully man, her womb the place where heaven and earth meld into one.

At the heart of Mary's worthiness is her obedience, not to a man, not to a culture, not even to a cause or a religion, but to the creative work of a God who lifts up the humble and fills the hungry with good things.

Madeleine L'Engle connects this type of obedience to our own everyday acts of creation. "Obedience is an unpopular word nowadays," she wrote, "but the artist must be obedient to the work, whether it be a symphony, a painting, or a story for a small child. I believe that each work of art, whether it is a work of great genius, or something very small, comes to the artist and says, 'Here I am. Enflesh me. Give birth to me.' And the artist can either say, 'My soul doth magnify the Lord,' and willingly become the bearer of the work, or refuses; but the obedient response is not necessarily a conscious one, and not everyone has the humble, courageous obedience of Mary."[7]

The same applies to faith. One need not be a saint, or even a mother, to become a bearer of God. One needs only to obey. The divine resides in all of us, but it is our choice to magnify it or diminish it, to ignore it or to surrender to its lead.

"Mary did not always understand," wrote L'Engle, "but one does not have to understand to be obedient. Instead of understanding—that intellectual understanding which we are so fond of—there is a feeling of rightness, of knowing, knowing things which you are not yet able to understand."[8]

Like a good Protestant should, I think Mary's act of radical obedience means more when she is one of us. Imperfect. Afraid. Capable of feeling all the pain and doubt and fear that come with delivering God into the world. But I suspect I may also be a bit of a Catholic, for on the rare occasion that I yield myself fully to the will of God, when I write or speak or do the dishes to magnify the Lord, I start to see Mary everywhere.

January: Valor

Will the Real Proverbs 31 Woman Please Stand Up?

A wife of noble character who can find?

—PROVERBS 31:10

IN THE EVANGELICAL CHRISTIAN SUBCULTURE, THERE ARE three people a girl's got to know about before she gets her period: (1) Jesus, (2) Ronald Reagan, and (3) the Proverbs 31 woman.

While the first two are thought to embody God's ideal for all mankind, the third is thought to represent God's ideal for women. Wander into any Christian women's conference, and you will hear her name whispered around the coffee bar and lauded from the speaker's podium. Visit a Christian bookstore, and you will find entire women's sections devoted to books that extol her virtues and make them applicable to modern wives. At my Christian college, guys described their ideal date as a "P31 girl," and young women looking to please them held a "P31 Bible Study" in my dormitory lounge at 11 p.m. on Mondays. She's like the evangelical's Mary—venerated, idealized, glorified to the level of demigoddess, and yet expected to show up in every man's kitchen at dinnertime. Only unlike Mary, there is no indication that the Proverbs 31 woman actually existed.

The subject of a twenty-two-line poem found in the last chapter of the book of Proverbs, the "wife of noble character" is a tangible expression of the book's celebrated virtue of wisdom. She appears in an oracle attributed to the mysterious King Lemuel that the text says was taught to him by his mother. Although the genre of royal instruction is a familiar one in ancient Near Eastern literature, this poem stands out in its representation of the queen mother as the source of wisdom and remains the longest, most flattering tribute to women of its time. Packed with hyperbolic imagery, the poem is an acrostic, so the first word of each verse begins with the next consecutive letter of the Hebrew alphabet. This communicates a sense of totality as the poet praises the everyday achievements of an upper-class Jewish wife, a woman who keeps her household functioning day and night by buying, trading, investing, planting, sewing, weaving, managing servants, extending charity, providing food for the family, and preparing for each season. She is so accomplished, in fact, that translators can't seem to agree on an adjective to describe her. Depending on who you ask, a lucky man will find (v. 10):

+ "a good wife" (New Century Version)
+ "an excellent wife" (New American Standard)
+ "a competent wife" (Common English Bible)
+ "a capable wife" (Good News Translation)
+ "a virtuous and capable wife" (New Living Translation)
+ "a wife of noble character" (New International Version)
+ "a virtuous woman" (King James Version)
+ "a worthy woman" (American Standard Version)
+ "a valiant woman" (Douay-Rheims American Edition)
+ "a capable, intelligent, and virtuous woman" (Amplified Bible)

However, most scholars seem to think that the Hebrew *eshet chayil* is best translated "valorous woman," for the structure and diction employed in the poem closely resembles that of a heroic poem celebrating the exploits of a warrior. Lost to English readers are the militaristic nuances found in the original language (*emphasis added*): "she provides *food* for her family" (literally, "prey," v. 15); "her husband . . . lacks *nothing of value*" (literally, "booty," v. 11); "she *watches* over the affairs of the household" (literally, "spies," v. 27); "she *girds herself with strength*" (literally, "she girds her loins," v. 17 kjv); "she can *laugh* at the days to come" (literally, "laugh in victory," v. 15). According to Erika Moore, "the valorous wife is a heroic figure used by God to do good for His people, just as the ancient judges and kings did good for God's people by their martial exploits."[1]

Like any good poem, the purpose of this one is to draw attention to the often-overlooked glory of the everyday. The only instructive language it contains is directed toward men, with the admonition that a thankful husband honor his wife "for all that her hands have done" (Proverbs 31:31). Old Testament scholar Ellen F. Davis notes that the poem was intended "not to honor one particularly praiseworthy woman, but rather to underscore the central significance of women's skilled work in a household-based economy." She concludes that "it will not do to make facile comparisons between the biblical figure and the suburban housewife, or alternately between her and the modern career woman."[2]

And yet many Christians interpret this passage prescriptively, as a command to women rather than an ode to women, with the home-based endeavors of the Proverbs 31 woman cast as the ideal lifestyle for all women of faith. An empire of books, conferences, products, and media has evolved from a subtle repositioning of the poem's intended audience from that of men to that of women. One of the more popular books is titled *Becoming the Woman God Wants Me to Be: A 90 Day Guide to Living the Proverbs 31 Life*. No longer presented as a song through which a man offers his wife praise, Proverbs 31 is presented as a task list through which a woman earns it.

The Proverbs 31 woman looms so large over the biblical womanhood ethos that I knew I had to work her into my project somehow. So I decided to take a page from the literalists and turn the whole chapter into a to-do list, based on various Bible translations, divided into daily tasks and tasks to be accomplished by the end of the month. I combed through every line of the poem and went through several drafts before generating the final list, which I stuck on the refrigerator:

EVERY DAY

- ☐ Get up before dawn—"She gets up while it is still dark" (v. 15).
- ☐ Practice contemplative prayer—"A woman who fears the LORD should be praised" (v. 30)
- ☐ Work out those arms—"She girds herself with strength and makes her arms strong" (v. 17)
- ☐ Make every meal and keep the house clean—"She provides food for her family" (v. 15); "She watches over the affairs of the home" (v. 27)
- ☐ Do something nice for Dan—"She does him good and not evil" (v. 12); "Her husband has full confidence in her" (v. 11)
- ☐ Avoid TV, Facebook, and Twitter—"[She] does not eat the bread of idleness" (v. 27)
- ☐ Keep working until 9 p.m.—"Her lamp does not go out at night" (v. 18)

TO DO THIS MONTH:

- ☐ Learn to sew—In her hand she holds the distaff and grasps the spindle with her fingers (v. 19); She selects wool and flax and works with eager hands (v. 13)
- ☐ Make a purple dress to wear—She makes coverings for herself; her clothing is fine linen and purple (v. 22)
- ☐ Knit a red scarf and/or hat for Dan—"When it snows, she has no fear for her household, for all of them are clothed in scarlet" (v. 21)

- ☐ Make pillows for the bedroom—"She makes coverings for her bed" (v. 22)
- ☐ Create a Proverbs 31 beauty queen sash to auction on eBay for charity—"She makes linen garments and sells them, and supplies the merchants with sashes" (v. 24); "She opens her arms to the poor and extends her hands to the needy" (v. 20)
- ☐ Make Martha Stewart's chicken curry—"She is like merchant ships, bringing her food from afar" (v. 14)
- ☐ Invest in real estate or community-supported agriculture—"She considers a field and buys it; out of her earnings, she plants a vineyard" (v. 16)
- ☐ Praise Dan at the city gate—"Her husband is respected at the city gate, where he takes his seat among the elders of the land" (v. 23)
- ☐ Work once a week at the health clinic—"She opens her arms to the poor and extends her hands to the needy" (v. 20)

You will notice that sewing projects occupy a disproportionate space on the list. This was cause for considerable concern, seeing as I didn't know how to sew . . . at all. I couldn't attach a button to a blouse if my life depended on it, and I'd never hemmed a pair of pants with anything besides duct tape. I owned very few sewing supplies. I'd never read a pattern. I thought thimbles only existed in fairy tales.

My mother took one look at the list and declared matter-of-factly, "You can't do this."

Which I took as my cue to gird up my loins and give it a go.

She selects wool and flax and works with eager hands.

—Proverbs 31:13

Page 14 of *Sewing for Dummies* warns that when it comes to selecting a machine, novice sewers have an unfortunate tendency to "drag out Aunt Millie's 75 year old clunker from the garage or basement thinking it's good enough for a beginner," which according to Jan Saunders is a huge mistake, because "just like your car, you want your sewing machine to be dependable."[3]

Well, I'll have you know I did no such thing.

Instead we dragged out my sister-in-law Debbie's twenty-five-year-old Simplicity 8130 from the attic, knowing perfectly well that it was good enough for a beginner, especially one who can't afford a dependable car, much less a sewing machine that costs about as much. The instruction manual was nowhere to be found, but an orange pouch containing a tiny screwdriver, three spools of thread, and a pin cushion had been taped to the side. I heaved the machine onto the dining room table, consulted the diagram in my *Dummies* book, and plugged it in. The little lightbulb glowed brightly. When I stepped on the pedal, the machine issued a gentle humming noise, and the needle started hopping up and down like a jackhammer. It worked.

Well, now. That seems like enough sewing for one day, I thought.

My aversion to crafting goes way back to an incident in kindergarten during which, upon gluing something like the fortieth Cheerio to the inside of a giant O-shaped construction paper cutout, I was suddenly struck by the futility of human existence. I must have cried about it because I was sent home with a note saying that I'd misbehaved during craft time. Mom should not have been surprised. I think I inherited my resistance to all glue-related activities from her. She rarely crafted, except for a short period of time in the late '80s when she earned extra money making giant hair bows that have rendered every photo taken of me between the years 1988 and 1992 too mortifying to frame. Mom had been forced to cut out patterns on many a Saturday afternoon as a kid, so she never pushed Amanda or me into sewing or knitting, and in fact spoke rather darkly about the old days of fabric and needles and seams, the way veterans speak of 'Nam.

This was fine by me. Precision has never been my strong suit, and the skills required for sewing just happen to include four things I habitually stink at—patience, cutting a straight line, working with machinery, and fractions.

I'm especially insecure about fractions. Fractions make me feel scattered and panicked, like I'm about to forget something important. Add a couple of fractions together incorrectly and you'll end up with an 800 on your SAT or too much onion powder in your casserole. Either way, you're just a few decimal points away from disaster.

Sure enough, taunting me from the inscrutable pattern for my Simplicity Misses Lounge Dress was a call for 3 1/8 yards of fabric, 2 5/8 yards of 3/8-inch-wide flat lace, and 5/8 yards of fusible interfacing. I chose the pattern because it promised to be easy, "sew easy," according to the package, that I could make it in a few hours. The fact that the dress made the wisp of a model in the photo on the front look like an overstuffed piñata in floral didn't bother me. At the time I was more concerned about making the dress than wearing it.

I purchased the dress pattern and a pillow-making kit at Wal-Mart, but the rest of my materials required a trip to Chattanooga and the nearest Hobby Lobby. If ever one should wish to see a modern incarnation of the Proverbs 31 woman in her natural habitat, Hobby Lobby would be the place to start. Jazzy worship music played over the PA, while petite, white-haired ladies carrying homemade totes glided through the fabric rolls, humming along and smiling politely at the raccoon-eyed crafting hipsters who darted across their paths.

When Dan first came to Tennessee, he'd never heard of Hobby Lobby and was in for an epic letdown when he saw for himself that the big-box store contained seven aisles of scrapbooking materials but not an RC plane in sight. I left him behind for this trip, on account of the sheer magnitude of my shopping list: dressmaker's shears, needles, thread, a tape measure, double-sided fabric tape, size 17 knitting needles, bulky red yarn, two 6 x 26-inch pieces of bridal satin, iron-on letters, 72-inch trim ribbon, a decorative pin, an 18-inch square pillow form, 3 1/8 yards of purple fabric, 2 5/8 yards of 3/8-inch-wide flat lace, and 5/8 yard of fusible interfacing, whatever the heck that was.

I drove out to Hobby Lobby on a cold January morning, one of those days when the sky is low and gray, and you feel like the whole world's stuck in a Tupperware container. I asked Jesus to give me a sweet, grandmotherly clerk at the fabric counter, but apparently Jesus had more important things to do because when I approached the table with a crumpled list in my hands and a jaunty grin on my face, a stern woman in her sixties looked back at me with a frown and asked, "How can I help you?"

Now, my mother may have skipped the sewing lessons, but she passed along to Amanda and me an uncanny ability to schmooze our way through customer service encounters until we get exactly what we want, with no hurt feelings on either side. Mom's exploits in this arena are legendary. She recently convinced Lowe's to replace all the blinds in her house for free, with an upgrade, because she was concerned that the cords on her old blinds could be a choking hazard for grandkids. (She doesn't even have any grandkids yet . . . and she told them so!)

So I took a deep breath, glanced at the lady's name tag, and turned on the Held charm.

"Hi . . . *Maude* . . . How's it going?"

No response.

"Well, you are not going to believe this," I said, leaning in closer, as if I had a secret, "but I have never sewed a thing in my life. Never even picked up a needle and thread."

Nothing.

"So anyway, I have three significant sewing projects to finish by the end of the month for a book I'm working on—I'm an author, by the way—and a list of supplies that I don't even understand, so I'm really glad you're here, because I desperately need an expert—"

"Did you have a question?" she interrupted.

So maybe I wasn't as good at this as my mom. I probably should have stuck with basic self-deprecation without veering into desperation.

"Yeah. What the heck is fusible interfacing?"

Turns out Maude is more of a get-down-to-business kind of girl. I handed her my list, and she helped me select and measure my fabric and thread (both plum purple to fulfill Proverbs 31, and both 100 percent cotton to fulfill Leviticus 19:19), pick out the right-sized knitting needles and yarn, find a package of iron-on letters for my Proverbs 31 sash, choose better material for the aforementioned sash, stock up on supplies, and gather 5/8 of a yard of fusible interfacing, which according to Maude would give my "lounge dress" a little more body and shape. We weren't exactly best friends at the end of it, and I didn't get anything for free, but I think I saw a smile creep across the corner of Maude's mouth when I asked where they kept the duct tape, just in case.

She gets up while it is still dark . . . She
sees that her trading is profitable, and
her lamp does not go out at night.
—PROVERBS 31:15, 18

By the second week of January, the Proverbs 31 woman and I were not on the best of terms.

Our friendship was doomed from the start, really, because the two of us have nothing in common. The Proverbs 31 woman has children; I don't. She is rich; I drive a '94 Plymouth Acclaim. She loves to work with her hands; I can't make a row of stitches without dropping one. And worst of all, the Proverbs 31 woman is a morning person, and I am most assuredly not.

As a writer, my body's been conditioned to mimic the sleep cycle of artists, evening news anchors, and potheads. I may be on Eastern Standard Time, but my muse is on Pacific. Dan, on the other hand, leaps out of bed every morning with a smile on his face and a song in his heart, a habit that would probably destroy our marriage if I didn't normally sleep through it. On the rare occasions that I join him, it takes four rounds of screeches from the alarm clock, three cups of coffee, and one hour of wandering the house in my bathrobe to get my bearings . . . which is why, in hindsight, my resolution to combine my early mornings with twenty minutes of contemplative prayer was ill-advised. If I can't have a civil conversation with my husband before 8 a.m., why should I expect to have a civil conversation with God?

There seems to be a universal consensus among people of faith that God is a morning person. The Dalai Lama rises at 3:30 a.m. to meditate. Pope Benedict begins his day around 5. I don't know what time Oprah gets up, but I bet it's before 7. Even as a kid, I remember hearing stories about our pastor's "morning quiet time," that magical space between dawn and breakfast when God told him exactly what the Bible meant and what to say about it on Sunday morning. But I didn't experience any magic or inspiration when I rose with the sun to meet God. Instead my Proverbs 31 morning routine went something like this: wake up, make coffee, choose a centering word for meditation, fall back asleep, wake up again, feel guilty, drink coffee, lift my five-pound weights for three minutes, practice knitting, give up, write. After just a few days, I ditched the centering prayer altogether to revert to the old standby—a hurried, half-awake Lord's Prayer while I washed my hair.

The five-pound weights represented yet another difference between the valorous wife and me. While the Proverbs 31 woman "girds herself with strength and makes her arms strong" (v. 17 NASB), I'm more of a cardio girl. I run three miles a day, five days a week, but the generic Bowflex in our garage hasn't seen any action since the third season of *Lost*. I tried doing just fifteen minutes of strength training three days a week, but soon enough my third resolution went the way of centered prayer . . . as did my resolution to stay off Facebook to avoid eating the "bread of idleness" (v. 27).

The big projects weren't going much better. Before my friend

Tiffany mercifully loaned me her copy of a helpful how-to book titled *Stitch 'n Bitch* (which supplied both a much-needed laugh and the useful suggestion that I start my first knitting project with extra-big needles and extra-bulky yarn so as to avoid tying my fingers in knots), I'd been fumbling around with my grandma's old size 8 needles, super-thin yarn, and a YouTube instructional video that featured a creepy nursery rhyme about a guy named Jack peeking through a window. The tedium of this exercise nearly drove me mad. Let's just say I dropped more than a stitch.

"Hon, do you really think that kind of language reflects Proverbs 31?" Dan asked as gently as possible when he came upstairs to find me sitting upright on the edge of the couch, elbows out like a penguin attempting flight, wrestling a row of stitches from one needle to the other—and cussing.

"I can't do this," I said, throwing the mangled heap of yarn to the floor. "How am I supposed to make an entire scarf and hat if I can't make three rows of stitches without it getting all . . . scrunched? I'm doing such a slap-bang job with this whole month."

"Slap-bang" is a phrase long employed by my mother. Slap-bang is when you pull a comforter over a disheveled wad of blankets and sheets and call it making the bed. Slap-bang is when you stick a plate caked with mashed potatoes into the dishwasher, or write a book report based on the illustrations. Slap-bang is when you promise to knit your husband a scarf and hat and then ask if he'd be okay with a pot holder instead. I have no idea if any of us are using this expression correctly, but everyone in the Held family knows just how guilty to feel when we're confronted with it.

Each time I let a writing project take priority over a sewing project or ordered pizza instead of making an exotic meal, the shame of my slap-bang tendencies overtook me. I hated that all my carefully chosen fabric sat in its Hobby Lobby bag untouched and that I'd already skipped a week at the local health clinic where our church volunteered. On days that I remembered to work out, I neglected to do something nice for Dan. Weeks in which I volunteered, I let the house get dirty. When my knitting improved, the sewing machine sat idle. When I got up early, I crashed at night. I wasn't conquering Proverbs 31; I was piddling around with it.

On top of all that, I'd run into a little snafu regarding my Proverbs 31–inspired real estate venture: mainly that I couldn't afford it. The downside to having the one job in America that lets you sleep late and work in your pajamas is that you don't get paid a lot for it. And since Dan and I are both self-employed, we tend to get big checks spaced far apart. The next big check would come in late February, but we needed that to stretch through April, so my prospects for buying a field and planting a vineyard within the next thirty days dwindled with every visit to the mailbox that didn't yield a sudden windfall. Even my alternate plan, to invest in community-supported agriculture, cost a whopping five hundred dollars. Apparently, locally grown radishes are worth as much as an iPad. I hated that the most liberated qualities of the valorous wife—her business savvy and financial prowess—proved as out of my reach as the domestic ones.

I had to hand it to her. In less than 14 days, the Proverbs 31 woman had made me feel guilty, inadequate, and poor.

The whole exercise had brought to the surface one of my most persistent insecurities—the fact that, despite having breasts and ovaries, I can't multitask to save my life. I've always hated this about myself because the prevailing theory is that nature created all women everywhere to be accomplished multitaskers, so they can care for their young while simultaneously fighting off predators, searching for water, and talking on their cell phones. Well, somebody forgot to let me in on this one. When confronted with a long and varied to-do list, I react more like a squirrel in the path of a car, frantically darting one direction and then another without actually getting anywhere besides the backside of a tire.

I knew from my research that Proverbs 31 was never meant to be turned into a to-do list, but there was something about the spectacularity with which I was blowing this that beleaguered my confidence. Most women walk around with the sense that they are disappointing someone. This year, I imagined that Someone to be God. Though Proverbs 31 represented a poetic ideal, I couldn't shake the feeling that if these were indeed the accomplishments of a competent, capable, virtuous, valiant, and worthy wife, then I must be none of those things.

Her children arise and call her blessed; her husband also, and he praises her: "Many women do noble things, but you surpass them all."
—PROVERBS 31:28–29

Seeing as how the Jews have several thousand years on us when it comes to interpreting Scripture, Christians might consider listening to them more often. I arrived at this conclusion shortly after I began corresponding regularly with Ahava, the rabbi's wife from Israel, whom God sent to me through the Internet. Witty, candid, and surprisingly chatty, Ahava grew up in the U.S. and knew a lot more about Christianity than I knew about Judaism. When I asked her what salutations would be most appropriate in an e-mail, she suggested *Kol Tuv*, which means "all the best."

"But please, whatever you do," she said, "don't start off with Shalom. It sounds like a serious affectation from a non-Jew. I can't even tell you how many times I've been 'shalomed' by a well-meaning Christian tourist. It mostly makes us laugh and roll our eyes a little."

This little insight helped explain why the rest of the rabbis weren't returning my messages. I needed to keep this lady around.

With a spiritual seeker for a mother and a devout atheist for a grandmother, Ahava was unaware of her Jewish heritage until her teens, when research revealed that her great-grandmother was an observant Jew. According to Orthodox law, which determines Jewish identity through matrilineal descent, this made Ahava a Jew too. And it's a good thing. As Ahava embraced her heritage and became more observant, friends connected her to a Jewish dating service, through which she met Michael, whose priestly descent required that he marry a Jewish-born virgin.

"He also wanted a redhead," she confessed. "So I fit the bill on all accounts."

Michael and Ahava married, had three children, and emigrated to Israel in 2007.

I asked Ahava what she considered to be the most common misconceptions about Orthodox Jews.

"When we travel, people seem to think we are Amish," she said. (Orthodox women typically cover their heads and wear modest clothing.) "There is this assumption that Jews are into a throwback/Hutterite/granola-type lifestyle, but most of us own cell phones and use computers. Last winter, while visiting friends in Ohio, I finally got to go gawk at the Amish, and you know what? They gawked right back!"

Another big misconception, according to Ahava, is that eating kosher is healthy.

"WRONG!" she said. "Ever heard of schmaltz? Well, Jews invented it."

After a few e-mails back and forth, I asked Ahava if Jewish women struggle as much as Christian women to live up to the Proverbs 31 ideal. For the first time in our correspondence, Ahava seemed a bit perplexed:

Here's the thing. Christians seem to think that because the Bible is inspired, all of it should be taken literally. Jews don't do this. Even though we take the Torah literally (all 613 commandments!), the rest is seen differently, as a way of understanding our Creator, rather than direct commands. Take Proverbs 31, for example. I get called an *eshet chayil* (a valorous woman) all the time. Make your own challah instead of buying? *Eshet chayil!* Work to earn some extra money for the family? *Eshet chayil!* Make balloon animals for the kids at *Shul*? *Eshet chayil!* Every week at the Shabbat table, my husband sings the Proverbs 31 poem to me. It's special because I know that no matter what I do or don't do, he praises me for blessing the family with my energy and creativity. All women can do that in their own way. I bet you do as well.

I looked into this, and sure enough, in Jewish culture it is not the women who memorize Proverbs 31, but the men. Husbands commit each line of the poem to memory, so they can recite it to their wives at the Sabbath meal, usually in a song.

"*Eshet chayil mi yimtza v'rachok mip'ninim michrah*," they sing in the presence of their children and guests. "A valorous woman, who can find? Her value is far beyond pearls."

Eshet chayil is at its core a blessing—one that was never meant to be earned, but to be given, unconditionally.

"It's like their version of 'You go, girl!'" I explained to Dan at the dinner table that night, glowing from the nerdy high of learning a foreign-sounding phrase.

"How do you say it again?" he asked.

"E-shet-hi-yil," I responded with my stubborn Southern accent and all the confidence of someone who has no idea what she's talking about. "You say the *h* from the back of your throat."

"Yeah, I'm not going to remember that," he said. "What does it mean exactly?"

"It means 'woman of valor.'"

"Well, that's what you are to me," Dan said. "You're a woman of valor!"

My heart swelled in my chest, as it would again and again in the months to come as Dan found ways to invoke the new blessing in the midst of our daily routines. When my blog sold enough ads to become profitable, he looked up from the computer, smiled, and declared, "Woman of valor!" When I finally got around to cleaning out the guest room closet, he high-fived me and shouted, "Woman of valor!" When I stumbled through the front door after a long day with nothing but takeout pizza to show for dinner, he stretched out his arms in absolute delight and cried, "Pizza? Woman of valor!"

It's amazing what a little poetry can do for a marriage.

Ahava said that women use the blessing to encourage one another as well, so I started trying it out with friends, family, and readers. Sure enough, it caught on. When Tiffany's pharmacy aced its accreditation, I congratulated her with a hearty *Eshet chayil*! When Amanda beat out about a million applicants for the job she wanted in North Carolina, I called her up and shouted, "Woman of valor!" When a fellow blogger went on national television to speak boldly against child abuse in fundamentalist churches, I sent her an e-mail with the subject line *Eshet chayil*! When I learned that three women had won the Nobel Peace Prize, I shared the news with my readers in a blog post entitled "Meet Three Women of Valor."

Before long, I overheard friends repeating the blessing to one another in response to news of pregnancy, promotions, finished projects, and final cancer treatments. I saw it exchanged in tweets and on Facebook walls. Readers sent me links to dozens of articles about women of valor from around the world who had built hospitals in Africa, launched successful micro-financing initiatives in India, been elected to public office in Afghanistan, and staged protests in Egypt. Never before had I considered how many acts of raw bravery occur every day in the lives of women. One friend told me she was thinking of getting an *Eshet chayil* tattoo!

As I saw how powerful and affirming this ancient blessing could be, I decided it was time for Christian women to take back Proverbs 31. Somewhere along the way, we surrendered it to the same people who invented airbrushing and Auto-Tune and Rachel Ray. We abandoned the meaning of the poem by focusing on the specifics, and it became just another impossible standard by which to measure our failures. We turned an anthem into an assignment, a poem into a job description.

But according to Ahava, the woman described in Proverbs 31 is not some ideal that exists out there; she is present in each one of us when we do even the smallest things with valor.

*She gets up while it is still dark; she provides food for
her family and portions for her female servants.*
—PROVERBS 31:15

I hoped it wouldn't come to this.

But when the third week of January arrived and I still had no dress, no pillow, no sash, and no scarf, I was forced to succumb to the last resort, to subject myself to that which is most dreaded and despised among women, an act we suffer to avoid and fear above all else:

I had to ask for help.

Even the Proverbs 31 woman didn't do it all on her own. According to verse 15, the valorous wife provided food for her family and portions for her "female servants." So instead I sought help in the form of a "Proverbs 31 Sewing/Knitting Party," with the promise that it was "in exchange for food as well as my eternal thanks and some good old-fashioned fellowship." Participants could stop by my house anytime between 10 a.m. and 9 p.m. on Saturday to help me with "my unfinished Proverbs 31 sewing projects." Missing from the invitation was any mention of servitude or the fact that in most cases "unfinished" was just an optimistic way of saying not started yet. Within forty-eight hours, I received fifteen RSVPs from an assortment of good-hearted souls ranging from neighbors to blog readers to church ladies with legendary reputations as seamstresses. It suddenly occurred to me that some people might actually consider this fun.

I rose early that morning to make yellow cupcakes with strawberry icing for my guests, who began arriving at 9:30 a.m., many with their own sewing machines, fabric, and supplies in tow. Darlene, an artistic sixty-something with more sewing expertise than the rest of us combined, lugged through the front door an emerald green restored Singer Featherweight, which even to the untrained eye was a beautiful piece of machinery. She was followed by Betty, a matriarch in the church and the sort of person you feel naturally inclined to spill your guts to on account of the fact that she is slow to judge, quick to listen, and quick to offer help. I suspect everyone in Dayton has been blessed by Betty at some point—(she basically coordinated my sister's wedding free of charge)—and yet no one seems to feel that they owe her anything.

Mom, who, in a true act of sacrificial love, had come over the night before to help me cut out the pattern for my purple dress, arrived at the house shortly after Betty, along with Jan, Dayna, Kristine, my friend Robin, and Robin's grandmother. I felt a little out of my element playing host when most of these ladies were my mom's age or older. But soon enough, a system emerged, and the dining room bustled with chatter, laughter, and the incessant hum of multiple sewing machines. Mom and Betty worked on the dress at the main table while Darlene and Dayna worked on the pillow on the foldout. Kristine knitted, Jan did some hand sewing, and Robin and her grandmother ironed. I mostly hid in the kitchen.

By lunchtime, both the decorative pillow and Dan's scarf were finished. I managed to sew but one crooked seam on the pillow and knit a grand total of three rows of stitches on the scarf. At some point Mom and Betty called me over to carefully pull a pinned-together version of my lounge dress over my head.

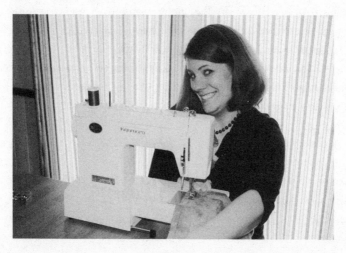

"How does it look?" I asked.

The room got quiet and everyone cocked their heads.

"Maybe if we make it shorter . . ." Betty offered tentatively, reaching for the hem with a fistful of pins.

"Or took off the sleeves," Robin added.

I looked down at the billowing tent of purple fabric hanging like a droopy bell from my shoulders. I may as well have been wearing a potato sack.

"I look pregnant, don't I?"

The silence was broken by uproarious laughter. We grabbed the pillow and stuffed it under the dress just in time for Dan to come home from wherever he'd escaped to find his pregnant-looking wife surrounded by giggling women, fabric, and half-eaten cupcakes.

"Looks like a lot happened while I was gone," he said with eyebrows raised.

Folks began trickling out after noon, but Saint Betty wouldn't leave until that dress was finished, which happened around four o'clock. It still looked like an oversized smock on account of the homely pattern and cheap fabric, but I hugged Betty's neck and promised I'd wear it out at least once.

"Was it cheating to delegate the majority of my sewing projects to other people?" I asked Dan as we surveyed the day's booty: the dress, pillow, and scarf from my list, along with four homemade car seat covers, a rice-filled therapy sack, and two knit scarves for the auction.

I was like Tom grinning at his whitewashed fence.

"I didn't marry a woman who knew how to sew," Dan replied with a mix of amusement and incredulity. "I married a woman who knew how to get things done."

Her husband is respected at the city gate, where
he takes his seat among the elders of the land.

—PROVERBS 31:23

Spurred by the support of my friends and the encouragement of progress, I set about crossing the final items on my January to-do list . . . two weeks into February. The tasks that remained included:

☐ Make Martha Stewart's chicken curry—"She is like merchant ships, bringing her food from afar" (v. 14).
☐ Create a proverbs 31 beauty queen sash to auction on eBay for charity—"She makes linen garments and sells them, and supplies the merchants with sashes" (v. 24); "She opens her arms to the poor and extends her hands to the needy" (v. 20).
☐ Invest in real estate or community-supported agriculture—"She considers a field and buys it; out of her earnings, she plants a vineyard" (v. 16).
☐ Praise Dan at the city gate—"Her husband is respected at the city gate, where he takes his seat among the elders of the land" (v. 23).

The easiest of these was the chicken curry. I nixed it the minute Dan informed me he didn't like chicken curry and would prefer that our regular ole Thursday-night taco salad count as the "food from afar" instead. Can't argue with Commandment #1.

The sash took all of 45 minutes to finish. I took a wide white ribbon, ironed onto one side sparkly pink letters that read "PROVERBS 31 WOMAN," and then added a hot-pink decorative pin that could attach the two pieces like a beauty queen sash. It was pretty fabulous actually. I auctioned it off on eBay along with the scarves, therapy sack, and car seat covers for $75 to benefit World Vision, thereby "supplying the merchants with sashes" and "extending my hand to the poor" all in one task. Before I shipped everything off, Dan took a picture of me holding my homemade pillow and wearing the dress, scarf, and Proverbs 31 sash. I made it my profile picture on Facebook.

We decided to put off an investment in community supported agriculture until we were independently wealthy and could afford luxuries like babies, iPads, and locally grown radishes.

I never made a knit hat or a second pillow. Most days I only accomplished three or four of my seven daily tasks, but I shoveled snow out of the driveway and bought the right kind of lightbulbs at Lowe's to ensure that Dan had "full confidence" in me as a wife. Halfway into February, I had just one more task between myself and unmitigated valor: to praise Dan at the city gate.

And so on a cold Friday afternoon, right at Dayton's four o'clock "rush hour," Dan took me to the giant Welcome to Dayton sign off Highway 27, where I stood for thirty minutes holding a poster that declared DAN IS AWESOME! to all thirty-five people who drove by. No one honked or waved or crashed their car in surprise. I suspect that most of them thought I'd simply lost a bet. It was a bit anticlimactic, but we had a good time with it, and the month from hell was finally over. We laughed victoriously all the way home.

I suppose that the moral of this story is that trying to copy another woman, even a woman from the Bible, is almost always a bad idea. As Judy Garland liked to say, "Be a first rate version of yourself, not a second rate version of someone else." When I tried to conform my lifestyle to that of an ancient Near Eastern royal Jewish wife, I was a second-rate version of the Proverbs 31 woman, which misses the entire point of the passage.

The Proverbs 31 woman is a star not because of what she does but how she does it—with valor. So do your thing. If it's refurbishing old furniture—do it with valor. If it's keeping up with your two-year-old—do it with valor. If it's fighting against human trafficking . . . leading a company . . . or getting other people to do your work for you—do it with valor.

Take risks. Work hard. Make mistakes. Get up the next morning. And surround yourself with people who will cheer you on.

READ MORE AT ONLINE:

"Dear President Obama . . ."— http://rachelheldevans.com/ dear-president

VASHTI, THE OTHER QUEEN

But when the attendants delivered the king's command, Queen Vashti refused to come.
—ESTHER 1:12

Just about everyone has heard of Queen Esther, the beautiful young maiden who saved the Jewish nation by capturing the affections of a Persian emperor and then daring to enter his presence to plead for their cause. But not so many know of Vashti, the other queen, whose defiance enabled Esther to fulfill her destiny and without whom there would be no story to tell.

According to the book of Esther, Vashti was the wife of King Xerxes of Persia. At the height of his glory and wealth, Xerxes threw a lavish, seven-day banquet for all of the nobles of his court. Feasts were held day and night in the palace garden, where fine blue and white linen hung from marble pillars, and merrymakers lounged on couches made of gold and silver and precious stones. Wine was so abundant that the king allowed each guest to drink without restrictions. Servants were told to give each man as much as he wished, and as the days wore on, the party grew wilder and wilder.

On the seventh day, when Xerxes was "in high spirits from wine" (Esther 1:10), he commanded the seven eunuchs who served him to bring Queen Vashti to the garden. He wanted to display her body before all the men of the court, for she was beautiful to behold. Tradition holds that he wanted her to strip naked of all but her royal crown.

When the attendants delivered the king's command, Vashti refused to obey. Her defiance infuriated the king, who consulted his closest advisers on how to respond to his wife's disobedience. A confidant named Memukan replied, "Queen Vashti has done wrong, not only against the king but also against all the nobles and the people of all the provinces of King Xerxes. For the queen's conduct will become known to all the women, and so they will despise their husbands and say, 'King Xerxes commanded Queen Vashti to be brought before him, but she would not come.' This very day the Persian and Median women of the nobility who have heard about the queen's conduct will respond to all the king's nobles in the same way. There will be no end of disrespect and discord" (vv. 16–18).

At Memukan's suggestion, Xerxes issued a royal decree to be written into the laws of Persia and Media, that Vashti would never again enter the presence of the king and that the king would bestow her royal position on someone else, someone who was "better than she" (v. 19). The decree, delivered to every province and in every language of the empire, proclaimed that "all the women will respect their husbands, from the least to the greatest" and that "every man should be ruler over his own household" (vv. 20, 22).

To fill the position vacated by the queen, King Xerxes ordered that all the virgin women of Susa be brought into his harem. Under the care of the royal eunuchs, the women underwent twelve months of beautification, adorning them-selves with oil, myrrh, spices, and lotions, before each took a turn in the king's bed to see who would please him best. (We didn't get that version in Sunday school.) The women received just one night with the king, after which they were transferred to the eunuchs in charge of the concubines, with the instruction not to return to the king's chamber unless summoned by name, under the penalty of death. The lovely

Esther, whose Jewish name was Hadassah, won the heart of King Xerxes, and he made her his queen.

We never learn of Vashti's fate. Many midrashic interpretations suggest that she was formally executed. Others propose that she was killed by Xerxes in a drunken rage. Still others, less sympathetic of the plight of pagan queens, contend that Vashti grew a tail. Few suggest she met a happy end.

Esther would go on to boldly defy Xerxes's edict and appear before him without a summon to plead on behalf of her people, who were about to be slaughtered by the king's evil vizier. To this day, Jews commemorate Esther's bravery and the salvation of their ancestors with the annual festival of Purim.

Only recently have feminist interpretations reminded readers that it took the defiance of *two* queens to save the Jews—Esther by appearing before the king, Vashti by refusing to.

February: Beauty

My Breasts Are Like Towers

I am a wall, and my breasts are like towers. Thus I have become in his eyes like one bringing contentment.

—SONG OF SONGS 8:10

TO DO THIS MONTH:

- ☐ Find out what the Bible *really* says about beauty and sex
- ☐ Interview a couple who practiced "biblical courtship"
- ☐ Give Dan a "Sex Anytime" coupon (1 Corinthians 7:4–5)

Shortly before Dan and I married, we attended the summer wedding of two college classmates in which the officiating minister offered an ominous charge to the young bride.

"The Bible requires that a wife be available to her husband," he said. "This means keeping yourself beautiful for him. Unfortunately, many women let themselves go after having children, giving little thought to their weight or appearance. It is your responsibility to delight your husband throughout all stages of life, so that he has no reason to stray."

I jabbed Dan in the ribs with my elbow and hissed, "HE JUST TOLD HER NOT TO GET FAT!"

I waited for a similar charge to be issued to the groom, but no such instructions were given.

Later, in 2006, popular evangelical pastor Mark Driscoll made headlines when in response to Ted Haggard's confession that he'd had an affair with another man, Driscoll declared:

> At the risk of being even more widely despised than I currently am, I will lean over the plate and take one for the team on this. It is not uncommon to meet pastors' wives who really let themselves go; they sometimes feel that because their husband is a pastor, he is therefore trapped into fidelity, which gives them cause for laziness. A wife who lets herself go and is not sexually available to her husband in the ways that the Song of Songs is so frank about is not responsible for her husband's sin, but she may not be helping him either.[1]

Driscoll's comments drew fire, and I believe he eventually apologized, but the sentiment behind the remarks—that the Bible holds women to a certain standard of beauty that must be maintained throughout all seasons of life and that wives must devote themselves to pleasing their husbands in bed—remains a popular one, even among women.

In *Recovering Biblical Manhood & Womanhood*, Dorothy Patterson wrote that "God's woman gives time and effort to her appearance" and hails the wife of seventeenth-century theologian Jonathan Edwards as the perfect example of a godly woman because "she stayed attractive, and fifteen years later she was still able to entrance men much younger than she was."[2]

Similarly, Martha Peace instructs women in *The Excellent Wife* to remain beautiful and sexually available for their husbands, declaring that "the husband should be so satisfied that even if another woman entices him, he won't be tempted."[3]

At the last Christian women's conference I attended, several speakers mentioned the importance of keeping a beauty routine so that husbands will not be tempted to "look elsewhere." The message is as clear as it is ominous: Stay beautiful, or your husband might leave you . . . and if he does, it's partially your fault.

The notion that buried somewhere in the sacred texts of Scripture is a verse directed at women that says "Thou shalt not let thyself go" has gained considerable traction within the Christian community in recent years. I wrote about the phenomenon in my blog, and the post broke traffic records, generating nearly three hundred comments from women and men alike. Many reported similar experiences:

- "My husband recently started seminary, and they had a special orientation for the married couples. In that orientation, they exhorted wives to be sexually available to their husbands and to keep up their appearance—again, this 'don't let yourself go' mentality. I wouldn't have had a problem with this if they had exhorted the husbands to do the same thing, but they didn't. Why is it okay for the guys to let themselves go, but not the wives? It makes guys seem like base creatures, unable to deal with any temptation from a pretty young woman."—Alias The Vault
- "The pastor that officiated my wedding presented this exact idea in one of our premarital counseling sessions. He mentioned his wife as an example, explaining that throughout their marriage she had always made an effort to dress nicely with her hair and makeup done when he arrived home in the evening. That idea stuck in my head, and for the longest time I felt guilty if my husband arrived home to find me in loungewear and a ponytail."—Jessica
- "Anytime we get into 'biblical' looks, it's going to be a losing proposition for women. If you don't look good enough, your husband will lust after women who look better. If you look too good, you make other men cheat on their wives in the hearts. So you're out of luck no matter what."—Alise

In addition to fighting unrealistic standards of beauty, many women said they struggled with the Christian culture's expectations regarding their sexuality:

+ "I was told by my church that having sex before marriage was like buying a car and crashing it and trying to resell it. No one would want me anymore because having sex even once meant I was totaled."—Sara

+ "In church I learned that, before marriage, it was my job to say, 'no,' to never think or talk about sex at all, and then, on my wedding night, flip a magic switch and turn into a sex goddess who magically knows what she wants, is comfortable with her body, and knows just how to please her husband."—Laura

+ "I went into marriage thinking that my husband wanted a 'girl next door in the living room but a tiger in the bedroom'—as I was told in the psychology classes at the small Christian college I attended . . . Then I had a child and found myself physically damaged from the birth and deep in postpartum depression. I turned to the local mother's group at a church for support, and what did they tell me? You need to make yourself beautiful for your husband, take time away from your kids, and make a special night in the bedroom every week. All I heard was 'you're broken, you're damaged, you're an awful wife.' They never actually said those things to me, but that's the message I heard. I never felt comfortable enough to share my struggles with any of them because they kept harping on the 'be a good wife by being amazingly beautiful and sexual' routine."—Regina

I, too, felt enormous pressure from the Church to meet certain expectations regarding sex and beauty.

I signed my first abstinence pledge when I was just fifteen. I'd been invited by some friends to a fall youth rally at the First Baptist

Church, and in the fellowship hall one night, the youth leader passed around neon blue and pink postcards that included a form letter to God promising to remain sexually abstinent until marriage. We had only a few minutes to add our signatures, and all my friends were signing theirs, so I used the back of my metal chair to scribble my name across the dotted line before marching to the front of the room to pin my promise to God and my vagina onto a giant corkboard for all to see. The youth leader said he planned to hang the corkboard in the hallway outside the sanctuary so that parents could marvel at the seventy-five abstinence pledges he'd collected that night. It was a pretty cheap way to treat both our bodies and God, come to think of it. Studies suggest that only about 12 percent of us kept our promise.[4]

Upon reaching her wedding night, a Christian woman is expected to transform from the model of chastity into a veritable sex goddess, ready to honor God by satisfying her husband's sexual needs without fail. I was told that, according to 1 Corinthians 7:4, I had no authority over my own body, but was responsible for yielding it entirely to my husband, who needed regular sex in order to remain faithful to me.

Wrote Debi Pearl, "Wife, it is your God-ordained ministry to your husband to be his totally enthusiastic sex partner, ready to enjoy him at all times . . . If you don't score high points here, you are providing an opening for your husband to be tempted by other women."[5]

Pointing to the Song of Solomon, also called the Song of Songs, Pastor Driscoll issued a blunt declaration to the women in his megachurch audience: "Ladies, your husbands appreciate oral sex. They do. So, serve them. It's biblical. Jesus Christ commands you to do so . . . Let me assure you of this: if you think you're being dirty, he's pretty happy."[6]

Jesus Christ commands oral sex?

It seems there are enough rumors floating around the Christian community about what the Bible says about sex and beauty to put the average junior high boys' locker room to shame.

So my first task for the month of February was to do some research, to sort fact from fiction and see what, if anything, the Bible required of women in the bedroom and in front of the mirror. Then I needed to find out how many of these instructions I could authentically reproduce for a book that I was pretty sure my mother would read.

Charm is deceitful and beauty is passing,
But a woman who fears the LORD, she shall be praised.
—PROVERBS 31:30 NKJV

Sometimes there's as much to learn from what the Bible doesn't say as there is to learn from what it does say. I discovered this one Saturday afternoon when I broke out my concordances to see what sort of advice the Bible actually gives women about beauty:

+ Of the occurrences in which the words *beauty, beautiful, lovely,* or *attractive* appear in conjunction with references to women, most are applied to specific Old Testament figures (Sarah, Rebekah, Rachel, Abigail, Bathsheba, Tamar, Vashti, Esther, the Shulammite princess in Song of Songs) or to groups of women (Job's daughters, the daughters of Jerusalem). While many Old Testament matriarchs are described as being beautiful, others, like Leah, are said to be plain. The gospel writers never rated the hotness of Jesus' female disciples.

+ The majority of verses that include woman and beauty in the same sentence are found in the book of Proverbs and appear in warnings to young men about the dangers of adultery. "Like a gold ring in a pig's snout is a beautiful woman who shows no discretion," says Proverbs 11:22. "Do not lust in your heart after her beauty or let her captivate you with her eyes," says Proverbs 6:25.

- While young love is certainly celebrated in the Bible, particularly in Song of Songs, there is nothing in Scripture to suggest that a woman is expected to maintain a youthful appearance throughout all phases of life. Nowhere does the Bible teach that a woman shares responsibility for her husband's infidelity because she "let herself go." And nowhere does it teach that outer beauty reflects inner beauty.

- The Bible consistently describes beauty as fleeting. "Charm is deceitful and beauty is passing," goes the famous line in Proverbs 31, "but a woman who fears the LORD, she shall be praised" (v. 30 NKJV). The apostle Peter told the women of the early church, "Your beauty should not come from outward adornment, such as elaborate hairstyles and the wearing of gold jewelry or fine clothes. Rather, it should be that of your inner self, the unfading beauty of a gentle and quiet spirit, which is of great worth in God's sight" (1 Peter 3:3–4 UPDATED NIV).

So for all of its complexity and incongruity, its mysteries and its dark stories, the Bible consistently presents us with a realistic and affirming view of female beauty. The writers of ancient Scripture seemed to acknowledge what all women instinctively know—that our bodies change as we get older, as we bear children, when we get sick, and as we experience joy, pain, life, death, victory, heartache, and time. And frankly, the suggestion that men are too weak to handle these realities is as emasculating as it is unbiblical.

Warning young men against adultery, the author of Proverbs 5 wrote:

> *Drink water from your own cistern,*
> *running water from your own well . . .*
> *May your fountain be blessed,*
> *and may you rejoice in the wife of your youth.*
> *A loving doe, a graceful deer—*

> *may her breasts satisfy you always,*
> *may you ever be intoxicated with her love.*
>
> (vv. 15–19 updated niv)

Both husbands and wives bear the sweet responsibility of seeking beauty in one another at all stages of life. No one gets off the hook because the other is wearing sweatpants or going bald or carrying a child or battling cancer. Any pastor who claims the Bible says otherwise is lying. End of story.

While Scripture has very little to say about beauty, it has quite a lot to say about sex. And when it comes to sex, the Bible is full of surprises. It includes erotic poetry and explicit sex scenes along with meticulously detailed laws about copulation and cleanliness. The Bible repeatedly warns against sexual immorality, yet some of its most celebrated heroes boasted sordid sex lives. The apostle Paul urged some Christians not to marry and instructed others to settle down. While Deuteronomy calls for the public stoning of women who fail to remain virgins before marriage, it is unclear whether the young lovers of Song of Songs were married at the time of their first sexual encounter. Hosea married a prostitute to make a point.

Far from idealizing the nuclear family, Jesus identified his disciples as his brothers, sisters, and mothers (Matthew 12:48) and insisted that his followers prioritize faith over family bonds (Luke 14:25–26). When the disciples asked Jesus if it is better not to marry, Jesus conceded that celibacy may be preferable for disciples and that some may choose to castrate themselves "for the sake of the kingdom of heaven" (Matthew 19:12 updated niv). And when the Sadducees tried to trip him up with a trick question about marriage after resurrection, Jesus responded, "When the dead rise, they will neither marry nor be given in marriage; they will be like the angels in heaven" (Mark 12:25).

Many early Christians took these teachings so seriously that they remained celibate, sometimes even castrating themselves, in anticipation of Christ's coming kingdom. Paul himself never married, praising the celibate lifestyle as free from distraction and heartache in a world where many followers of Jesus were being persecuted by Rome (1 Corinthians 7:32).

Apparently, Paul's teachings caused some confusion in the Corinthian church, where misinterpretations of one of his previous letters, now lost to history, required a follow-up letter from Paul for clarification. It seems that some Christians were teaching "it is good for a man not to have sexual relations with a woman" (1 Corinthians 7:1 UPDATED NIV) and applying this across the board, even to married couples. This was causing an increase in divorce, adultery, and marital unhappiness among these early Christians (particularly, we can surmise, when one partner in a marriage wanted to devote himself or herself to asceticism, while the other did not). So Paul spent a good deal of time in 1 Corinthians clearing things up. In chapter 7 he offered these instructions:

> Each man should have sexual relations with his own wife, and each woman with her own husband. The husband should fulfill his marital duty to his wife, and likewise the wife to her husband. The wife does not have authority over her own body but yields it to her husband. In the same way, the husband does not have authority over his own body but yields it to his wife. Do not deprive each other except perhaps by mutual consent and for a time, so that you may devote yourselves to prayer. Then come together again so that Satan will not tempt you because of your lack of self-control. (vv. 2–5 UPDATED NIV)

In other words, no one should withhold sex from his or her spouse out of misguided religious devotion. Paul added, "I say this as a concession, not as a command. I wish that all of you were as I am, [single,] but each of you has your own gift from God; one has this gift, another has that" (vv. 6–7 UPDATED NIV).

The apostle's elevation of singleness as the ideal stands in stark contrast to the modern Church's fixation on marriage and family. Singles were celebrated in the Church then, and they should be now.

Given this context, it seems odd that 1 Corinthians 7 is cited by so many Christians as a command from God to women everywhere to "just say yes" to whatever a husband initiates in the bedroom.

For example when I first announced that I would be following the Bible's commandments for women as literally as possible for a year, Dan received playful ribbings from friends who declared, "Dan, you lucky man! You get sex whenever you want!"

According to Debi Pearl, the Bible says that even physical pain is no excuse for a woman to take a rain check on sex one night. "Don't talk to me about menopause," she wrote in *Created to Be His Help Meet*. "I know all about menopause, and it's a lame excuse. Don't talk to me about how uncomfortable or painful it is for you. Do you think your body is special and has special needs? Do you know who created you, and do you know he is the same God who expects you to freely give sex to your husband? Stop the excuses!"[7]

Such an interpretation fails to take into account the specific context of 1 Corinthians 7 in which the "deprivation" in question relates to religious asceticism. Worse yet, it overlooks the passage's striking emphasis on mutual satisfaction between husband and wife. Paul never placed women in the role of submissive sex slaves to husbands, who get to call all the shots. The pleasures of sex are meant to be mutual.

I like Eugene Peterson's paraphrase of 1 Corinthians 7:4–5 in *The Message*: "The marriage bed must be a place of mutuality—the husband seeking to satisfy his wife, the wife seeking to satisfy her husband . . . Marriage is a decision to serve the other, whether in bed or out."

Sometimes you serve by getting in the mood for your spouse. Sometimes you serve by waiting. But when sexuality gets relegated to the realm of religious absolutes, the focus tends to shift from serving one another to servicing one another. And that's no way to love.

For the project this month, I had originally planned to bestow upon Dan a homemade "SEX ANYTIME" coupon for Valentine's Day, (along with some other coupons that shall remain undisclosed on account of the fact that my mother will read this book). But this proved biblically, and practically, unnecessary.

Sex is fun for both of us; no one "owes" the other anything. When one of us isn't in the mood, the other lets it go. We don't keep tallies or make demands. We don't throw Bible verses at each other to get our way. And believe it or not, we have a great sex life . . . mainly, I'm told, because we don't have kids yet.

> Place me like a seal over your heart,
>   like a seal on your arm;
> for love is as strong as death,
> its jealousy unyielding as the grave.
>   It burns like a blazing fire,
>   like a mighty flame.

—SONG OF SONGS 8:6

It is a hallmark of Southern evangelical culture that the youth group has its own reserved seating on Sunday mornings. These two rows of pews are typically located to the extreme left or right of the sanctuary, far enough from the front to avoid eye contact with the preacher and far enough from the back to escape the cries of fussy babies. The Sunday after my first week of high school, I was invited to join the motley assemblage that made up "the youth": rebellious missionary kids, pimply outcasts, Goths, Goody Two-shoes, pretty girls whose Sunday skirts violated public high school dress codes, and awkward teenage boys whose arms and legs hung over the pews like the limp limbs of forgotten marionettes. The boys were spaced exactly four feet apart from one another, the girls exactly two. On Easter, when the nominally religious suddenly showed up and we all had to scrunch together to make room for the "lukewarm," the whole enterprise would collapse into a seething cauldron of sexual tension.

Although I fit rather definitively in the Goody Two-shoes category, having signed my name to a virginity pledge that was stuck to a corkboard at the Baptist church and all, sometimes, when the pastor preached from the book of Isaiah, and my Bible sat open across my lap, I'd sneak a glance at the pages that preceded the prophet's dire warnings to Israel. And there, right in the middle of my Holy Bible, was this:

> *My beloved is to me a sachet of myrrh*
> *resting between my breasts. . . .*
> *How handsome you are, my beloved!*
> *Oh, how charming!*
> *And our bed is verdant. . . .*
> *Your stature is like that of the palm,*
> *And your breasts like clusters of fruit.*
> *I said, "I will climb the palm tree;*
> *I will take hold of its fruit."*
>
> (SONG OF SONGS 1:13, 16; 7:7–9)

Filled with guilt, I'd flip back to Isaiah, desperate to ignore the way the gangly guy to the right suddenly didn't seem so gangly after all.

How can this be in the Bible? I wondered. *Does the pastor know it's there? Do my parents know it's there? Does God know that I'm thinking about . . . fruit . . . right in the middle of church?*

Apparently I wasn't the only one stirred by these words.

Although it never mentions God, prayer, worship, or religion, Song of Songs is rivaled only by Genesis and the Psalms in the number of commentaries that have been written about it. The eight chapters that make up this small book between Ecclesiastes and Isaiah contain a titillating love poem that invites readers to listen in on the impassioned romantic exchange between a young Shulamite girl and her handsome lover. The Hebrew title Song of Songs means "the most superlative, or best, of songs."

The poem is drenched with rich imagery from the time of Solomon's reign, but most scholars believe that the linguistic evidence points to a later date of composition and that the nod to Solomon in the title and the references to his kingdom throughout are employed by the author to recall that glorious period in Israel's history. I always used to think that the male subject of the poem was Solomon himself, but that is unlikely, which is fine by me. Nothing ruins a good love poem like knowing the hero went out and got himself a harem.

Jewish philosopher Saadia Gaon said, "Know, my brother, that you will find great differences in interpretation of the Song of Songs. In truth they differ because the Song of Songs resembles locks to which the keys have been lost."[8]

Indeed, sometimes it seems like all a person requires to take a stab at interpreting Song of Songs is a vivid imagination.

On the one hand, we have centuries of medieval Christian theologians who went to great lengths to render the poem entirely allegorical, interpreting the intimacy between the man and the woman as the love between Christ and the Church. This required some interpretive gymnastics that at times preclude common sense. According to Origen, the two breasts that the suitor is so eager to grasp represent the Old Testament and the New Testament. The lips he longs to kiss represent the Eucharist, noted another medieval scholar. The luxurious bed on which the lovers lie represents the convents of the Church, said Saint Bernard.

Sure. And Hooters represents the American affinity for owl culture.

On the other hand, we have contemporary readers who essentially treat the book as soft porn, mining every last metaphor for Freudian insinuations. Some pastors have gone so far as to turn the poem into a Christian sex manual. Pastor Driscoll took this approach and says he owes much of his early success to it.

"I assumed the students and singles were all pretty horny," he wrote in his memoir, "so I went out on a limb and preached through the Song of Songs . . . Each week I extolled the virtues of marriage, foreplay, oral sex, sacred stripping, and sex outdoors, just as the book teaches . . . This helped us a lot because apparently a pastor using words like 'penis' and 'oral sex' is unusual, and before you could say 'aluminum pole in the bedroom,' attendance began to climb steadily to more than two hundred people a week."[9]

Now, I've got nothing against aluminum poles, sex outdoors, "sacred stripping," and that sort of thing, but you should be able to tell your spouse that you'd like to try it in the backyard without insisting your instructions come directly from God. Poems were never meant to be forced into commands.

I think Ellen Davis offers the best advice for making sense of the Song of Songs when she says we must "learn it from the poets"—not psychoanalysts, not theologians, not pastors using sex sermons to fill the pews. Like any good poem, the Song should tickle the imagination. It should deliver its meaning indirectly, through metaphor and rhythm and rhyme. It should speak to the heart, not the mind. It "should not mean, but be."[10]

But what interested me the most about Song of Songs was the fact that it presents us with the longest unmediated female voice in the entire Bible. Where much of the Old Testament seems to regard female sexuality as something to be regulated and feared, Song of Songs unleashes a vivid and erotic expression of woman's desire. In fact, the female perspective so dominates the poem that some scholars believe it may have been written by a woman.

So what does this ancient, uninhibited female voice say?

To sum it up, she says she's beautiful, and she knows what she wants. (Basically, the lyrics to Beyoncé's next hit.)

"Do not stare at me because I am dark, because I am darkened by the sun," she tells the Daughters of Jerusalem, who act as a sort of chorus throughout the poem. "Dark am I, yet lovely" (Song of Songs 1:6).

"I am a rose of Sharon, a lily of the valleys," she insists (2:1). "I belong to my beloved, and his desire is for me" (7:10 UPDATED NIV).

When the Daughters of Jerusalem make a remark about her small breasts, the Shulamite counters, "I am a wall, and my breasts are like towers. Thus I have become in his eyes like one bringing contentment" (8:10).

In addition to speaking boldly about her own unconventional beauty, the Shulamite girl initiates much of the action in the romance. She is the first to speak in the poem, declaring, "Let him kiss me with the kisses of his mouth" (1:1). She actively seeks out the handsome shepherd in his fields, saying "Why should I be like a veiled woman beside the flocks of your friends?" (v. 7). When the two are separated, she goes out into the streets, looking for him, and at one point is accosted by the city guards. When she finds him, she brings him into a private room. There, she says, "I held him and would not him go" (3:4).

It is she who initiates a sexual encounter in a vineyard in the countryside, and it is she who offers her lover a frank invitation to drink her wine and to enter her "garden" to taste its choice fruits. Indeed some of the most beautiful lines of the poem—and arguably of the Bible—are hers: "Place me like a seal over your heart, like a seal on your arm; for love is as strong as death" (8:6).

Her suitor is more than happy to oblige, showering her with a litany of compliments that I'm sure would drive any Ancient Near Eastern girl wild, but which lose a little of their potency to the modern reader.

Her eyes are like doves (1:15).

Her hair is like a flock of goats (4:1).

Her teeth are like a flock of sheep recently shorn; "each has its own twin, not one of them is missing" (6:6 NIV UPDATED)

Her cheeks are like halves of a pomegranate (4:3).

Her neck is like the tower of David (4:4).

Her nose is like the tower of Lebanon (7:4).

Her breasts are like two fawns (4:5).

Her legs are like jewels (7:1).

Her navel is like a rounded goblet (7:2).

Her waist is like a mound of wheat (7:2).

While most girls these days would insist that under no circumstances should their waist be compared to a mound of wheat, these images held cultural and poetic significance that proves the young man took seriously the ancient proverb about delighting in the love of your youth. He didn't care what the Daughters of Jerusalem said. The beauty of his beloved surpassed every other woman's.

All in all, the Song of Songs struck me as surprisingly liberating this time around. I had much more fun reading it as a married woman than as a guilt-ridden teenager afraid of her own libido.

The Song reminds me of another biblical poem, this one from the book of Proverbs:

> *There are three things which are too wonderful for me,*
> *Four which I do not understand:*
> *The way of an eagle in the sky,*
> *The way of a serpent on a rock,*
> *The way of a ship in the middle of the sea,*
> *And the way of a man with a maid.*
>
> (30:18–19 NASB)

Believers should be wary of overzealous attempts to prescribe "biblical sex," when sex—like beauty and like God—remains shaded with mystery. Paul likened it to the mystery of Christ's love for the Church, the writer of Proverbs to the inscrutable way of an eagle in the sky. If Christians have learned anything from our rocky two-thousand-year theological history, it's that we make the most beautiful things ugly when we try to systematize mystery. Even the writers of Scripture knew that some things were simply beyond their grasp.

RUTH, THE MOABITE

No Ammonite or Moabite or any of their descendants may enter the assembly of the LORD, *not even in the tenth generation.*
—DEUTERONOMY 23:3 UPDATED NIV

By far the most common qualification for a good wife found within the pages of Scripture is that she not be a foreigner. Endogamy was a recurring concern in the narrative of Israel's history, the writers of Scripture insistent that the descendants of Abraham eschew any form of assimilation to foreign customs and gods. Of all the threats to national security, beautiful foreign women were seen as the most surreptitious, blamed, at least in part, for everything from King Solomon's downfall to the Babylonian captivity.

The Law includes a command that when God delivers a nation to Israel, the Israelites must "destroy them totally. . . . Do not intermarry with them," it states. "Do not give your daughters to their sons or take their daughters for your sons, for they will turn your children away from following me to serve other gods, and the Lord's anger will burn against you and will quickly destroy you" (Deuteronomy 7:2–4 UPDATED NIV).

Foreign wives, young Israelite boys were warned, were seductive, idolatrous, and the demise of kings. For the sake of their lives, they must stay away.

And so it is ironic, perhaps even poetic, that the Bible's exemplary daughter-in-law and one of the most celebrated women in Jewish and Christian history is a Moabite by the name of Ruth.

Ruth, like so many of the Bible's heroines, was a widow. In the violent and uncertain days when judges ruled Israel, a woman named Naomi and her husband, Elimelech, left a famine in Bethlehem for the hill country of Moab, where their sons married Moabite women—Orpah and Ruth. Tragically, both Elimelech and his sons died, leaving Naomi and her childless daughters-in-law with no male family members to protect their future and preserve their name. Grief-stricken and penniless, Naomi decided to journey back to Bethlehem. On the way, she urged her daughters-in-law to leave her.

"Go back, each of you, to your mother's home," she said. "May the LORD grant that each of you will find rest in the home of another husband" (Ruth 1:8, 9).

The women wept together, and Orpah took her leave. But Ruth refused to go back home.

"Where you go I will go, and where you stay I will stay," she declared. "Your people will be my people and your God my God" (v. 16).

It was a bold declaration of both loyalty and liberation, for Ruth would not concede their future to despair simply because of an absence of men. When Naomi saw that she could not convince her daughter-in-law to leave her, she allowed Ruth to come along, and the pair finally reached the city of Bethlehem, just as the barley harvest began. The narrative continually refers to Naomi's companion as "Ruth the Moabite." (See, for example, Ruth 1:22 and 2:2.)

Perhaps the only thing more surprising than Ruth's stubborn loyalty to her mother-in-law is her unconventional love story.

Once settled in Bethlehem, Ruth went to the nearby fields to glean the barley left behind by the reapers for the poor to gather, a provision stipulated by Jewish law

(Leviticus 19:9). Ruth found herself working a field owned by a wealthy and respected man from Bethlehem, named Boaz. When Boaz came out to greet his harvesters one day, he took notice of Ruth and asked his workers about her. They told him that she was a Moabite and companion to Naomi who gleaned from the field each day, working tirelessly for long hours.

Intrigued, Boaz spoke to Ruth, encouraging her to continue gleaning in his field and to avail herself of his water and the help of his servants. He invited her to share lunch with him, and warned the men working in the field not to harm or harass her in any way.

And so Ruth gleaned daily from Boaz's field until the barley harvest was finished. One night, Naomi pulled Ruth aside. She told her daughter-in-law that Boaz was a close relative and may therefore function as a *go'el*, (often translated "kinsman-redeemer"), a male relative who would undertake a levirate marriage, so family property remained in the family and the widows wouldn't be forced to enter into slavery.

"Tonight he will be winnowing barley on the threshing floor," Naomi divulged. "Wash, put on perfume, and get dressed in your best clothes. Then go down to the threshing floor, but don't let him know you are there until he has finished eating and drinking. When he lies down, note the place where he is lying. Then go and uncover his feet and lie down. He will tell you what to do" (3:2–4 UPDATED NIV).

Naomi offered a rather brazen plan, for uncovering a man's feet was a euphemism for uncovering his genitals, and the threshing floor was commonly associated with extramarital activity (Hosea 9:1). But Ruth agreed, prepared herself as Naomi had suggested, and at midnight, after Boaz had enjoyed much to drink and fallen asleep, she sneaked down beside him on his bed of barley. He awoke, startled, and Ruth asked him to spread his cloak over her. (In contrast to her mother-in-law's instructions, Ruth told Boaz what to do.)

Boaz was overjoyed, but confessed that he was not technically Naomi's closest relative.

"Stay here for the night," Boaz said, "and in the morning if [the closest kin] wants to do his duty as your guardian-redeemer, good; let him redeem you. But if he not willing, as surely as the LORD lives I will do it. Lie here until morning" (3:13 UPDATED NIV).

Ruth slept at Boaz's feet until morning, and left before the sun rose, so she wouldn't be recognized. When she told Naomi what happened, Naomi wisely noted, "The man will not rest until the matter is settled today" (v. 18).

For all her wisdom, charm, and hard work, Ruth's fate was left to a group of men. Fortunately, Boaz skillfully negotiated the terms of the redemption with his relatives and acquired Ruth, along with some property left to the family, for his own. The townspeople rejoiced, blessing Ruth and Boaz with high hopes, saying, "May the LORD make the woman who is coming into your home like Rachel and Leah, who together built up the family of Israel" (4:11 UPDATED NIV). Their praise welcomed Ruth, the Moabite, fully into the family of Abraham. She was called *eshet chayil*—a woman of valor!

The two married and had a son named Obed. But Obed is referred to as Naomi's son, for Ruth had successfully negotiated her own version of the law of levirate, allowing her mother-in-law to live in hope of leaving a distinguished family legacy once again.

The book of Ruth, one of only two books of the Bible named after a woman, concludes with a genealogy that reveals Ruth and Boaz's son Obed to be the father of Jesse, and Jesse the father of King David. In Matthew's genealogy of Jesus, Ruth is one of the five women mentioned, four of whom, the keen reader might notice, were foreigners.

March: Modesty

Hula-Hooping with the Amish

*I also want the women to dress modestly, with
decency and propriety, adorning themselves,
not with elaborate hairstyles or gold or pearls or
expensive clothes, but with good deeds, appropriate
for women who profess to worship God.*

—1 TIMOTHY 2:9–10 UPDATED NIV

TO DO THIS MONTH:

- ☐ Dress modestly (1 Timothy 2:9)
- ☐ Wear a head covering (1 Corinthians 11:6)
- ☐ Wear only dresses and skirts; no slacks or jeans (Deuteronomy 22:5)
- ☐ Abstain from wearing jewelry (1 Timothy 2:9)
- ☐ Hang out with the Amish

"You look like a hippie," Dan said, "But it's not that bad. I promise."

I stood in front of the bedroom mirror in a billowing brown peasant skirt, matching brown tights and flats, a simple lavender cardigan buttoned all the way to my collarbone, and a white, loose-knit beret on my head. No makeup. No jewelry. No product in my nest of hair.

"I look like a religious freak," I wailed. "I can't go out like this. People will think I'm—I don't know—homeschooled."

Dan sighed. (Have I mentioned that he was homeschooled?) "Hon, this was your idea, remember."

"How can I forget when you bring it up every time I get discouraged?" I grumbled back. "It's all MY fault. The project was MY idea. I am responsible for my own misery. I GET IT, OKAY?"

We would engage in this same exact argument approximately seventeen times before the end of the year. It usually began with me in the fetal position on the floor somewhere, crying about how much I had to do and how desperately I hated housework and how insufferable I found the apostle Paul's rambling prose. I'd trawl around for pity until Dan, exasperated and powerless to help, reminded me that my affliction was the result of a contract I willingly signed with a publisher, rather than the mysterious scourge of God—a pretty unsympathetic way to look at it, if you ask me. A cold distance would fall between us until a good night's rest or a couple episodes of *The Twilight Zone* extracted me from my stupor.

We were right smack-dab in the middle of the project. And it felt like it.

The arrival of March put me in a special kind of funk because it forced me to confront a subject of particular sensitivity to women of religious breeding—modesty. Drop the m-word around the wrong girl and she'll be environed by ugly flashbacks—rulers against bare legs, turtlenecks under homemade jumpers, swimsuits hidden beneath

T-shirts and shorts, and red-faced pastors blaming the fall of Western civilization on the exposure of cleavage.

On my blog I posed the question, "What first comes to mind when you hear the word 'modesty'?"

My readers had some opinions about that:

+ "Selfish Hypersexuality. The word 'modesty' to me rarely implies anything about actual clothes but more about the sexuality (availability, intention, allusion) of the wearer as seen by those who look."—Sandra
+ "'Modesty' rings a whole lot of negative bells in my mind to do with 'controlling how women dress and behave' and 'blame the victim' attitudes. Something about the word 'modest' just yanks my chain. It smacks of imposed restrictions and judgmental tastes, and making women take responsibility for the thoughts of men."—Elizabeth
+ "Humility. That's the first word to come to mind."—Verity
+ "When I hear 'modesty,' I flash back to my childhood and shorts that came to my knees and a list of things that 'good girls don't wear.' And I think of the freedom of choosing my own swimsuit my freshman year in college and the lecture I got because it was immodest (French cut legs), with my mother insisting I purchased it to get men to look and me insisting that I got it because it was beautiful with black and turquoise flowers and I felt good in it."—Rea

In Judaism, the term used for modesty is *tzniut,* and it refers to both the inward traits of humility and the outward observance of laws pertaining to dress. I asked Ahava about this and she said, "Tzniut is more than just a list of rules about how to dress. It's a state of mind. The idea is to avoid dressing in a way that draws attention to your outer self, but instead to dress so that your inner self is allowed to shine through. You should try to be pretty, but not alluring. You do a huge disservice to modest dress if you wear the same outfit over and over again, particularly if it's frumpy. Nobody wants to be around a schlumpy dresser."

Schlumpy. I love these useful Jewish words.

"*Tzniut* is also about how you act," Ahava added. "You don't want to try to make people notice you or force yourself to the forefront for attention. Having the newest and nicest things is a way that many people try to get attention, but that is not the way of tzniut."

The apostle Paul seemed to be getting at the same idea when he wrote to young Timothy, "I also want the women to dress modestly, with decency and propriety, adorning themselves, not with elaborate hairstyles or gold or pearls or expensive clothes, but with good deeds, appropriate for women who profess to worship God" (1 Timothy 2:9–10 UPDATED NIV).

The Greek word translated "modesty" here is *kosmios*. Derived from kosmos (the universe), it signified orderliness, self-control, and appropriateness, with its closest antonyms being disorder or chaos. It appears only twice in the New Testament, and interestingly, its second usage refers specifically to a godly man, who is expected to be "above reproach, faithful to his wife, temperate, self-controlled, respectable, hospitable, able to teach" (1 Timothy 3:2 UPDATED NIV). In that context, *kosmios* is typically translated as "self-controlled."

The King James Version for 1 Timothy 2:9 says that women are to wear "modest apparel, with shamefacedness and sobriety." These instructions closely resemble those given by Peter in his first epistle, where he also warned against "gold jewelry" and "elaborate hairstyles," which were apparently the Ancient Near Eastern equivalent of diamond-encrusted teeth grilles. Similarly, the Amish speak of modesty in terms of the contrast between *Hochmut* (pride), and *Demut* (humility), citing Proverbs 11:2, which says, "When pride comes, then comes disgrace, but with humility comes wisdom."

Given the sensitive nature of this whole modesty issue, I knew that the dress code I chose for the month would be highly controversial. From the Amish to evangelicals, cloistered nuns to Hasidic Jews, women from a variety of religious groups claim biblical modesty as their standard of dress, and yet none of them dress exactly the same.

What the Bible says about what (not) to wear is clearly open to interpretation. I figured my best bet was to borrow from a variety of traditions to make my own dress code. So beginning on March 9, the first day of Lent, I resolved to observe six new rules of dress for my month of modesty:

1. Wear a head covering at all times.

By far the most ubiquitous item in the world's religious wardrobe is the head covering. We recognize Sikhs by their dastars, the Amish by their white bonnets, Jewish men by their kippas, and Muslim women by the hijab. Although the Bible often mentions women's veils (Genesis 24:65; Song of Songs 4:1), there are no explicit Old Testament commandments requiring women to wear them.[1] However, it has long been a Jewish custom for married women to cover their hair, and in rabbinic literature, the veil functions as an important symbol of modesty, for it signifies that a woman is married and unavailable to all except her husband.

Like most Orthodox Jews, Ahava usually wears a simple headscarf over her hair. "It's a mystical thing," Ahava explained to me. "Since the time of my *kiddushin* [marriage] my hair has become as much a private part as my breasts."

The importance of the head covering in ancient Jewish and Christian worship is underscored in the apostle Paul's first letter to the Corinthians, where he declares that "every woman who prays or prophesies with her head uncovered dishonors her head—it is the same as having her head shaved. For if a woman does not cover her head, she might as well have her hair cut off; but if it is a disgrace for a woman to have her hair cut off or her head shaved, then she should cover her head" (11:5–6 UPDATED NIV).

Modern manifestations of the biblical veil take many different forms. Traditional Catholics often wear the mantilla, a lacy black veil that falls over the head and shoulders. Orthodox Jewish women may wear a *tichel* (headscarf), *sheitel* (wig), or *mimkhatah*. Amish and Old Order Mennonite women refer to their trademark white bonnets simply as "coverings," with styles varying from region to region. Orthodox nuns wear a long head covering called an *apostolnik* that covers the head, neck, and shoulders, while Catholic nuns typically wear a black veil over a white coif, (unless, of course, they intend to fly and instead opt for a cornette).

I'd been tossing scarves and bandannas over my head during prayer for six months, but for Lent I resolved to wear a head covering at all times. Fortunately for me, slouchy, loose-knit berets were all the rage that winter, so I found a cute, cream-colored beret at Target that wasn't too warm and that looked good with both casual and business attire. I'd wear it so often that, before the year was finished, it looked more beige than cream.

2. Wear only full-length dresses and skirts; no slacks or jeans.

Deuteronomy 22:5 says that "a woman must not wear men's clothing, nor a man wear women's clothing, for the LORD your God detests anyone who does this."

While some Jewish scholars see this commandment as a prohibition against cross-dressing, others interpret it to mean that women should not carry weapons of war, a view sometimes cited in debates about exempting women from military conscription in modern Israel. Growing up in an Independent Fundamentalist Baptist Church, my mom was forbidden to wear pants to church because of this verse, and St. Padre Pio famously refused to hear the confessions of women wearing anything other than skirts that fell at least eight inches below the knee.

In the 1960s, Cardinal Giuseppe Siri warned that the increasing popularity of women's trousers threatened "feminine psychology proper to women" and signaled "the flattening out of all mankind."

"When we see a woman in trousers," he declared, "we should think not so much of her as of all mankind, of what it will be when women will have masculinized themselves for good. Nobody stands to gain by helping to bring about a future age of vagueness, ambiguity, imperfection and, in a word, monstrosities."

That's right. Monstrosities.

So for Lent I gave up my dress pants, sweatpants, khakis, and jeans in exchange for the three cotton peasant skirts I'd been holding on to since 2003. This wasn't much of a sacrifice because I love peasant skirts; they're like wearing air. The only problem was that skirts are a bit cool for early March, which meant I had to wear tights underneath them. Also, someone who loves the Cracker Barrel as much as I do generally requires a more constrictive waistband material than elastic for the purposes of self-control in the face of breakfast-all-day specials. I must have gained five pounds during the month of March.

3. No short skirts, short sleeves, or V-necks.

The Catholic Church took the concept of modesty to a new level of specificity in 1944 when Fr. Bernard A. Kunkel launched the "Marylike Modesty Crusade," an effort to codify Pope Pius XI's instructions regarding immodest dress. In addition to producing the perfect name for an indie garage band, the Marylike Modesty Crusade issued the following seven standards of dress for Catholic women[2]:

1. Marylike is modest without compromise, "like Mary," Christ's Mother.
2. Marylike dresses have sleeves extending at least to the elbows; and skirts reaching below the knees . . .
3. Marylike dresses require full coverage for the bodice, chest, shoulders and back; except for a cut-out about the neck not exceeding two inches below the neckline in front and in the back, and a corresponding two inches on the shoulders.
4. Marylike dresses do not admit as modest coverage transparent fabrics, laces, nets, organdy, nylons, etc. unless sufficient

backing is added. However, their moderate use as trimmings is acceptable.

5. Marylike dresses avoid the improper use of flesh-colored fabrics.

6. Marylike dresses conceal rather than reveal the figure of the wearer; they do not emphasize, unduly, parts of the body.

7. Marylike dresses provide full coverage, even after jacket, cape or stole are removed and after assuming a sitting position.

I figured my own dress should be as Marylike as possible, at least for the month. This meant topping off my peasant skirts with long-sleeved, loose-fitting sweaters and sticking with high jewel necklines—not the most flattering look for my figure, especially with a veritable tent around my waist.

4. No jewelry.

In his list of God's grievances against Israel and his warnings of Jerusalem's imminent destruction, the prophet Isaiah wrote:

> *The women of Zion are haughty,*
> *walking along with outstretched necks,*
> *flirting with their eyes,*
> *strutting along with swaying hips,*
> *with ornaments jingling on their ankles.*
> *Therefore the Lord will bring sores on the heads of the*
> *   women of Zion;*
> *the LORD will make their scalps bald.*

> *In that day the Lord will snatch away their finery: the bangles and headbands and crescent necklaces, the earrings and bracelets and veils, the headdresses and anklets and sashes, the perfume bottles and charms, the signet rings and nose rings, the fine robes and the capes and cloaks, the purses and mirrors, and the linen garments and tiaras and shawls.*
>
> (ISAIAH 3:16–23 UPDATED NIV).

At first glance, this passage would suggest that Westboro Baptist Church has it wrong: what God *really* hates is accessories. But the larger context reveals that what so troubled Isaiah and his fellow prophets was the blatant materialism among Israel's rich to the neglect and disenfranchisement of its poor.

In biblical times, gold jewelry signified wealth, and although several of the Bible's heroines wore it (Genesis 24:22–31; Song of Songs 1:10–11), jewelry was far more commonly associated with excess and idol worship (Genesis 35:2–4; Exodus 32; 33:4; Jeremiah 4:30; Ezekiel 7:18–20; 16:9–15; Hosea 2:13). This sentiment carries over into the New Testament, where both Paul in his letter to Timothy and Peter in his letter to the churches of Asia Minor discouraged women from wearing gold jewelry and pearls in the context of a Christian community that prioritized simplicity and charity.

In fact, it seems that most of the Bible's instructions regarding modesty find their context in warnings about materialism, not sexuality . . . a pattern that has gone largely unnoticed by the red-faced preacher population. I've heard dozens of sermons about keeping my legs and my cleavage out of sight, but not one about ensuring that my jewelry was not acquired through unjust or exploitive trade practices.

Some conservative religious communities, such as the Amish and Old Order Mennonites, continue to forbid women to wear any sort of jewelry at all. Others simply discourage excess. I'm a bit of a jewelry fanatic—not so much of the gold and pearl variety, but of the beads and hemp variety—so I figured it would be a healthy exercise in self-discipline to ditch my necklaces, bracelets, and rings for Lent. I wore only my wedding band, not my engagement ring, and I avoided the items in Isaiah's list: bangles, headbands, earrings, bracelets, anklets, sashes, perfume, charms, rings, nose rings, fine robes, capes, shawls, and, of course, tiaras.

5. Dress and speak plainly.

The Amish prefer the word "plain" to "modest," and a spirit of plainness informs not only their style of dress, but also their customs, lifestyle, relationships, and way of looking at the world. Adopting a plain lifestyle, according to many Amish, Mennonite, and Quaker traditions, means placing a higher value on the inward traits than on outward appearance. It means living simply, without excess, and prioritizing the good of the community over the good of oneself. For those of the Old Order traditions, plainness may require forgoing cars, electricity, modern farming equipment, and modern clothing. For those in more progressive denominations, plainness may simply mean reducing carbon footprints, rejecting designer labels, and not posting a bunch of mirror self-portraits to Instagram.

I resolved to prioritize plainness in my dress and manners, which meant sticking to muted, solid colors and unembellished fabrics, speaking as honestly and plainly as possible, and resisting the urge to flaunt status symbols, like my second-generation Kindle and my Acclaim.

All said, my Lenten dress code left me with a grand total of one outfit—a lavender button-up sweater paired with one of three peasant skirts. I went to Marshalls and picked up a black skirt and a couple more tops, which brought my options to four. You would think I'd find this constrictive, but I confess there's something nice about getting up in the morning and knowing exactly what you're going to wear that day. There's also something nice about hiding your crazy hair beneath a cute, slouchy beret. I may have looked like a cross between a hippie, a homeschooler, and an Old Order Mennonite, but I'd cut my morning prep time in half, and the results weren't so schlumpy after all.

But the thing about sporting an über-modest look in this day and age is it attracts a lot of attention. Children stared at me at the grocery store. Men avoided making eye contact. Friends struggled to come up with compliments. I think a lady took a picture of me with her cell phone at a rest stop near Lancaster, Pennsylvania.

Even Dan treated me differently.

"I feel like I can't swear around you," he confessed. "You project so much . . . conservativism. It's like I'm afraid you'll be offended."

What bothered me the most about my new look was the feeling that strangers were judging me as a religious fundamentalist based solely on my appearance. I faced this insecurity each time I walked into church, wandered the mall, sat in a boardroom, or approached a speaker's podium, and it forced me to confront the fact that the reason I feared this particular judgment so acutely was because I'd grown accustomed to issuing it myself. When I saw women at the airport wearing the hijab, the first word that came to my mind was oppressed. When I saw families at the park boasting long denim skirts and tennis shoes, I labeled them sheltered. When I saw Amish buggies creeping down a busy street, I rendered their drivers legalistic, outdated. When I saw a perky coed donning a pro-life T-shirt and a "What Would Jesus Do?" bracelet at a concert, I filed her under Bible-thumper. Now I feared that all those harsh words were being mentally lobbed at me. There's perhaps no better way to foster empathy for those whose appearances you judge than to spend a few weeks walking in their shoes.

By mid-March, I'd grown tired of the double takes followed by quick glances away, tired of hurried explanations about my head coverings and skirts, tired of the way other women seemed annoyed by my presence, tired of sticking out in the crowd for trying to be plain.

But I'd soon find myself in good company.

Dan's Journal
March 22, 2011

This month has been a little weird. Not bad, just weird. Rachel has been dressed in her modesty garb. I find myself feeling like I should talk to her differently. I also wonder what people think about me—Am I an oppressive chauvinist? Do I control her and yell at her behind closed doors?

Then I realize, maybe that's how I view other people. Maybe those thoughts are what go through my mind when I see people wearing conservative clothing. I automatically suspect abuse and control. I realize it's shallow to simply assume you know a person by the clothes they are wearing, but at the same time, aren't we taught that we should "dress for the position you want?" And how many business owners would hire the interviewee with the ripped jeans and dirty T-shirt? There are reasons we associate certain clothing (or lack thereof) with certain behaviors and lifestyles. Isn't clothing a form of nonverbal communication? If so, should we be allowed to judge others by what they "say"?

It's interesting to see people's responses to Rachel. Some people, after seeing a picture of her online, asked, "Are you mocking those who dress like that?" So apparently I'm not the only one making judgments based on appearances.

"You may need to find a better Amish lady," Mary yelled over the roar of the generator powering her clothes dryer. "I'm afraid I've gotten rather fancy."

"Fancy" is how the Amish describe things like cars, electricity, blue jeans, and people who aren't Amish. But Mary wasn't fancy. Plump and grandmotherly, she spoke with a charming "Dutchy" accent and wore all the traditional accoutrements of Amish life—a black apron pulled over a muted purple blouse, a simple black skirt, a heart-shaped bonnet, wool sweater, and black Crocs. (Yes, Crocs are all the rage in Amish country right now, along with Transitions lenses.)

Mary was giving me, my friend Janet, and Janet's friend Kathy a tour of her sprawling ranch-style farmhouse, which sat on sixty gorgeous acres in Gap, Pennsylvania. Noonday light poured through the windows, but Mary showed us how the house was equipped with gas-powered lamps built into oak stands that looked like normal end tables but hid propane tanks inside. The décor was simple, though not sparse, with framed embroidery and Thomas Kinkade prints decking the walls. The playroom, for Mary's grandchildren and neighbors, was littered with blocks and coloring books and, somewhat ironically, nearly naked Barbie paper dolls.

Mary was Kathy's aunt and an acquaintance of Janet's. Janet

grew up in the Gap area but in an Old Order Mennonite community. Though she left the Mennonite tradition as an adult, she still knows just about everyone there is to know in rural Pennsylvania, and had arranged our meeting that day, as well as several additional stops in what I'd come to call the "Amish Paradise Tour of 2011." Dan and I made the ten-hour drive from Tennessee a few days before and were staying with Dan's brother and his family in Downingtown, where, despite the fact that it was late March, we were greeted with snow flurries and ice—a friendly reminder of exactly why we choose to live down south. Fortunately, the weather cleared up by the time I arrived with Janet and Kathy on Mary's farm, but it was still freakishly cold outside. Mary hurried the three of us inside and to a large kitchen table covered with a lace tablecloth, where we talked and snacked on pretzels, cheese, and freshly baked chocolate chip cookies. Two brown-eyed little girls wearing simple beige dresses and long, brown braids crept shyly to the table to watch us.

"Tell me about your own courtship," I prompted Mary after we'd chatted for a while about Amish weddings.

"We dated for about two and a half years," she responded, "which is probably not that different from the length of worldly courtships. We spent the first few months of our marriage visiting with family and living with his parents, which I suppose some might think is strange, but that is traditional in our community."

"Do you remember what you wore on your wedding day, Aunt Mary?" Kathy asked.

"Oh, it would have been something like this," Mary said, looking down at her clothes with a smile and a shrug. "Nothing fancy."

"In Amish and Mennonite weddings, girls can wear any color except for white," Janet explained to me.

"Why's that?"

"Because white is what the worldly girls wear on their wedding days," Janet said with a wry smile.

Mary nodded in agreement.

"And Amish girls can get married in any month except June," Janet continued.

"Because . . ."

"Because that's when worldly girls get married."

At one point in the conversation, Kathy pointed to a hinged leaf on the far side of the table where the two little girls were playing.

"Is this for family that has been shunned?" she asked Mary.

"Yes," Mary said with a grin. "Many of us have them now."

"What do you mean?" I asked, fingering the hinge. "What does this have to do with shunning?"

In the Amish community, shunning—or *medung*—occurs when someone who committed him- or herself to the Amish way of life as a young adult decides to leave the community later on. The severity of *medung* varies from community to community, but Mary said that each generation seems to grow more tolerant of family and friends who have left Amish life.

"We're not allowed to share a table with family members who have left the Amish way," Mary answered. "That's why we add the extra leaf, so that when such family comes to visit, they can eat with us without being at the same table."

I confess I was a little taken aback. As an outsider, it seemed rather obvious to me that it was the rule that needed to be changed, not Mary's kitchen table. At the same time, I found this odd little workaround surprisingly moving, a bizarre expression of unconditional love that spoke to the lengths to which people will go to maintain fellowship with their dearest family and friends. One is hard-pressed to find a culture in which a mother allows a law to stand between herself and her children.

"Did you ever consider leaving the Amish life?" I asked Mary.

"No, not once," she responded. "This is how it has always been for me. I can't imagine it any other way."

Mary and her husband have five children, a relatively small family for that community, and all of them remained solidly Amish, which is a source of much joy to Mary.

"So what do you think of Rachel's outfit, Mary?" Janet asked. "Is it plain enough?"

Mary chuckled, looking over my lavender button-up sweater, black A-line skirt, black boots, and beret.

"The covering is just about right," she said, "but the buttons are a little fancy." (Amish women typically use pins to fasten their clothing. Buttons are considered ornamental.)

We talked awhile longer about shoofly pie, children, and the reputation of Amish "gangs" (youth, but I swear the phrase "Amish gangs" made me want to laugh out loud every time it was said), before grabbing lunch together at a nearby café.

On our way out, Janet noticed a multicolored weighted Hula-Hoop propped up against Mary's fireplace.

"What do you use that for?" she asked

"For keeping trim!" Mary said cheerily, patting her belly.

So of course we each took a turn, giggling like schoolgirls as we swung our hips—Janet in jeans and tennis shoes, Kathy in a flowered skirt and heels, me in my A-line and boots, Mary in her apron and Crocs.

The next stop on the Amish Paradise Tour was a one-room schoolhouse just down the road from Mary's place. Mary knew the teacher and most of the students well, and I was delighted by the prospect of witnessing an Amish school in session, something tourists visiting Lancaster County rarely get to see.

When we pulled into the schoolyard,

we were greeted by an austere blond llama nibbling on the grass between a row of seesaws, and by an Amish boy, about eight or nine, tucking in his shirt and dashing from an outhouse to the front door of the modest frame schoolhouse.

We sat in the back of the classroom, where a row of benches was reserved for guests. Inside we found twenty-six students, their ages ranging from seven to fourteen, sitting at large wooden desks. The desks faced a chalkboard covered with multiplication tables and a message in neat cursive writing that said, "Salvation is free for you because someone paid for it."

A busy but ordered energy filled the room, and it appeared that different age groups were working on different subjects, some collaborating with one another, others listening to the teacher, still others working quietly by themselves. Only the littlest ones looked back and studied our faces with curiosity before returning to their work.

At the front of the classroom was a raised platform upon which sat the teacher's desk and a cast-iron stove. Gaslights hung from the ceiling, and a warm afternoon light streamed through the windows, casting a movielike glow over the quaint scene that reminded me of my favorite moments from *Anne of Green Gables*, the one where Anne slams the slate over Gilbert's head. Girls wore colored blouses covered by black jumpers or aprons, their hair pulled back with bobby pins into neat buns. Boys donned colored shirts, black pants, and suspenders. The wooden pegs on the coatrack by the door held a myriad of straw hats, bonnets, kerchiefs, and coats.

Presiding over all of this like a master conductor was an energetic and confident eighteen-year-old teacher. When we arrived, she was leading the third graders in a geography game, while answering questions from the sixth graders about their reading work, while keeping a cautious eye on a couple of fourth graders sticking their coloring sheets to the wall with putty. It was the most orderly classroom I'd ever seen.

"Eshet chayil!" I whispered to Janet.

The Amish only educate their children through eighth grade, a religious liberty that is protected by the Constitution. They reason that all a person needs to live a simple Amish life is basic elementary school education and some practical life skills. This severely limits the career options available to girls, who are expected to marry, have children, and tend a home shortly after they are baptized into the faith as young adults.

As I watched the children run around makeshift baseball bases at recess, heads bent down against the cold wind, I wondered how many of them would continue in this way of life as adults, and how many would forge their own paths. I wondered what would have happened to a girl like me—curious, skeptical, and strong-willed—had I grown up Amish in Gap, Pennsylvania, instead of evangelical in Dayton, Tennessee. It was one of those moments when you realize just how much of your own life is out of your control, how little of it you actually choose for yourself . . . right down to the day that you marry and the clothes you wear.

"I kept my head covering in the glove compartment of my car for years," Janet said with a sigh. "I put it on before family gatherings, even though everyone knew I was long gone."

It was just the two of us now. We were in Janet's car, taking a winding highway from Gap to Morgantown to pay a late afternoon visit to Janet's cousin Sarah.[3] We drove through little towns and long stretches of farmland, past general stores and horse-drawn carriages. We stopped to look at the old farmhouse where Janet grew up, and the grocery store her parents once owned. At one point we spotted a woman jogging in a knee-length skirt, apron, and head covering.

"I don't think I could finish the half-marathon in that!" Janet laughed.

Janet was one of those girls—curious, skeptical, and strong-willed. The Old Order Mennonite tradition is similar to Amish, though typically less conservative. Most Old Order Mennonites use electricity, and some drive cars. Her family initially disapproved of her leaving the Mennonite tradition, but Janet was not shunned for it. One of seven children, the rest of whom remained in the faith, she married a fellow Mennonite, and they left the tradition together.

"It was all the rules," Janet explained. "I had so many questions, and no one had any good answers to them. I think it's something you're born with—that need to inquire and to make sense of things. I just never really fit in here."

Janet's a writing buddy I got to know through the Internet. When she heard about my month of modesty, she volunteered to give me a comprehensive look at Amish country, from Zimmerman's store (where Harrison Ford made phone calls in *Witness*) to Angela's I (where I had the best sweet potato fries of my life) to the full-sized biblical tabernacle reproduction at the Mennonite Information Center in Lancaster (where a woman appropriately named Miriam gave us the grand tour).

"People are people," Janet said as we pulled past a stable full of horses into her cousin's gravel driveway. "You can be Mennonite and be just as self-centered and arrogant as the next guy, or you can be Mennonite and be generous and loving and kind. It's about the heart—not the clothes, not the rules."

Jane's cousin Sarah is famous for both her baked goods and her green thumb. Though she and her husband drive a horse and buggy, they use electricity and even own a fax machine to help Sarah keep up with bagel and bread orders.

"No computer, though," Sarah noted after we'd joined her at her kitchen table to talk. "Though I've been told I'd sell more if I had a web

page, probably more than I could handle."

Sarah was soft-spoken and warm, with a pretty face and gentle brown eyes. She looked like Emily Dickinson to me, exuding an energy of mystery and peace. Unlike the Amish, Mennonites are allowed printed fabric, so Sarah wore a simple floral dress under a black apron. Her head covering resembled Mary's but sat further back on her head, without the distinctive heart shape. Her house was smaller than Mary's, but homey and full of light. A Crock-Pot simmered on the kitchen counter.

"What do you call the ribbons attached to your covering?" I asked Sarah, pointing to the two black ties resting on her shoulders.

"We just call them ribbons," Sarah said.

"Why are some of them white and some of them black?"

"Unmarried women wear white. Then several years after marriage, they switch to black."

"Is it to mark some sort of occasion?" I asked. "Like an anniversary or the birth of a child?"

"I don't know," Sarah answered. "Someone once told me that women with children switch over to black because black shows less dirt . . . which makes sense, especially with toddlers, but still, I don't know. There are a lot of traditions like that. We keep them, but no one seems to know exactly why."

She paused for a moment and then told us a story:

"Once there was a new bride who wanted to prepare a special roast for her husband. Before putting the roast in the oven, she cut half an inch of meat off each of the two ends, just as she had always seen her mother do. When her husband asked why on earth she would cut off the best part of the roast, the only thing she knew to say was 'because my mother always made it that way.' So the next day, the bride went to her mother's house to ask why she cut the ends off the roast. Just like her daughter, the mother shrugged her shoulders and said, 'Because my mother always made it that way.' Now they were both curious. So the two found the bride's grandmother and together asked, 'Why do we cut off the ends of a roast before putting it in the oven?' Shocked, the grandmother cried, 'You've been doing that all these years? I only cut off the ends of my roasts because they never fit into my tiny pan!'"

We laughed, and Sarah confessed that sometimes Mennonite life seems a bit like that recipe for roast. Traditions stick around for reasons that have long been lost to history.

"But our traditions give us our community," she said. "They set us apart, so there is value to them."

Sarah isn't naive. She knows that the laws that govern her way of life aren't perfect, but she submits to them willingly, with her eyes open, because she believes they are good for her and her family. You might say she embodies the spirit of *Gelassenheit*, a German word that the Amish use to speak of yieldedness and peace, a willingness to let things be.

As Janet had observed, there's no typical Amish woman. As in any culture, there are some women who wrestle with the rules, some who uncritically accept the rules, and some who thrive within the rules. There are those who flourish under the creative constraints of tradition, and those who struggle to find their voice. There are women for whom the bonnets and aprons foster humility and women for whom the same things foster pride.

That's because true modesty has little to do with clothing or jewelry or makeup. The virtue that is celebrated in Scripture is so elusive we struggle to find words to capture its spirit—humility, self-control, plainness, *tznuit*, *Gelassenheit*.

And so we codify. We legislate. We pull little girls to the front of the class and slap rulers against their bare legs and try to measure modesty in inches. Then we grow so attached to our rules that they long outlive their purpose, and the next thing we know, we're adding leaves to our tables and cutting the ends off our roasts. We cling to the letter because the spirit is so much harder to master.

More often than not, this backfires, and our attempts to be different result in uniformity, our attempts to be plain draw attention to ourselves, our attempts to temper sexuality inadvertently exploit it, and our attempts to avoid offense accidentally create it.

Perhaps this is why Paul encouraged women to "adorn themselves" with good deeds, why he instructed all Christians, "Clothe yourselves with the Lord Jesus Christ," and why the valorous woman of Proverbs 31 is praised because she "clothes herself in strength and dignity."

It's not what we wear but how we wear it.

And like clothing, modesty fits each woman a little differently.

MARY MAGDALENE, THE WITNESS

Mary Magdalene went to the disciples with
the news: "I have seen the Lord!"
—JOHN 20:18

The story of how Mary Magdalene became known as a prostitute is a complicated one. One of six Marys that followed Jesus as a disciple, she was distinguished from the others through identification with her hometown of Magdala, a fishing village off the coast of the Sea of Galilee. According to the gospels of Mark and Luke, Jesus cleansed Mary of seven demons, (a backstory infinitely more complicated and mysterious than prostitution, if you ask me), after which Mary became a devoted disciple, mentioned by Luke in the same context as the Twelve, who traveled with Jesus and helped finance his ministry.

In 597 Pope Gregory the Great delivered a homily on Luke's gospel in which he combined Mary Magdalene with Mary of Bethany (Martha's sister), suggesting that this Mary was the same woman who wept at Jesus' feet in Luke 7, and that one of the seven demons Jesus excised from her was sexual immorality. The idea caught on and was perpetuated in medieval art and literature, which often portrayed Mary as a weeping, penitent prostitute. In fact, the English word maudlin, meaning "weak and sentimental," finds its derivation in this distorted image of Mary Magdalene. In 1969, the Vatican formally restated the Gospels' distinction between Mary Magdalene, Mary of Bethany, and the sinful woman of Luke 7, although it seems Martin Scorsese, Andrew Lloyd Webber, and Mel Gibson have yet to get the message. A cynic might suggest that this mistake and its subsequent popularity represent a deliberate attempt to typecast and

discredit a woman whose role in the gospel story is so critical and so revolutionary that the Eastern Orthodox Church
refers to Mary Magdalene as Equal to the Apostles.

Although she appears to have been a critical part of
Jesus' early ministry, Mary Magdalene's extraordinary faithfulness shines most brightly in the story of the Passion.
After Jesus' arrest in the Garden of Gethsemane, his male
disciples abandoned him. Judas delivered him over to the
authorities for a bribe. Peter denied him three times. And
only John, described as "the apostle whom Jesus loved,"
was present at the crucifixion.

But Mary Magdalene and the band of women who followed Jesus and supported his ministry are described by all
four gospel writers as being present during the Savior's darkest hours. Even after Jesus took his last breath, and all hope of
redemption seemed lost, the women stayed by their teacher
and their friend and prepared his body for burial. It is precisely because they were present, loyal even through failure,
that the women who followed Jesus were the first to witness
the event that would define Christianity: the resurrection.

Gospel accounts vary, but all four identify Mary
Magdalene as among the first witnesses of the empty
tomb. According to the Synoptic Gospels, she and a group
of women rose early that fateful morning, three days after
Jesus had died, to anoint the body with spices and per-
fumes. When they arrived at the tomb, they were met by
divine messengers guarding the entrance, who declared
that Jesus had risen from the dead, just as he said he would.
The women immediately left the tomb behind and, "with
fear and great joy" (Matthew 28:8), ran to tell the other
disciples. Luke notes that on their way, they remembered

what Jesus had taught them about resurrection, confirmation of the fact that these women had been present for some of Christ's most important and intimate revelations and that they took these teachings to heart.

But when the breathless women arrived at the home where the disciples had gathered, the men did not believe them. Women were considered unreliable witnesses at the time (a fact that perhaps explains why the apostle Paul omitted the women from the resurrection account entirely in his letter to the Corinthian church), so their proclamation of the good news was dismissed by the men as an "idle tale," the type of silly gossip typical of uneducated women. Perhaps the men invoked the widely held belief that, just like their sister Eve, women were easily duped.

A few, however, were curious enough to take a look at the tomb, and so, according to John's account, Mary returned with Peter and another disciple to the place she had encountered the messengers. The men saw for themselves an empty grave and a pile of linen wrappings folded neatly within it, and conceded to the women that the tomb was indeed empty. However, John 20:9 notes, "they still did not understand from Scripture that Jesus had to rise from the dead."

The men returned to report what they had seen to the rest of the disciples, leaving Mary behind. Perhaps disciples posited the theory that Jesus' body had been stolen, for John wrote that Mary, once so full of breathless excitement and impassioned belief, now stood outside the tomb, crying.

Angels appeared and asked her what was wrong.

"They have taken my Lord away," she told them, fully accepting the disciple's dismissal of her "idle tale" of resurrection, "and I don't know where they have put him" (v. 13).

The angels were then joined by a mysterious man, whom Mary assumed to be the gardener. He, too, asked why she was crying.

"Sir, if you have carried him away, tell me where you have put him, and I will get him," she pleaded (v. 15).

Only when he called her by her name did she recognize the man as Jesus.

"Mary," he said.

"Rabboni!" she cried.

"Do not hold on to me," Jesus urged as she fell before his feet, "for I have not yet ascended to the Father. Go instead to my brothers and tell them, 'I am ascending to my Father and your Father, to my God and your God'" (vv. 16–17 UPDATED NIV).

And so again, Mary Magdalene ran to the house where the disciples were staying and told them she had seen the risen savior face-to-face. "I have seen the Lord!" she declared. But it was not until Jesus appeared to the men in person, allowing them to touch the wounds in his hands and side, that they finally believed. Far from being easily deceived, women were the first to make the connection between Christ's teachings from Scripture and his resurrection, and the first to believe these teachings when they mattered the most. For her valor in twice sharing the good news to the skeptical male disciples, the early church honored Mary Magdalene with the title of Apostle to the Apostles.

That Christ ushered in this new era of life and liberation in the presence of women, and that he sent them out as the first witnesses of the complete gospel story, is perhaps the boldest, most overt affirmation of their equality in his kingdom that Jesus ever delivered. And yet too many Easter services begin with a man standing before a congregation of Christians and shouting, "He is risen!" to a chorused response of "He is risen indeed!" Were we to honor the symbolic details of the text, that distinction would always belong to a woman.

April: Purity

The Worst Time of the Month to Go Camping

"When a woman has her regular flow of blood, the impurity of her monthly period will last seven days, and anyone who touches her will be unclean till evening."

—LEVITICUS 15:19

TO DO THIS MONTH:

- ☐ Observe the Levitical Purity Laws by undergoing twelve days of ritual impurity during menstruation (Leviticus 15:19–31)
- ☐ Camp out in the front yard for first three days of impurity (Leviticus 15:19)
- ☐ Eat only pure (kosher) food
- ☐ Eliminate every trace of leavened bread from the house for Passover (Exodus 13:6–10)
- ☐ Host a Passover Seder (Exodus 12:17)
- ☐ Take a true Sabbath (see supplemental material)

Laban was pretty much the worst father-in-law of all time.

When Jacob fell in love with Laban's beautiful daughter Rachel, Jacob promised seven years of work on Laban's land in Paddan Aram in exchange for her hand.

"So Jacob served seven years to get Rachel," says Genesis 29:20, "but they seemed like only a few days to him because of his love for her."

Finally, the wedding day arrived. Laban held a feast, friends and family gathered, wine flowed with abundance . . . and somehow, amid all the revelry, Laban switched out his younger daughter, Rachel, for his older daughter, Leah, and Jacob consummated the marriage with the wrong girl.

Must have been a lot of wine.

"When morning came," the Bible says, "there was Leah!" (v. 25).

Jacob demanded an explanation. Laban said he simply wanted to marry off his older daughter first, but if Jacob would pledge to work for him another seven years, he would give him Rachel within the week. Jacob agreed, married Rachel, and spent another seven years working Laban's land. All told, Jacob ended up with four women—Leah; Leah's servant, Zilpah; Rachel; and Rachel's servant, Bilhah—whose twelve sons would become the ancestors of the Twelve Tribes of Israel.

After more than fourteen years, Jacob asked to be released from Laban's charge, so he could return with his wives and children to his homeland. Jacob argued that while his expertise had dramatically increased Laban's livestock and wealth, he had nothing of his own to show for it. But Laban refused to let Jacob go, saying he had "learned by divination" that Jacob had a special way with animals that would continue to increase the family's wealth (30:27). He told Jacob to name his price.

So Jacob, who was apparently Paddan Aram's goat-whisperer, made a deal in which he divided the family's livestock, allowing Laban and his sons the keep the animals with solid fleeces, while keeping the animals with spotted or irregular fleeces for himself. Laban probably thought he was getting the better end of this deal, as the solid-colored animals were more numerous and valuable at the time, but he forgot to take into account Jacob's mad breeding skills. Within six years, Jacob's flocks were flourishing while Laban's were feeble.

This ticked Laban off big-time. Sensing his father-in-law's anger, Jacob called together Leah and Rachel and told them to prepare for a secret departure. Leah and Rachel had little affection for their father, noting that they themselves had been treated as mere currency by him. "Surely all the wealth that God took away from our father belongs to us and our children," they said. "Do whatever God has told you" (31:16).

So Jacob's sprawling family gathered together their livestock and goods and left Paddan Aram by a camel train, crossing the Euphrates River and heading for the hill country of Gilead . . . But not before Rachel could sneak onto Laban's property and steal his precious household idols.

No one really knows what motivated Rachel's crime. Rabbinical literature contends she was merely trying to save Laban from his idolatry, while other sources suggest she may have wanted the idols for herself, as fertility charms, having struggled for so long to conceive a child. Or maybe she just wanted to stick it to the guy who'd snuck her sister into her marriage bed on her wedding day.

It took Laban three days to realize that Jacob and his family were gone. He gathered together an army of relatives and pursued the troupe for a week until he caught up with them in Gilead. Leah, Rachel, and their children must have been terrified, for Laban's force outnumbered their own. Laban angrily confronted Jacob, crying, "What have you done? You've deceived me, and you've carried off my daughters like captives in war. . . . You didn't even let me kiss my grandchildren and my daughters good-bye. . . . Why didn't you tell me, so I could send you away with joy and singing to the music of tambourines and harps?" (vv. 26, 28, 27).

(Because Laban was all about sending Jacob away with music and dancing.)

Jacob pleaded his case, but Laban would not relent until he'd recovered his stolen idols. Unaware of what Rachel had done, Jacob declared, "If you find anyone who has your gods, that person shall not live. In the presence of our relatives, see for yourself whether there is anything of yours here with me; if so, take it" (v. 32 UPDATED NIV).

Furious, Laban stormed from tent to tent, turning each one inside out in pursuit of his idols, until he reached Rachel's.

There he found his daughter sitting on a camel saddle and some blankets.

"Let it not displease my lord that I cannot rise before you," Rachel said demurely. "For the manner of women is with me" (v. 35 NKJV).

In ancient Mesopotamia, "the manner of women" was a mysterious and frightening event and the subject of much regulation and superstition. So Laban did not protest, but went about searching her tent for his idols. When he turned up short once again, Jacob got angry and demanded, "What is my crime? How have I wronged you that you hunt me down? Now that you have searched through all my goods, what have you found that belongs to your household?

Put it here in front of your relatives and mine, and let them judge between the two of us" (vv. 36–37 UPDATED NIV).

Laban finally relented, released Jacob from his charge, and the two made a covenant of peace together, marking the moment with a heap of stones.

It must have seemed to Rachel that her heart pounded louder than each clash of the altar rocks, for she had hidden the idols in her camel saddle.

Believe it or not, "the manner of women"—or, in case you still haven't caught on, "that special time of the month," "the visit from Aunt Flo"—is a popular topic in Scripture. The Torah repeatedly forbids men to have sexual relations with menstruating women with the penalty of being "cut off from their people" (Leviticus 20:18). The book of Leviticus relays specific instructions from God regarding what a woman must do during her monthly flow of blood. Most of these instructions appear in the context of ritual cleanliness, or purity, which should be distinguished from the modern concept of cleanliness as hygiene and understood instead as a ceremonial or ritualistic purity that allows full participation in religious life.

The Bible specifies several instances in which a person comes into a state of ritual impurity—skin diseases where the skin is broken or oozes any kind of fluid (Leviticus 13:1–45), the emission of semen (Leviticus 15:16), any abnormal discharge of bodily fluids (Leviticus 15:2), contact with a corpse (Numbers 19:11), childbirth (Leviticus 12:2), and menstruation (Leviticus 15:19).

Rabbi Wayne D. Dosik notes that "these circumstances all revolve around loss—loss of bodily fluid, loss of potential life, loss of life itself. In a state of loss, a person was not considered whole, and thus was not able to participate in ritual observances (in those days, the bringing of sacrifices to the sanctuary) with a full and complete heart."[1] Interestingly, Leviticus 12 stipulates that when a woman gives birth to a boy, she is considered ceremonially impure for forty-one days, but when she gives birth to a girl, she is considered ceremonially impure for more than seventy days.

To reenter a state of ritual purity, a person must bathe in natural, flowing water as a symbolic act of purification. This is why Orthodox Jewish communities today always include a *mikveh*—a specially designed bathing pool for ritual immersion that looks a bit like a whirlpool but is connected to some kind of reservoir of natural water.

For ancient Israelite women and for modern-day Orthdox Jewish women, a ritualized bath marks the end of a monthly time of separation called *niddah* (literally, "separate"). When a woman is *niddah*, she is prohibited from having any physical contact whatsoever with men, including her husband. The time of separation varies from tradition to tradition, but most Orthodox Jews, like Ahava, observe it for a total of twelve days.

The restrictions surrounding *niddah* are outlined in Leviticus 15:

> When a woman has her regular flow of blood, the impurity of her monthly period will last seven days, and anyone who touches her will be unclean till evening. Anything she lies on during her period will be unclean, and anything she sits on will be unclean. Anyone who touches her bed will be unclean; they must wash their clothes and bathe with water, and they will be unclean till evening. Anyone who touches anything she sits on will be unclean; they must wash their clothes and bathe with water, and they will be unclean till evening. Whether it is the bed or anything she was sitting on, when anyone touches it, they will be unclean till evening. If a man has sexual relations with her and her monthly flow touches him, he will be unclean for seven days; any bed he lies on will be unclean. . . . When she is cleansed from her discharge, she must count off seven days, and after that she will be ceremonially clean. On the eighth day she must take two doves or two young pigeons and bring them to the priest at the entrance to the tent of meeting. The priest is to

sacrifice one for a sin offering and the other for a burnt offering. In this way he will make atonement for her before the LORD for the uncleanness of her discharge. (vv. 19–24, 28–30 UPDATED NIV)

For millions of modern Jewish women, the principles outlined in this passage are not antiquated curiosities of an ancient time, but rules for living that still apply today. Leviticus 15 explains why the characters in *Fiddler on the Roof* grasp handkerchiefs between them while they dance. In Jewish communities where the *taharat hamishpacha*, or "laws of family purity," are still observed, a husband and wife must avoid the slightest touch during a woman's period.

"From the first sign of blood, you start counting the days," Ahava explained to me in an e-mail. "Until the end of the time, all physical contact between husband and wife is forbidden, as well as passing objects (he gets his own saltshaker!) and any kind of 'sexual' talk. We sleep in separate beds and aren't supposed to look at each other undressed."

By this point in my relationship with Ahava, chatting about sex and saltshakers seemed perfectly natural. I was constantly e-mailing her with questions, especially as I prepared for the month of April, which for me would include eating kosher, celebrating Passover, and observing the laws of family purity. As our exchanges got more personal and substantive, I grew increasingly thankful for her friendship and advice, and I realized how anemic my Christian faith had been without context, without a connection to the people from whom my Bible came.

"Then, five days to bleed," Ahava continued, "hopefully not more. I start checking for traces of blood twice daily. As soon as I get a clean check, I count seven days, and on the final day I begin to prepare for going to the mikveh (ritual bath). That is a process designed to remove foreign substance from your body—from dirt under your nails, to loose hairs, to things stuck between your teeth. It can take anywhere from forty-five minutes to two hours. Once I'm ready to go, I call the *mikveh* attendant, and she also checks me over. Then

I step down into the (thankfully) heated pool. It's about five square feet in most places, with the water chest-high. You are supposed to push your breath out and dunk yourself under as best you can. When you come up, the attendant says, 'Kosher!' if all your hair went under, and you stand there in the water and say the blessing that translates, 'Blessed are you L-rd our G-d,[2] king of the universe who has sanctified us with the commandments and has commanded us concerning immersion.' You can also take a moment for personal prayer.

"In the past, when I was ready to get pregnant again, I prayed for my future kids; sometimes I pray for my husband or for our financial situation. After that, you can dunk again any number of times, depending on your custom, and then you get to go home and kiss your husband again! Usually my husband has been getting the kids to bed and showering himself, and possibly making dinner. So, yeah, coming home is pretty romantic.

"I have mixed feelings about *niddah* these days," Ahava confessed. "Sometimes it's a nice break to not have any physical expectations in our relationship, but there have been extremely emotional times when a hug would have been nice, but it couldn't happen. This is especially hard after giving birth, which is a hugely emotional time."

No hugging after the birth of a baby?

This seemed unreasonable, even cruel. I wondered about women who miscarried and whose blood represented a deeply painful loss. Could the law not be broken to offer them comfort? What kind of God would be offended by that?

Orthodox Jews like Ahava adhere to the laws of family purity simply because they are taught in the Torah. They need no other explanation or incentive to obey. However, many say that practicing *taharat hamishpacha* does have its advantages. For one thing, the timing of a couple's reunion after *niddah* corresponds exactly with the time most women are ovulating, so couples hoping for children are in luck. In addition, word on the street is that Orthodox sex is super-steamy, that the forced separation ignites all the fantasies and longings of a couple about to embark on their honeymoon. Throw in a few readings from Song of Songs, and you've got the makings of some sweet post-*mikveh* lovemaking.

In an article for YourTango.com titled "Why Orthodox Jews May Have the Hottest Sex Lives," Lynne Meredith Schreiber wrote, "I chose this way of living because I liked the way Orthodox husbands looked at their wives—with smoldering sensuality, hidden knowing, and reverence. They spoke sweetly and didn't play games, and I never saw the flicker of distance in their eyes.

"As for those 12 days of separation," she continued, "they're hard, but the mandated time off is a gift . . . I look at him with the yearning I felt when we were dating. I start to fantasize. My husband's hands look stronger to me, and I think of his touch. Here's what we'll do; here's how he'll touch me . . . In my world, every touch is electric."[3]

At the more popular level, modern impressions of biblical menstruation are largely informed by the success of Anita Diamant's best-selling novel, *The Red Tent,* an imaginative retelling of the story of Jacob's family through the eyes of Dinah, the daughter of Leah. In *The Red Tent,* menstruation is portrayed as a time of rest, repose, and female bonding as the women of the house of Jacob gather together each month to mark the new moon and the arrival of their cycles beneath a secluded red tent. While many cultures use huts or tents for the purpose of secluding menstruating women, there is no solid biblical or archaeological evidence to suggest this happened among tent-dwelling family groups in Bronze Age Mesopotamia, though it is certainly possible. Ahava called the entire book "nonsense," but I read it anyway and loved it.

Despite the promise of some hot post-niddah sex, I was nervous about my plans to observe *taharat hamishpacha.* I still had some questions about what I could and could not touch and about how to avoid rendering every chair or bench I sat on unclean. Also, upon looking at the calendar, I realized we were scheduled to attend a wedding during the latter half of my *niddah.* How would that work exactly? The whole thing felt a bit like getting caught in the tampon aisle at Walgreens. Before long, everyone in Dayton would know that the "manner of women" was upon me.

"I just hope you don't plan to camp out in a red tent," Ahava said before signing off of chat one night.

Unbeknownst to Ahava, I'd already begun gathering the disparate pieces of camping gear we had stowed about our house.

But first, Passover . . .

∞

> *"Celebrate the Festival of Unleavened Bread,*
> *because it was on this very day that I brought your*
> *divisions out of Egypt. Celebrate this day as a*
> *lasting ordinance for the generations to come."*
> —EXODUS 12:17

Not unlike Christmas, the Jewish holidays are pulled off almost entirely by women, so making the traditional foods, preparing for company, and seeing that all the proper candles are lit and proper prayers recited seemed an integral part of "biblical womanhood" to me.

There are five Jewish holidays mentioned specifically in the Torah: Rosh Hashanah, Yom Kippur, Shavuot, Succot, and Pesach (Passover). Because the dates are different each year, only three of these overlapped with my project. The first to arrive on the calendar was Passover, which I decided to mark with a traditional Passover Seder—a ritualized feast celebrated on the first evening of the holiday in memory of the Israelites' exodus out of Egypt.

In addition to hosting a

seder, I would spend the week observing the biblical dietary laws of *kashrut* (kosher), which are significantly stricter during the Passover holiday.

My Passover Seder was scheduled for Tuesday, April 19. The Friday before, I was running a little close on time but feeling oh-so confident with my oh-so-kosher grocery list and the relative orderliness of my house that I e-mailed Ahava to brag about my progress.

"That's wonderful!" she replied. "Just let me know if you need help eliminating all the chametz from your house. That's always a challenge."

Chametz refers to leavened bread, any food made of grain and water that has been allowed to ferment and rise. This includes bread, cereal, cookies, pizza, pasta, beer, and just about every processed food on the market. The Bible instructs Jewish people to eliminate *chametz* from their diets during Passover to commemorate the haste with which their ancestors fled Egypt (Exodus 13:3; 12:20; Deuteronomy 16:3). As the story goes, the Israelites left in such a hurry, their bread didn't have time to rise, so it was brought with them as flat, unleavened cakes called matzah. The penalty for intentionally eating a piece of *chametz* the size of an olive or bigger during Passover was to be "cut off from Israel" (Exodus 12:15).

I knew about eliminating *chametz* from my diet, but this was the first I'd heard about eliminating it from my house. I asked Ahava for more details.

"Oh we get rid of all the chametz" she said, "down to the last crumb. Some women literally spend weeks cleaning. I have devoted this entire week to cleaning, but I did some sorting prior. All I have left is to do is clean out the fridge and kasher the kitchen. Then, after Shabbat, I'll kasher the dining room table and floor."

Kashering for Passover is the process of deep-cleaning dishes, pots, pans, flatware, glassware, countertops, appliances, and floors with scalding hot water, so as to completely purge them of any traces of chametz. Some Orthodox Jews even take select dishes to a *mikveh* for ritual immersion. After *kashering*, all these items must be covered in plastic wrap so they are not exposed to *chametz* between the *kashering* and the start of the holiday.

"The run-up to Passover and the seder is killer," Ahava continued. "I actually saw one panicked woman running through the grocery store on the day before the holiday last year. Passover tends to make us all a little crazy."

This didn't sound like fun anymore. It sounded like Christmas, and I needed a way out of it fast.

"The part about eliminating the chametz from your house is not in the Torah, right?" I wrote Ahava hopefully. "It's rabbinic tradition, but not really part of the law." (After all, this was my year of living biblically, not my year of living Talmudically.)

Ahava responded with a link to Exodus 13:6–10:

> For seven days eat bread made without yeast and on the seventh day hold a festival to the LORD. Eat unleavened bread during those seven days; nothing with yeast is to be seen among you, nor shall any yeast be seen anywhere within your borders. On that day tell your son, "I do this because of what the LORD did for me when I came out of Egypt." This observance will be for you like a sign on your hand and a reminder on your forehead that this law of the LORD is to be on your lips. For the LORD brought you out of Egypt with his mighty hand. You must keep this ordinance at the appointed time year after year.

Well, that settled it.

I started by vacuuming every room in the house that might contain crumbs . . . which turned out to be all of them, even (for reasons I'd rather not get into here) the bathrooms. Then I mopped the kitchen floor and cleaned all counters and tabletops with hot water. But when it came time to throw all our boxed food into a giant garbage bag, along with all our bread, flour, rice, and pasta, I just couldn't do it. We weren't in a financial position to restock our entire kitchen, especially when only half of us were supposed to be living biblically anyway. So instead, I divided everything up, designating some cabinets, drawers, and refrigerator shelves "kosher" and others "not kosher," attaching yellow sticky notes with all-caps warnings about not mixing anything up, lest the offender be "cast out" of the home.

As it turns out, my strategy wasn't completely unprecedented. Although rabbinic tradition forbids Jews from even owning *chametz* during Passover, the rabbis created a legal process that allowed some *chametz* to be "retained" during the holiday if finances or logistics make total elimination impractical. In this process, a family authorizes a rabbi to sell their *chametz* to a non-Jew for the duration of Passover. At the end of the holiday, the sale becomes null and void, and the *chametz*, which more than likely never left the property, returns to its owners.

The whole endeavor was a bit slap-bang, but I felt like I'd made a sincere effort, so after a handshake with Dan, I went ahead and recited the traditional pledge: "Any leaven that may still be in the house, which I have not seen or have not removed, shall be as if it does not exist, and as dust of the earth."

With the house prepared on Saturday, I made the forty-five-minute drive to Chattanooga on Sunday in search of ingredients for our Seder feast and food to fit my kosher diet. In addition to eliminating *chametz* for Passover, I decided to stick to the rest of the dietary laws found in the Old Testament as well, in order to eat only that which is considered pure. This meant, among other things, no pork, no shellfish, no mixing of meat and dairy, no wine or grape-juice products made by non-Jews, and no meat, except that which comes from animals slaughtered and prepared according to biblical law.

According to the Chabad Jewish Center of Chattanooga Web site, the best place in town to find kosher foods was the Publix on East Brainerd Road, so there I went, braving a spring downpour that I hoped wouldn't stick around for my "tent time." Sure enough, at Publix I found kosher-for-Passover honey, sea salt, and grape juice, as well as parve butter (parve describes food without any meat or dairy products in it, which can be eaten with meat) and chocolate, and a shelfful of matzo meal, matzo ball soup mix, and matzah bread.

The matzah (unleavened bread), came in large flat sheets like giant saltine crackers. Publix offered traditional matzah, whole wheat matzah, and egg matzah, so I got two boxes of each for good measure. I even found colorful Passover napkins covered in illustrations of the ten plagues of Egypt so we could wipe our mouths across swarms of locusts and frogs while remembering the deliverance of the Israelites from Egypt. I'd crossed most the items off my list within thirty minutes. *Eshet chayil!*

But what about the meat?

I'm at a distinct disadvantage when it comes to selecting good cuts because I get painfully shy around butchers. It's got something to do with never wanting to bother people, which I guess has something to do with low self-esteem, which I guess has something to do with a repressed childhood memory or something.

Kosher meat is a complicated affair. Only animals that chew their cud and have cloven hooves are allowed, which rules out pigs and rabbits and a bunch of other animals no one should eat anyway, but which thankfully includes cattle and sheep. Domesticated birds, like chickens and turkeys, are in, but wild fowl and birds of prey are out. Popular cuts of meat, such as sirloin, porterhouse steak, T-bone steak, and filet mignon, are not considered kosher because the Torah forbids the children of Israel from eating the hindquarters of any animal, to honor the story in the Bible where Jacob wrestles with God, limping away from the altercation with a leg injury (Genesis 32:32). A kosher animal must be subjected to a ritual slaughter in keeping with biblical law, providing the swiftest and most humane death possible. The blood must then be removed (Leviticus 7:26) through a process called "soaking and salting," and the excess fat trimmed off (Leviticus 7:23).

I had yet to decide what sort of meat I wanted to serve at our Passover Seder. I figured I'd get a look at the selection first. My initial instinct was to roast a leg of lamb, but this turns out to be a common rookie mistake. Jews actually avoid eating roasted meat at Passover, particularly lamb, because they don't want their guests to think they might be eating the Paschal sacrifice—a lamb traditionally sacrificed and eaten on the eve of Passover in a ritual that ended with the destruction of the Second Temple in AD 70.

I scanned the meats, looking for a tag or sign that said, "KOSHER MEAT HERE!" or that at least included the OU (Orthodox Union) symbol I'd grown accustomed to identifying. No luck. Finally I worked up the courage to ring the bell on the counter and ask the butcher.

"Do you have any kosher meat?" I asked sheepishly when a stout, middle-aged man in a white apron came out from behind the swinging doors.

"We sure do!" he said, pointing to the frozen food section. "Right over there."

"Oh. You mean you don't have any fresh kosher meat?"

"Not here," he responded with a polite laugh that convinced me I'd just asked a totally stupid question.

"Well then, where the heck do all the Jews in Chattanooga get their meat?!" I wanted to shout, but didn't because I hate bothering people.

So I wandered over to the frozen food section, where I nearly died of cold searching high and low for anything labeled kosher. After about fifteen minutes, I finally saw it: "Meal Mart Breaded Chicken and Turkey Cutlets: Passover Edition." The food came in a bright-blue box with an enlarged picture of the cutlets on the front and the words "Kosher for Passover" stamped prominently across the bottom along with all the proper kosher labels.

That little box created a big dilemma. On the one hand, if I served this chicken (and/or turkey) for Passover, I could rest assured that I wasn't breaking any biblical laws. On the other, we planned to invite guests to our Seder, and what kind of "biblical woman" serves frozen chicken (and/or turkey) cutlets to guests? I knew I should go back to the butcher and ask him if he knew of a local shop that sold kosher meats, but then I read the directions: "Preheat oven to 375 degrees. Arrange cutlets on a baking sheet. Cook for 40 minutes and serve."

My Passover Seder had just gotten a lot easier.

The next stop was the liquor store on the north side of town.

The Talmud requires that Jews remember their ancestors' exodus out of Egypt with "no less than four cups of wine." These four cups symbolize the four redemptions promised by God in Exodus 6:6–7 (paraphrased)—"I will take you out of Egypt," "I will deliver you from slavery," "I will redeem you with a demonstration of my power," "I will acquire you as a nation." Because Exodus 6:8 includes yet another promise from God—"I will bring you into the land of Israel"—a fifth glass of wine is poured. But the rabbis who wrote the Talmud could not agree on whether this glass should be consumed, because the land of Israel had yet to be restored to them. So they decided to leave the matter to the prophet Elijah; that is, to wait until Elijah returns ahead of the Messiah to clarify issues related to the Law. This compromise is symbolized by a fifth glass of wine, which is poured and left out for Elijah. Traditionally, children present at the Seder open the front door of the house to let Elijah in.

"Watch Elijah the Prophet enter," say the Seder instructions at Chabad.org. "Can't see him? That's precisely why you need another cup of wine."

This sounded like fun.

I walked through the door of the liquor store to find a giant sheepdog lying across the entrance . . . because this is East Tennessee, after all . . . and a skinny blond woman sitting on a stool, reading last week's edition of *Us Weekly.*

"Hi. Can I help you?" she said in a long, raspy sigh without looking up from her magazine.

"Yeah, do you have any kosher wine, like, for Passover?"

"Max!" the woman suddenly shrieked. "MAX!!"

I figured she was talking to the dog and looked to see what sort of trouble he'd gotten into.

"MAX! We got anything kosher besides the Mogen David and the Manischewitz?"

A voice from somewhere in the store shouted back, "Naw, that's it."

"This way," she said, slouching off her stool and taking me to the aisle with the fruity wines.

"Them two shelves there," she said, pointing to a row of bottom shelves filled with dark wine bottles, about half of which boasted a bunch of Concord grapes surrounded by a gold Star of David on the label. I kneeled down to study the selection, and the labels on each bottle said "Kosher for Passover," a good sign. Varieties included Concord grape, pomegranate, and blackberry. A little fruity for dinner, I thought. Big bottles of Mogen David cost eleven dollars each. Small bottles cost seven. That seemed a bit on the cheap side.

I realized then that the clerk was gone and I needed a cart—yes, a cart—for my bulk purchase. As I got up to find a cart, a short, curly-haired man with thin-rimmed glasses and a quiet voice passed by and offered gently, "You might want to try the Golan Moscato over by the dessert wines. It's kosher, but very good."

"Thank you," I responded politely, with no intention of following up. The *Us Weekly* chick with the dog told me this was the only kosher wine in the store; why ever should I believe the nice man with the New York accent?

I drove home with the windows down and the radio on, feeling like a real woman of valor with my peasant skirt fluttering in the breeze, six boxes of matzah, and three bottles of Mogen David wine rolling around in the trunk. I didn't even think to test the wine to see how it would pair with my chicken (and/or turkey) cutlets until the night before our Passover Seder, when I poured myself half a glass of Concord, took a sip, and nearly threw up in the kitchen sink.

"Dan!!!" I cried out in despair.

Dan came running, expecting to confront something truly disastrous, like the end of the paper towel roll.

"This stuff is awful," I cried. "I can't serve this!"

He took my glass and tried it himself. His nose did that thing it does when his senses are overloaded. He tried to control his face, but to no avail.

"Well, it's a little sweet," he finally said after clearing his throat.

"It's awful!" I cried. "It tastes like spiked Kool-Aid . . . only with more syrup! The Jews make HORRIBLE wine!"

"Well, now, you just sound like a racist," Dan said before taking another sip. "But you're right. It does kinda taste like Kool-Aid."

I fell to my knees to engage in a second round of kitchen floor crying that rivaled my previous bout with the butter-bleeding pie.

The next morning I got up early, drove back to Chattanooga, and bought a bottle of kosher Golan Moscato, like the man I now suspected to be Jewish had recommended, and a bottle of semisweet kosher pomegranate wine at the liquor store, without uttering so much as a word to the clerk. The sheepdog wagged his tail like we were old friends.

Fortunately, our friends Chris and Tiffany brought a bottle of Tishbi Cabernet when they showed up on our doorstep with their daughter, Early, a few hours later for the Passover Seder. The evening went beautifully. Every item at the table—from the wine to the matzah to the vegetables—carried special meaning, and assisted in the

retelling of the story of the Exodus. The chicken (and/or turkey) cutlets were a success, as was my homemade matzah toffee that served
as dessert.

Tiffany and I only made it through two glasses of wine, but Dan
and Chris managed to get down four. It was one of the best meals of
the project so far. At the end of the night, just as Chris, Tiffany, and
Early were headed out the door, I remembered to shout, "*L'shana
ha'ba-ah b'Yerushalayim!* Next time in Jerusalem!"

My period started three days later, on Good Friday. Dan was at
home, watching *The Universe* on Roku when I came out the bathroom and declared, "Honey, it's tent time!"

Dan had taken it upon himself the week prior to air out the purple-
and-beige umbrella tent that had been sleeping, undisturbed, in our
attic for the past seven years, and to find a suitable location for it in
our front yard. I guess I'd spent that morning in an undignified tizzy
because someone dared to disagree with me on the Internet, prompt-
ing Dan to gently mention that I might be needing my tent soon.

In East Tennessee, if it's April, it's either sunny, breezy, and seventy degrees outside, or your house is getting hit by a tornado—one or the other. Lucky for me, the forecast for Easter weekend called for partly cloudy skies, wind, and temperatures in the seventies. My plan was to camp out for the first three days of my period in order to truly separate myself as part of *niddah* and to pay homage to *The Red Tent*. I'd spend the remaining nine days of my "impurity" living in the guest room and using the guest bathroom (Leviticus 15:28), making sure to keep all my sheets, blankets, and clothes separate for washing (vv. 20–23).

To avoid sitting on something and rendering it unclean (v. 20), I'd be carrying my handy-dandy Rhea County High School Golden Eagles stadium cushion everywhere I went. Throughout the twelve days, I was forbidden to touching a man in any way: no handshakes, no hugs, no pats on the back, no passing the salt (v. 19). Obviously, this meant no sex with my husband. I'd allow myself to go to church, but not participate in rituals, like Communion, until I was ceremonially clean again (vv. 28–30).

So that afternoon we set the tent back up, and equipped it with an air mattress, sleeping bag, Coleman lantern, cell phone, and

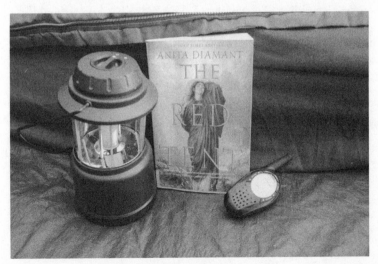

walkie-talkie. The walkie-talkie was to pacify my mother, who was convinced that putting me out in a tent in the front yard would invite every rapist in the tristate area to our neighborhood via some kind of untraceable telepathic system that they share. I gave her a hard time about it, but I confess that that night, when the wind was howling and the lantern light was flickering, I reached out to grasp that little transceiver in my hand, just to remember that it was there.

Earlier we'd gone to Mom and Dad's for dinner because my sister, Amanda, and her husband, Tim, were in town for the weekend. It was a classic Held affair: cheeseburgers, chips, homemade coleslaw, and theological discussions for dinner; Mom's famous "buster bar" layered ice cream and Trivial Pursuit for dessert. None of this being kosher, I was left to nibble idly on leftover matzah while the rest of the family scarfed down their buffet of abomination. I still wore my slouchy head covering and peasant skirt, and poor Tim blushed every time I adjusted my stadium cushion before sitting down. Somehow the liberal in the family had turned into the religious freak, and no one knew quite what to do about that.

It was weird not touching my own husband. I never realized, or appreciated, how often we communicated through the silent but assuring gestures of a squeeze of the hand, a head on a shoulder, a back-scratch, a high-five. The human touch is a powerful connective bond, and going without it can be strangely isolating. We kept forgetting about the rule, accidentally resting our arms on one another before one of us would suddenly shout, "No touching!" and we'd jerk our hands away like we were in a prison scene in *Arrested Development*.

When it came time for bed, I trudged through the front yard, pillow and lantern in hand, and settled into my tent. Dan and I checked the walkie-talkies a few times, but I'm not sure we needed them. He'd left the bedroom window open, and could apparently hear just about everything that happened outside, for, around midnight, when I caught a whiff of pollen and sneezed, he radioed in a cheery "Bless you."

This made me feel much better.

I wasn't scared so much as alert. My ears followed every snap of a twig or rustling in the bushes, transforming all the cats and squirrels of the neighborhood into rabid coyotes and mountain lions in my dreams. At one point, the motion-sensor light clicked on and I feared the worst. It didn't help that every bear within a one-hundred-mile radius was supposedly drawn to my scent.

No one likes to go camping during her period. In fact, I'd say that camping falls just below yoga, waterskiing, and tubing on my things-I'd-rather-not-do-with-Aunt-Flo list. The only thing worse than sleeping on a partially inflated air mattress on the ground is sleeping on a partially inflated air mattress on the ground with cramps . . . and a migraine . . . and an overactive imagination. And just when I'd finally start to drift off, the cursed train would barrel its way through downtown Dayton, announcing its arrival with a sudden shriek.

Between the train and the wildlife and the buzz of the streetlight, I got maybe three hours of sleep. And between the hormones and the paranoia and the stash of matzah toffee I'd downed before going to bed, I had some crazy dreams.

Dan's Journal

April 23, 2011

It was a bit awkward when Rachel carried around the stadium cushion. Granted, it was more practical than having to ceremonially cleanse each piece of furniture she sat on, but still, it was kind of weird.

As all adults know, women of a certain age have a period. It's normal. It's routine. It's just a little weird when it's public knowledge. Why? I don't know . . . and I don't really want to think about it anymore.

Oh yeah, and in case people didn't notice the stadium cushion, there was a tent in our front yard, so anyone familiar with the project who drove by probably figured it out.

This month I experienced some things I never experienced before:

1. We officially celebrated Passover.
2. We attended an Ash Wednesday service.
3. My wife camped out in the front yard.

Rachel won't know it until she reads this, but I slept with a crowbar and a hatchet under my bed, ready to fend off any attackers should the need arise.

Why a crowbar instead of a shotgun? Noise level. I wouldn't want to wake the neighborhood and have to explain why my wife was out in the tent in the first place . . . though I suppose it may have ended up in a police report. Yes. We guys think about that sort of stuff.

Once I moved from the tent to the guest room, the days of my *niddah* seemed to stretch on forever. I longed for my husband's embrace, and frankly, it wasn't sexy, like the magazine said it would be. It was lonely and isolating, one of the most difficult tasks of the project so far. When Easter brought back memories of a beloved friend who had recently died, I cried alone in my bed with only Dan's careful words, offered from the hallway, to comfort me.

It was also awkward. Near the end of my time of impurity, we attended a wedding in Chattanooga. (I "accidentally" left my stadium cushion at home for that one.) People get really touchy-feely at weddings, so I was constantly dodging the outstretched hands of warmhearted men, even giving the groom an "air hug" in the receiving line.

The upside was, Dan and I had an excuse not to dance. No one harassed us about seeing our (truly horrid) dance moves once we informed them that we couldn't touch because "the way of women" was upon me. In fact, no one really talked to us at all after that.

When the twelve days were finally over, I washed all my clothes and sheets, scrubbed down my stadium cushion, and took a long, hot shower meant to symbolize *tevilah.* (Non-Jews are not allowed to immerse themselves in a *mikveh,* and it was too cold to go skinny-dipping at the nearby state park.) Then I gave Dan a very long hug.

There's a story in the Gospels about a woman who had suffered from what appears to be a chronic uterine hemorrhage. "She had suffered a great deal under the care of many doctors and had spent all she had," notes Mark 5:26, "yet instead of getting better she grew worse."

The law makes no concession for women with bleeding disorders (Leviticus 15:25), so this woman was in a perpetual state of *niddah,* a condition that would have permanently cut her off from her husband and her religious community and that would prevent her from bearing children.

No wonder she spent all she had to try and heal her body; as long as she was *niddah,* she was not considered whole.

Jesus showed little regard for the Levitical purity codes. Word had spread around Galilee that he had recently healed someone with a skin disease by reaching out and touching him (Mark 1:41), an act forbidden by the purity laws that made lepers ceremonially unclean. Perhaps the woman had heard this rumor, for she gathered up the courage to join the large crowd that was following Jesus, pressing in around him.

If I but touch the hem of his garment, the woman resolved, as she fought her way closer to Jesus, *I will be made well* (from Mark 5:28).

So she stretched out her arm, and in an act of brazen defiance against the laws that made her unclean, touched Jesus' cloak with her fingertips.

"Immediately," Mark reports, "her hemorrhage stopped; and she felt in her body that she was healed of her disease" (v. 29 NRSV). Hers is the only healing in the Gospels that occurs without the express intent of Jesus.

At that same moment Jesus himself sensed that "power had gone forth from him," so he stopped, turned to the crowd, and asked, "Who touched my clothes?" (v. 30 NRSV).

The incredulous disciples reminded Jesus that he was in the center of a mob at the moment, so there was no way to know who had touched his clothes, but the woman, "in fear and trembling," fell down before Jesus and told him what had happened (v. 33 NRSV).

Jesus responded with words of tenderness.

"Daughter," he said "your faith has made you well. Go in peace, and be healed of your disease" (v. 34 NRSV).

It is no coincidence that immediately after encountering the "untouchable" man and the "untouchable" bleeding woman, Jesus rendered himself unclean yet again by bringing back to life the "untouchable" corpse of the daughter of Jairus, whom he "took by the hand," and told *"Talitha koum!"* ("Little girl, get up!") (v. 41).

There was a message behind these healings, and it sounded throughout all of Galilee, Judea, and the known parts of the world: When God became human, when he wrapped himself in our blood and skin and bones, his first order of business was to touch the ones that we would not touch, to fellowship in our sufferings, and to declare once and for all that purity is found not in the body, but in the heart.

READ MORE ONLINE:

"The Passover Seder"— http://rachelheldevans.com/ passover-seder

"A Sabbath for the Birds" — http://rachelheldevans.com/ sabbath-birds

LEAH, THE UNLOVED

Genesis reports that Rachel was beautiful, with a lovely figure, but that her sister, Leah, had "weak eyes" (29:17). The exact meaning of the word *rakot* (literally, "soft") is unclear. Some midrashic interpretations say that Leah had fair, beautiful eyes and that the text sought to contrast the sisters' best features. Others say that Leah's eyes were soft from weeping.

Leah was never as loved as Rachel, at least not by their shared husband. Jacob had wanted Rachel from the beginning, but he got Leah as part of a sour deal, and he made his dissatisfaction known to her, presumably through the quiet, lethal wounds that only a spouse can inflict. The writer of Genesis stated matter-of-factly what must have consumed Leah's thoughts and dreams, dragging like a millstone on her heart: "His love for Rachel was greater than his love for Leah" (v. 30 UPDATED NIV).

But Leah had a strategic advantage, a gift for which her sister so longed it nearly drove Rachel mad. Leah bore children.

"When the LORD saw that Leah was not loved," the text reports, "he enabled her to conceive, but Rachel remained childless" (v. 31 UPDATED NIV). The unloved wife was fertile, while the favored one was barren. Each wanted what the other had.

So when Leah gave birth to her first son, she named him Reuben, meaning "Look! A son," and said, "It is because the Lord has seen my misery. Surely my husband will love me now" (v. 32).

When she gave birth to her second, she called him Simeon, meaning "One who hears," and said, "Because the LORD heard that I am not loved, he gave me this one too" (v. 33).

Then, with the third, a boy named Levi, meaning "Attached," she declared, "Now at last my husband will become attached to me, because I have borne him three sons" (v. 34).

It was not until the birth of her fourth child, a boy she named Judah, meaning "Praise," that Leah was content in the validation of a higher lover. "This time," she resolved, "I will praise the LORD" (v. 35).

Meanwhile, Rachel struggled to conceive, at one point relinquishing a night with Jacob to Leah in exchange for a handful of mandrake roots, thought to aid in fertility. One can sense the tension between Leah and her husband when she informed him of the transaction. "You must sleep with me," she said. "I have hired you with my son's mandrakes" (30:16).

Leah delivered two more sons and at least one daughter. Rachel finally gave birth to Joseph, Jacob's favorite son, and Benjamin, whose life would mean her death. It was only in their burial that the women achieved the status they so desired, for Rachel's tomb on the road to Bethlehem would be regarded as a shrine to those seeking fertility, and Leah would be buried in the Tomb of the Patriarch, alongside her husband, Jacob.

May: Fertility

Quivers Full of Arrows and Sippy Cups

God said to them, "Be fruitful and multiply and fill the earth . . ."

—Genesis 1:28

TO DO THIS MONTH:

- ☐ Read a stack of parenting books (Genesis 1:28, Ephesians 6:4)
- ☐ Come clean about fear of motherhood (1 Timothy 2:15)
- ☐ Interview a Quiverfull daughter (Psalm 127:3–5)
- ☐ Babysit Addy and Aury for a day (Matthew 19:14)
- ☐ Care for a computerized "Baby-Think-It-Over" for three days (Titus 2:4)

People cope with fear in different ways.

Some prefer fight, others flight. Some get addicted to a substance; others watch a lot of TV.

When I'm afraid of something, I intellectualize it. I buy books.

I consult experts. I search to see if there are any TED talks on the topic. I memorize all the statistics about how you're more likely to get killed in a hippo-related incident than in a plane crash, and research what every religion from Buddhism to Sikhism says about death. I work my way through *Martha Stewart's Cooking School* with highlighters and sticky notes.

So it should come as no surprise that at the commencement of the month in which I was to focus on cultivating my motherly instincts, I went to town on Amazon and ordered a stack of books intended to help me think my way into maternal instincts:

+ *What to Expect When You're Expecting,* 4th ed., by Heidi Murkoff and Sharon Mazel
+ *The Baby Book: Everything You Need to Know About Your Baby from Birth to Age Two* by William Sears and Martha Sears
+ *On Becoming Baby Wise* by Gary Ezzo and Robert Bucknam
+ *How to Talk So Kids Will Listen & Listen So Kids Will Talk* by Adele Faber and Elaine Mazlish

- *Babyproofing Your Marriage* by Stacie Cockrell, Cathy O'Neill, and Julia Stone

I arrived at this list after posting what turned out to be a controversial question on Facebook: "What books would you recommend for someone interested in learning about parenting? (And no, I'm NOT pregnant!)"

The responses started out cordially enough, with a diversity of friends and acquaintances weighing in with their favorite titles on everything from pregnancy to discipline to "biblical parenting." But then someone recommended *On Becoming Baby Wise* by Gary Ezzo, and all hell broke loose.

"Whatever you do, DO NOT read ANYTHING from Gary Ezzo!" a young mom wrote in response. "He's not even a real doctor, and his cry-it-out approach is CRUEL to children."

"I used Ezzo's 'Baby Wise' and my baby was sleeping through the night long before most other babies," another wrote back. "Why should an entire family have to revolve around a baby's schedule? At least my son won't turn into a spoiled brat for getting coddled AP-style."

Apparently in his context, AP refers not to the Associated Press but to "attachment parenting," a parenting philosophy promoted by pediatrician William Sears that emphasizes the importance of parent-to-child bonding in developmental psychology. His approach stands in contrast to that of Gary Ezzo, who suggests that parents should exercise more control over a baby's sleeping and feeding schedule, allowing infants to cry it out if they get hungry or fussy out of schedule.

"Sears rules!"

"Trust Ezzo!"

"Rachel, you'll have to read them both and tell us which one you like better."

I wasn't even pregnant, and yet somehow I'd managed to get myself recruited into the Mommy Wars. Pretty soon I'd have to weigh in on breast or bottle, natural or epidural, cloth or disposable, canned or homemade, public or private, homeschool or circus. How

I responded to these questions would automatically place me into the category of "friend" or "enemy," depending on the company, and once I spoke out on an issue, there would be no turning back. This was one of about a hundred things that terrified me about motherhood. I'd spent enough time in the Bible Belt to want to keep my distance from fundamentalism, religious or otherwise.

It's no wonder books like these get referred to as "The Pregnancy Bible" or "The Baby Bible" or "The Sleep Bible," even when most of the authors make sure to note, as Dr. Sears does on his Web site, that their methods represent "an approach, rather than a strict set of rules."[1] Like the Bible, parenting philosophies are subject to differing interpretations and applications, and as with the Bible, no one seems to want to admit that.

The word on the street was that I had two options when it came to caring for my future baby: I could either eat, sleep, drink, bathe, walk, and work with my baby permanently affixed to my body until the two of us meld into one, or I could leave my baby out naked on a cold millstone to cry, refusing to hold or feed her until the schedule allowed. Apparently, there was no in between.

But upon reading both of the authors in question, I saw no instructions of the sort, but rather general guidelines for the loving care of a child, some of which made sense to me, others of which did not. When eager Facebook friends asked for a verdict, I told them, "I think I'll have to wait until when I have a baby before I decide what's best for our family," thereby successfully disappointing everyone except for my mother, who was just happy to see the phrase "*when* I have a baby" on my Facebook wall.

Sometimes our actions shape our beliefs, rather than the other way around, and I think this is especially true when it comes to raising families. We tend to take whatever's worked in our particular set of circumstances (big family, small family, AP, Ezzo, home school, public school) and project that upon everyone else in the world as the ideal. We do this, I think, to protect ourselves, to quiet those pesky insecurities that follow us through life, nipping at our heels. To declare that your way is the *only* way effectively eliminates any fear that you might be wrong, or at least pushes it below the surface for a time.

Things get even hairier when parenting philosophies and religion mix, and the folks dishing out the parenting advice are convinced that God is on their side. From contraception, to spanking, to family size, to the decision of a mother to work or stay at home, there is perhaps no arena in which women of faith are more subjected to the expectations of "biblical womanhood" than in their capacity to bear and raise children.

"Women should remain at home, sit still, keep house and bear and bring us children," Martin Luther wrote. "If a woman grows weary and at last dies from childbearing, it matters not. Let her die from bearing, she is there to do it."

"Contraception makes a prostitute out of the wife and an adulterer out of the husband," St. Augustine said.

"We need mothers who are not only family-oriented but also family-obsessed," wrote Dorothy Patterson in *Recovering Biblical Manhood & Womanhood*.[2]

"Woman's hope, the church's hope, the world's hope is joined to childbearing," says Walter Chantry. "Women, here is a life-long calling! It is the highest any woman can enter."[3]

Growing up in the Church, I must have heard a thousand times that my highest calling as a woman was to bear and bring up children. While men could honor God in varying capacities through work, family, and ministry, a woman's spiritual aptitude was measured primarily by her ability to procreate. Even as a child I noticed that the church deaconesses hosted dozens of wedding and baby showers each year, but never a housewarming party for a single woman or a celebration dinner for a woman who passed the bar or graduated from medical school. Subtly, the belief that I was incomplete without a husband and children crept into my subconscious. Without procreating, I believed, my contribution to the Church didn't really count.

It hasn't always been this way.

Both Jesus and Paul spoke highly of celibacy and singleness, and for centuries the Church honored the contributions of virgins and widows to the extent that their stories occupied the majority of Christian literature. The gory accounts of early Christian martyrdom included the celebrated heroics of unmarried virgins like Agatha (scourged, burnt, torn with meat hooks for refusing to marry the pagan governor of Sicily), Agnes (beheaded for refusing suitors and consecrating herself to Christ alone), Lucy (executed for distributing her wealth among the poor rather than marrying), and Blandina (a young slave thrown to wild beasts in the arena for professing Christianity), as well as women who chose martyrdom over motherhood, including Felicitas (executed along with her seven sons for withholding sacrifices to the Emperor) and Perpetua (thrown to wild beasts for refusing to renounce Christianity, despite her father's pleas for her to recant in the interest of her infant son).

The pendulum would swing back during the Reformation, when, as a reaction to the cloistered life, Luther and the Reformers elevated the virtues of homemaking and domesticity above those of rigid asceticism. "The word and works of God is quite clear," Luther wrote, "that women were made either to be wives or prostitutes."

Perhaps someday, all women, no matter their marital status or procreative prowess, will be equally honored by the Church.

I understand that many pastors elevate motherhood in order to counter the ways contemporary culture often dismisses the value of moms. This is a noble goal indeed, and the Church should be a place where moms are affirmed, celebrated, honored, and revered. But the teaching that motherhood is a woman's highest calling can be painful and isolating for women who remain unmarried or childless.

Carolyn Custis James said it well in her book, *Half the Church*:

> To define women solely in terms of marriage and motherhood simply does not fit the reality of most of our lives. Even for those women who enthusiastically embrace marriage and motherhood . . . a substantial part of their lives is without a husband and/

or children . . . Furthermore, the traditional message to women is tenuous at best—all it takes is a single tragic phone call for her to be dropped from that demographic. It happens every day.

A message that points to the marriage altar as the starting gate of God's calling for women leaves us with nothing to tell [unmarried women] except that God's purpose for them is not here and now, but somewhere down the road.[4]

As a Christian, my highest calling is not motherhood; my highest calling is to follow Christ. And following Christ is something a woman can do whether she is married, or single, rich or poor, sick or healthy, childless or Michelle Duggar.

Still, the religious accouterments of the past are not shed all at once, and so, for the past eight years, I'd been greeting the arrival of my period each month with a mixture of relief and guilt. I knew in my head that I didn't have to bear children to matter to God, and yet a sense of moral failure pervaded my growing collection of fears regarding motherhood. It could only be selfishness that kept me from happily ditching the laptop for a diaper bag, I reasoned. If only I had more faith, I could welcome my 30th birthday—now less than a month away—with no thought of biological clocks or bank accounts or "loosing myself" in a succession of birthday parties and play dates and Calliou reruns. Somehow, I'd known from the age of ten, with a cool and uncanny certainty, that I wanted to be a writer when I grew up, and yet I've never known with the same intensity that I wanted to be a mother. *What was wrong with me? Where were my motherly instincts? Should a person like me even consider having children when it doesn't feel natural?*

When the first set of parenting "Bibles" finally arrived in the mail, I scoured their pages for answers, but the only consensus they seemed to reach involved the importance of taking prenatal vitamins. While volumes have been written about how to care for children, little has been said about whether or not to have them to begin with. And so I found myself simultaneously resisting and revering a fundamentalist approach, squinting through the foggy gray for some sign of black-and-white. Like all who search for truth out of fear, I desperately wanted someone else to tell me exactly what to do.

> *People think we are overpopulating the world.*
> *We are just following our convictions.*
> —JIM BOB DUGGAR

The Bible often describes children as a gift from God.

"Behold, children are a heritage from the LORD," the Psalmist wrote, "the fruit of the womb a reward. Like arrows in the hand of a warrior are the children of one's youth. Blessed is the man who fills his quiver with them! He shall not be put to shame when he speaks with his enemies in the gate" (Psalm 127:3–5 ESV).

"Blessed is everyone who fears the LORD, who walks in his ways! You shall eat the fruit of the labor of your hands; you shall be blessed, and it shall be well with you. Your wife will be like a fruitful vine within your house; your children will be like olive shoots around your table" (Psalm 128:1–3 ESV).

Passages like these have long inspired the cultivation of large families among the religiously devout and most recently have given rise to what is called the Quiverfull movement.

Based on the aforementioned Psalm that describes children as arrows in a man's quiver, Quiverfull is a lifestyle in which parents keep an "open womb," discounting any form of family planning as patently immoral. The most famous "open womb" family is, of course, the Duggar family. Featured on the popular TLC reality show that began as *17 Kids and Counting*, then graduated to *18 Kids and Counting* and is now (at least the last time I checked my local listings) *19 Kids and Counting*, Jim Bob and Michelle Duggar proudly keep an open womb and appear to be loving every minute of it. With nineteen children, ages two to twenty-four, all of them with names beginning with the letter *J*, the family lives on a twenty-acre farm in Tontitown, Arkansas. Their 7,000-square-foot house includes an industrial kitchen, a cafeteria, a game room, and a laundry room, complete with four washers and four dryers. The show features the Duggars organizing their own orchestra, visiting Niagara Falls, going on a book tour, and celebrating Mother's Day. By all accounts, they seem like a happy, healthy, highly functional family.

My friend Hillary grew up in a Quiverfull home, but she says her childhood looked nothing like that of the Duggar kids.

"I'm the oldest arrow in a quiver of eleven," she said. "I can't speak for every Quiverfull household, but the strongest underlying principle of this lifestyle is trust. Adherents claim to trust God with their fertility and extend this faith to provision for all physical needs, which means that any consideration of economics often plays a secondary role, if one at all. But despite strong faith, most Quiverfull families don't have the luxury of financial freedom, and many fathers (or older siblings) work from dawn to dusk to provide for the many mouths to feed and many bodies to clothe and educate and keep warm. Most of the Quiverfull women I speak with report living arrangements in stark contrast to the abundance that the Duggars enjoy."[5]

Hillary, now thirty-two, grew up in a small farmhouse down South. She says there were times when she went nearly two weeks without a bath so the family could conserve water, and her house never had heating or air-conditioning.

"I can't remember when our toilet worked," she recalls. With just one bathroom for twelve people, the septic tank backed up again and again. "We kept a bucket in the tub to flush it when it got bad . . . The stench, the smell of un-flushed waste, permeated the house."

Still, there was much that Hillary loved about the Quiverfull lifestyle.

"In a large family, there's always someone to make you laugh, someone to cry with, someone to tell secrets to, someone to get in trouble with, someone to make memories with," she told me. "Having these relationships brought much richness and beauty to my life. But being the oldest became an endless cycle of pouring out to meet needs while my own basic needs went largely unmet. Burnout was perpetual, because on top of this was the spiritual teaching that our own needs are not important and we should die to ourselves daily."

Part of the problem, Hillary explained, is that Quiverfull turns what the Bible describes as a blessing into an implicit command, requiring women to bear as many children as possible, regardless of whether their health or finances can support those children. According to Quiverfull advocates, the Duggar lifestyle is "biblical" and therefore desirable for Christian women everywhere.

"Michelle Duggar is the real deal," noted Doug Phillips, President of Vision Forum Ministries when Michelle received the Mother of the Year award at the organization's annual Baby Conference in 2010. "She embodies the very best of a Christian role model for women."[6]

Interestingly enough, I could find no single woman in Scripture responsible for bearing more than 15 children on her own. Men like Jacob, Gideon, and Solomon had multiple wives, slaves, and concubines contributing to their large families (A possible exception is Job's wife. If she is the same wife he had before his scourge, then she would have had a total of twenty children.)

Even in the Bible, the degree to which parenthood is a blessing appears to be somewhat conditional. Speaking of the future tribulation of the Church, Jesus said, "But woe to those who are pregnant and to those who are nursing babies in those days! (Matthew 24:19).

War, famine, persecution, and instability bring us face-to-face with the sobering reality that the children we bring into the world are capable of being hurt by it. The blessing of parenthood carries enormous risk.

"One of the most astonishing and precious things about motherhood," writes Kathleen Norris, "is the brave way in which women consent to give birth to creatures who will one day die."[7]

I am not so brave. Far more frightening to me than the threat of interrupted plans or endless to-do lists is the threat of loving someone as intensely as a mother loves her child. To invite into the universe a new life, knowing full well that no one can protect that life from the currents of evil that pulse through our world and through our very bloodstreams, seems a grave and awesome task that is at once unspeakably selfish and miraculously good. I am frightened enough by how fervently I love Dan, by my absolute revolt against the possibility—no, the inevitable reality—that he will get hurt, that he will experience loss, and that one day he will die. I'm not sure my heart is big enough to wrap itself around another breakable soul.

I was once waiting in an airport next to a woman whose six-year-old daughter suffered from a rare heart defect that could take her life at any moment. In spite of mounting medical bills and the pressures of raising both a child with special needs and another younger daughter, the woman said she and her husband planned to adopt a boy from Ethiopia later that year.

"What made you want to grow your family in the midst of all this turmoil?" I asked.

"Why did the Jews have children after the Holocaust?" she asked back. "Why do women keep trying after multiple miscarriages? It's our way of shaking our fists at the future and saying, you know what?—we *will* be hopeful; things *will* get better; you can't scare us after all. Having children is, ultimately, an act of faith."

Dan's Journal
May 31, 2011

Since we don't have kids of our own, Rachel's been researching and writing a lot this month. However, she did babysit some of our friends' kids. We had two little girls over for a day while their parents were in the hospital as their new baby sister came into the world. I felt that since this month Rachel was focusing on motherhood for the project, I wouldn't have to be as present as I might otherwise be for the babysitting part. I came in and played with the kids for a half hour or so, and then went back to what I was doing.

That didn't go over very well. Rachel got pretty upset. It turned into a "you-said-when-we-had-kids-you-would-help-raise-them" argument. This discussion started after we were both in bed, the lights were off, and I was almost asleep. Rachel started crying. It didn't help that when I asked, "What's wrong?" I asked with a tone of annoyance rather than concern. After a while, we resolved the issue. When she told me that she felt like the brunt of the caretaking fell on her, and that she wanted me more involved, I told her I thought that since this was part of the project, she was supposed to be the one caring for the kids. We both understood each other's position better and we were able to go to sleep. However, I think this will be a point of further enlightenment and self-discovery if we ever have children of our own

Bidden or unbidden, God is present.
—ERASMUS

After the babysitting ordeal, I decided to lay it all out there and confess to God and everybody that I was terrified of having children.

"I've been punished by fellow Christians for saying this out loud," I wrote on my blog, "but it's the truth: I'm afraid of motherhood.

"I'm afraid that having children will disrupt our happy marriage.

"I'm afraid that starting a family will put a swift end to my career.

"I'm afraid that I will never figure out how to use [D]iaper [G]enies.

"I'm afraid that my inability to multitask will make me a bad mom.

"I'm afraid of losing myself in a world of diapers and Dora and nursery themes and mommy wars.

"I'm afraid of being totally responsible for another life.

"I'm afraid of bringing into this world a little person who can and probably will be hurt and disappointed.

"And I'm afraid that I have to figure out my own faith before I can pass it along to a new generation."

As always, I felt a strange sense of relief upon giving all those amorphous fears a shape and parading them before the public like wild animals on a circus train. Blogging is an inexpensive form of therapy if you do it right, if you use it to tell the truth about something other than what you had for dinner that night. I asked for feedback and received hundreds of comments from readers, many of whom surprised me with their candor:

- "Oh yeah. Had all of those fears, plus some. (I mean, stretch marks? Nursing bras? Spit rags? YIKES.) I filled up an entire journal when I was pregnant with my oldest, recording every single fear, no matter how irrational. We had been married for six years before we got pregnant, so I was particularly concerned about what it would do to our marriage.

  "So how did I overcome the fears? I had me some babies! Aaaaaand, I'm still scared. And bonus: EXHAUSTED. And I'm still happily married, and I love my girls with a love that is in one moment smooshy and saccharine and in the next desperate and fierce. And I'm thankful for this path we are on."—Sorta Crunchy

+ "Motherhood is transformative, and traumatic, but one thing I wish I had been told more often is that in many ways you do get your old life back—piece by piece, a little more every year. So my career definitely suffered for a few years, but now it's mostly back on track. My sleep suffered for many years but now (with a 7-year-old and a 5-year-old), I get an uninterrupted 7 hours every single night. There are parts of me that have changed forever, and that feel natural and right to me now, but in many ways the biggest surprise is how much like my old self I am now that my kids are a bit older."—Bea

+ "I have 6 children and still fear a lot of the same things you do every day. I fear that I'm doing it all wrong, that I'm screwing them up every single day. I fear that I'm losing myself, and when I do my own thing (I'm pursuing my [master's]), I fear that I'm losing them. Kids complicate things but (and here's where I go and get sappy) they make things so much more amazing. Baby feet are the cutest thing ever, nursing has been my best experience, and the first time your baby smiles at you you'll fall apart and never be put back together the same way. They can drive you crazy all day and then when you sneak into their rooms at night you'll forget every awful moment and fall in love all over again. And your marriage will be so different but, in my opinion, watching your husband fall all over himself to impress his little girl/boy is twice as good as quiet dinners and weekend getaways."—Maria

+ "Thank you for this post! I'm a single woman with no children at 32. I want a family, but I am also slowly coming to terms with the idea that I can be OK whether or not that happens. However, the people around me don't seem to be coming to terms with that idea. They all say 'when you get

married' and 'when you have kids' as if those are the certain
next steps in my life. I feel like they are waiting for those
things to happen before I'm invited to sit at the 'grown up
table' of life."—Julie

What I loved about these responses was that they didn't read like
parenting books. They read like diaries, like real life. The thought-
fulness and honesty with which these women told their stories
reminded me that a woman only loses herself when she stops looking, that no role is too confining or too grand for a woman of valor.

I confess that a part of me had hoped that by the time I finished
this month of motherhood, I'd have overcome all my fears about
being a mom and that I'd know for certain when and if Dan and
I should start a family. But as hard as I looked, I didn't find the
answers in the Bible, and I didn't find the answers in my stack of
parenting books. There's a certain security that comes with feeling like you've found a magic text, be it authored by Sears, Ezzo, or
God Almighty, that tells you *exactly* when to have children, *exactly*
how to raise them, *exactly* how to love them, and *exactly* how to be
a good mom . . . right down to the very last detail. But no such text
exists because faith isn't about having everything figured out ahead
of time; faith is about following the quiet voice of God *without* having everything figured out ahead of time.

I didn't wait for certainty when I married Dan. I didn't wait for
certainty when I wrote my first book. I didn't wait for certainty
when I decided to follow Jesus—or when I started this project. I
just listened to my heart, and let love pull me through the unknown.

The moms on my blog helped me see that perhaps I had more
motherly instincts than I'd been giving myself credit for.

Two days after my thirtieth birthday, a baby arrived on our
doorstep.

It was delivered via UPS at 1 p.m. on Friday afternoon, just as expected, in a giant cardboard box labeled "Baby-Think-It-Over: Some Decisions Last a Lifetime."

(You could say we had a successful home delivery.)

I told the lady on the phone that she could surprise me with the gender and ethnicity of the child, so as soon as I pulled away the Bubble Wrap to reveal a life-size

baby doll in blue pajamas, with fair vinyl skin and glossy azure eyes staring blankly up at me, I called Dan.

"It's a boy!" I sang.

"Well, congratulations!" Dan said.

"I've just got to put in the batteries and he'll start working. Right now he's still a little creepy."

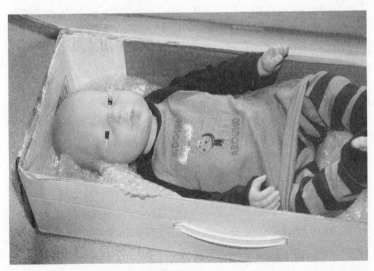

"Um, yeah . . . because adding batteries makes it a lot less creepy. I'll be home around five if you want to wait until then."

"No, I've got it under control," I said with cheery confidence. "We want to get our money's worth. Just be thinking of a good name—something playful. He's Caucasian, and looks more like you than me, but I won't be able to tell you much about his personality until—"

"You put the batteries in."

"It's material," I said, before hanging up.

Someone at the baby rental place must have dusted the little guy with baby powder for effect, because as soon as I lifted my Baby-Think-It-Over out of the box and smelled the top of his vinyl head, every latent maternal instinct inside of me kicked in and I immediately began nesting. I vacuumed the entire house, made a crib out of a laundry basket and towels, went to the dollar store to find a baby blanket and new set of clothes (they put the kid in long sleeves in the middle of June, for heaven's sake!), and read the Baby-Think-It-Over instruction manual cover to cover.

"Baby-Think-It-Over makes it possible for people to practice caring for an infant 24 hours a day, seven days a week," said the manual. "During simulation, Baby cries for care at all hours, day and night. The Caregiver has to figure out what Baby needs: feeding, burping, rocking, or diapering. The caregiver wears a unique wireless ID bracelet to ensure accountability while Baby's computer tracks its care and safe handling. Detailed data is downloaded after simulation, including exact times of missed care and specific mishandling . . . This simulation will be challenging for young adults. It will teach them more about the responsibilities of parenthood than any amount of lecturing ever could."

I bristled a bit at the suggestion that the only folks ordering Baby-Think-It-Overs were concerned parents and sex-ed teachers, but read on.

"Baby's activities are those of real infants . . . Parents of 50 newborns kept diaries of their infants' activities for several days. Baby's schedules re-create some of those days. Each 24 hours of your simulation may be the schedule of a different infant."

The doll came with a small diaper bag that included a bottle, a purple ID bracelet, and two cloth diapers. On the ID bracelet was a metal sensor that lined up with a sensor on the baby's back. Sensors on the neck, mouth, shoulder blades, arms, legs, and bottom would record every movement, from feeding to rocking to burping to changing. According to the manual, whenever the baby cried, I had to touch my sensor to the baby's back, wait for it to beep, and then offer care. The manual said the baby would let me know if he was satisfied by cooing.

I had trouble imagining how all of this would work out exactly, so I decided to just stick the batteries in and give it a go. It took about fifteen minutes to get everything activated according to the directions, and even after I was sure I'd done it right, the kid just lay there on the living room floor, looking up at me without making a sound.

I touched the sensor to his back.

Nothing.

I rocked him back and forth a little bit.

Nothing.

I placed him in his makeshift cradle.

Nothing.

He just looked up at me with that same glassy stare, his stiff little arms outstretched like a plastic mummy's.

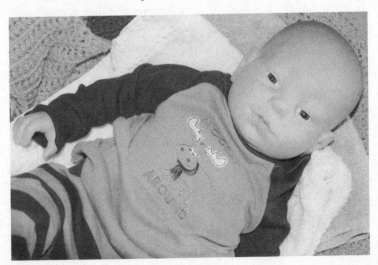

"Hello?" I asked, thumping his foot with my index finger. "Anyone there?"

I figured I might as well start dinner, so I went to the kitchen to boil the water for the spaghetti and dice up some garlic for the bread, peering around the corner every now and then to see how the kid was doing.

Nothing.

Finally, just as I was plopping a bunch of frozen meatballs into a saucepan, I was startled by a piercing scream.

He's awake!

I ran into the living room, picked the baby up, and immediately stuck the bottle in his mouth.

The cries continued.

So I ripped off his diaper and replaced it with a new one, careful to make sure the Velcro patch lined up with the proper sensor.

That didn't work either.

The noise (a rather convincing recording of a real infant's cries) kept coming, and it seemed to grow louder and more insistent by the second.

I picked the baby up, careful to support the head, and swung him

back and forth in my arms, hoping my exaggerated movements would let the sensors know I was rocking him.

He must have thought I was about to discus-throw him out the window, because his cries turned into hysterics. I stuck the bottle in his mouth again, but to no avail.

Right at this moment, I heard Dan pull into the garage.

Perfect. Just in time to catch me at my maternal finest.

Desperate to get it together

before Dan walked through the door. I turned to the instruction manual, and within seconds realized I'd forgotten to activate the main sensor on the baby's back with my ID bracelet when I provided care. As soon as I did, a loud beep issued from the baby's belly. He kept on crying, but when I grabbed the bottle for a third time and stuck it in his mouth, the screaming stopped and was replaced by the sound of sucking . . . just as Dan walked through the door.

"Look, sweetie! I'm feeding the baby!"

We decided to name him Chip after the bundle of silicon that made up his soul, a suggestion offered by a Facebook friend.

Chip cried about once every two hours. Most of the time he quieted down after a bottle or diaper change, but occasionally he just kept on screaming.

"Sometimes infants are just fussy and cannot be comforted," the manual said. "Baby simulates fussy times, but for no longer than three minutes. The real infant may have been fussy for much longer."

If folks are handing these things out to teenagers to keep them from having sex, I can personally attest to their effectiveness. As the night wore on, those "fussy times" occurred more and more frequently, as if the kid had been programmed to go nuts every fifteen minutes beginning at 8 p.m. This crying schedule meant another night in the guest room for me, just like the good ole days of *niddah* . . . Only this time I got a lot less sleep.

The moment I'd start to drift off, Chip would wake me up with his cries. Feeding sessions lasted at least twenty minutes each, and if the bottle slipped for a just second from Chip's lips, he'd punish me with a grating scream. Once, at about 3:30 a.m., when I lifted Chip out of the crib I'd pulled next to the bed, I let his head fall back just a little, and the kid went absolutely crazy, releasing a series of bloodcurdling screams that I'm pretty sure woke the dead and prompted Dan to knock softly on the guest room door to ask if everything was okay.

According to the instruction manual, failure to support the baby's head would result in one minute of crying, recorded as "neglect" in the baby's computer.

Great. I'd had the kid for less than twenty-four hours and already Baby-Think-It-Over's child protective services were on my back.

On top of all of this, Chip was a picky little fellow. If he wasn't properly burped after his feeding, he'd cycle through a pattern of three cries, followed by seven seconds of silence, followed by three cries, followed by seven seconds of silence . . . a pattern I listened to over and over and over again as I watched my alarm clock crawl from 3:00 a.m. to 3:30 a.m. to 4:00 a.m. to 4:30 a.m. I put his laundry basket crib on top of the chair next to the bed and tried to rock him while I dozed off, but the minute my arm stopped moving, he'd cry again. By 6 a.m., I could tell instantly from the tone and severity of his cries whether Chip needed a diaper change, a bottle, or rocking.

"We should change his name from Chip to Chucky," I said, with my head in my hands at breakfast the next morning.

"Maybe you should let me take him tonight," Dan offered.

"No, this was my idea," I insisted. "I want to prove to you and to myself that I can do this, that I can take care of a kid without going nuts."

"Hon, babysitting a computer is totally different from caring for your actual child," Dan said. "Don't get too carried away projecting all your insecurities about motherhood onto Chip. Just think how rewarding this would be with a real baby, a baby we created and that we actually love."

"You mean a baby that stays like this for weeks and weeks? I can't even get through one night! How am I supposed to handle years and years and years of this insanity?"

"Hon, I don't think babies cry like this for years and years," Dan responded with mild irritation. "You're being a little overdramatic. Why don't you take a nap?"

"IT'S SEXIST TO SAY I'M BEING OVERDRAMATIC!" I screamed, before storming to the bedroom to sob for forty-five minutes.

Fortunately, that afternoon Chip switched over to a different infant's sleeping cycle, because he kept quiet for longer periods of time and was easily pacified with bottles and diaper changes. I even managed to squeeze in a three-hour nap while Dan kept an eye on him.

That night, Chip woke me with his cries once or twice, but I got a lot more rest than the night before, so I felt my confidence and affection returning.

"I'm sorry I called you Chucky," I told Chip before drifting off to sleep, one arm draped across his crib. I could have sworn I saw a little grin creep across his vinyl lips, but I suppose that was just the delirium.

The next morning Dan took some photos of me and Chip to post on Facebook.

As soon as I shared them, I heard from a mom who expressed concern that I was bottle feeding . . . *my computer baby*.

(For the record, La Leche Leaguers, the Baby-Think-It-Over manual clearly states that "although you will be feeding Baby with a bottle, the recommended method for best nutrition is breast feeding.")

As the day wore on, Chip reverted back to hellion mode, crying every forty-five minutes and requiring longer and longer feeding times. The final night was as bad as the first.

I felt only a slight twinge of guilt the next afternoon when I removed Chip's batteries, swaddled him in Bubble Wrap, and placed him back in the box to return to the rental company, where he'll probably be sent to some irresponsible high school football player who will pay an opportunistic computer geek to deactivate him. Of course, real moms don't have the option to mail their kids to Virginia.

I never received the report from Chip's computer, and I got so busy with the next month's activities I forgot to follow up with the rental place.

"You were so stressed-out about that report," Dan said. "Now you're just going to wonder."

I surprised myself by responding, "I don't need some computer printout to tell me I'll be a great mom someday. I already know I will."

Dan's Journal
June 10, 2011

Part of last month's project bled over into this month. His name was Chip. After experiencing Chip, I decided we didn't need any more enlightenment and self-discovery for a while.

READ MORE ONLINE:

"Babysitting"— http://rachelheldevans.com/babysitting

THE SAMARITAN AT THE WELL

Praised be Thou, O Lord, who did not make me a gentile;
Praised be Thou O Lord, who did not make me a boor;
Praised be Thou, O Lord, who did
not make me a woman.
—R. JUDAH

There is neither Jew nor Gentile, neither
slave nor free, nor is there male and female,
for you are all one in Christ Jesus.
—GALATIANS 3:28 UPDATED NIV

In the Bible, important things happened at wells.

Rebekah earned the favor of Abraham's servant by tending to his camels at the well outside of Nahor, thereby securing Isaac's hand in marriage and her place among Israel's matriarchs. When Jacob stopped for water at a well in Paddan Aram, he encountered the shepherdess Rachel, whose beauty captured his heart. Moses, too, met his wife, Zipporah, at a well, and it was at a cool spring beside the road to Shur that the banished Hagar was promised a son by God. In ancient literature, water symbolized fertility, promise, and life, so when John told a story that began with Jesus by a well, it was intended to be momentous.

According to the fourth chapter of John's gospel, Jesus and his disciples were on their way from Judea to Galilee when they had to pass through Samaria. This route would have troubled any group of Jewish travelers, for it is well documented that in the first century, the Jews and the Samaritans absolutely hated each other. Upon reaching Jacob's well near a Samaritan town called Sychar, Jesus sat down for a rest while his disciples went into town to buy

some food. As he waited, a Samaritan woman approached
to draw water from the well.

"Will you give me a drink?" Jesus asked.

The woman was taken aback. "You are a Jew and I am a
Samaritan woman. How can you ask me for a drink?"

Here John reminded readers that Jews and Samaritans
did not associate with one another, but also implicit in the
woman's response is the fact that men in that culture, particularly rabbis, were discouraged from talking to women.

"If you knew the gift of God and who it is that asks you
for a drink," Jesus replied, "you would have asked him and
he would have given you living water."

"Sir, you have nothing to draw with and the well is deep,"
she responded. "Where can you get this living water? Are
you greater than our father Jacob, who gave us the well and
drank from it himself, as did also his sons and livestock?"

The Samaritan woman seemed to suppose this Jewish
traveler to be arrogant and self-righteous.

Jesus answered, "Everyone who drinks this water will
be thirsty again, but whoever drinks the water I give them
will never thirst. Indeed, the water I give them will become
in them a spring of water welling up to eternal life."

"Sir, give me this water so that I won't get thirsty and
have to keep coming here to draw water."

"Go call your husband and come back," Jesus said.

"I have no husband," she replied.

"You are right when you say you have no husband,"
Jesus answered. "The fact is, you have five husbands, and
the man you now have is not your husband. What you have
just said is quite true."

Traditionally, readers of the text have assumed that Jesus

called the woman out on her loose morals, confronting the aberrant nature of her sexual history in order to convict her of her sin. But such a confident interpretation reveals a certain level of bias, for John never actually revealed the reason *why* the Samaritan woman had five husbands. It is just as plausible, therefore, to assume that her marital history was a tragic one—women were not permitted to initiate divorce at that time, after all—and that Jesus sought to acknowledge the difficult set of circumstances facing a woman in first-century Palestine. She may have been a concubine or a slave, which would explain why the man she was with was not her husband.

Whatever Jesus' meaning, his words signal a significant change in the woman's banter with him.

"Sir, I can see that you are a prophet," she said.

Then, just like the Pharisee Nicodemus in the chapter before, she engaged Jesus in a theological conversation, asking him his opinion about the temple debate between the Samaritans and the Jews. Jesus transcended the debate entirely by telling the woman, "Believe me, a time is coming when you will worship the Father neither on this mountain nor in Jerusalem. . . . A time is coming and has now come when the true worshipers will worship the Father in the Spirit and in truth, for they are the kind of worshipers the Father seeks. God is spirit, and his worshipers must worship in the Spirit and in truth."

The woman responded by expressing confidence in the coming Messiah, who both Jews and Samaritans believed would settle all disputes regarding the Law.

"I, the one speaking to you—I am he," Jesus said.

She was the first person to whom he disclosed that he is the Messiah.

At that moment, the disciples returned with some food, and were "surprised to see him talking with a woman." But the Samaritan woman had taken to heart the words of this strange traveler, and so she ran back to the town to tell her family and friends, leaving her water jar, like the apostles' abandoned fishing nets, behind. Because of her testimony, many in Sychar came to believe that Jesus was not only the Messiah but the "savior of the world," and they welcomed Jesus and his disciples into their homes (John 4:7–42 UPDATED NIV).

With this unconventional well story, unique to John's gospel, Jesus establishes a new kind of family, a family that transcends marriage, endogamy, and fertility, to include the most despised and marginalized of first-century society. The Samaritan woman was nothing like the untouched Rebekah, the beautiful Rachel, or the pregnant Hagar, and yet she was the first to be presented with everlasting water, the kind available to all who thirst, no matter their status or station in life. Perhaps she is not named because the disciples could not be bothered to take her name down, or perhaps she is not named because she could be any one of us.

June: Submission

A Disposition to Yield

Wives, submit to your husbands as to the Lord.
—EPHESIANS 5:22

TO DO THIS MONTH:

- ☐ Submit to Dan "in everything" (Ephesians 5:22–24; see also Colossians 3:18–19; 1 Peter 3:1–2)
- ☐ Serve as Dan's executive assistant, based on Debi Pearl's understanding of "helpmeet" (Genesis 2:18)
- ☐ Observe the Good Wife Rules, circa 1950
- ☐ Find out what biblical submission really means

My mother says she's submitted to my father exactly three times: Once in 2004, when he preferred the gray Honda Pilot and she preferred the blue Honda Pilot. Once in 1995, when he preferred "silver stone" exterior paint and she preferred "peaceful sky." And once in 1976, when he was sure they could make it the rest of the way down a snow-covered mountain road, and she was convinced it would be their deaths.

Mom says she remembers every word the two of them exchanged in their '69 Camaro the night they almost died on Highway 226 through Spruce Pine, North Carolina. Having just survived a nasty slide that fortuitously sent them crashing into the side of the mountain rather than flying off of it, Mom had no interest in testing their luck twice. When you grow up in Florida, snow is not something you negotiate with.

"That's it. We're walking the rest of the way," she reportedly said, unbuckling her seatbelt and reaching for the door

"No. We can make it," Dad insisted.

"This is crazy! We're going to die."

"Robin, please. You need to stay in the car. I'm taking it down the hill, and I'm asking you to go with me."

"You mean you want me to submit?"

Mom wanted to make him say it, but I guess that in the time it took her to realize he wouldn't, she decided she'd rather die in the act of submitting to my father than to go on living without him.

Of course, my existence is a testimony to the fact that Mom and Dad made it down the mountain unharmed. When they reached the bottom, their car slid gently into the parking lot of Winters Motel, a run-down establishment that did remarkably good business in the months between Christmas and Easter. They walked to a nearby gas station to get dinner, called their coworkers in Salisbury to let them know they'd be coming in late on Monday morning, and watched the Steelers beat the Cowboys in Super Bowl X while the snow accumulated outside.

There are three New Testament passages that instruct wives to submit to their husbands (all quoted from the UPDATED NIV):

+ Colossians 3:18—"Wives submit yourselves to your husband, as is fitting in the Lord."
+ 1 Peter 3:1–2—"Wives, in the same way, submit yourselves to your own husbands so that, if any of them do not believe the word, they may be won over without words by the behavior of their wives, when they see the purity and reverence of your lives."

- Ephesians 5:22–24—"Wives, submit to your own husbands as you do to the Lord. For the husband is the head of the wife as Christ is head of the church, his body, of which he is the Savior. Now as the church submits to Christ, so also wives should submit to their husbands in everything."

Of the more than thirty thousand verses in the Bible, two of these passages are listed on the Council for Biblical Manhood and Womanhood Web site as being among the five "key texts" useful in understanding the relationship between men and women.[1] The belief that the womanly submission described in the epistles of Peter and Paul is normative, extending to all women everywhere, has led many conservative evangelicals to conclude that gender relationships are inherently hierarchal, that men must always lead and women must always follow.

"A man, by virtue of his manhood, is called to lead for God," wrote Raymond Ortlund in *Recovering Biblical Manhood & Womanhood*. "A woman, just by virtue of her womanhood is called to help for God."[2]

John Piper describes the spirit of submission as "a disposition to yield," and defines biblical femininity as "a freeing disposition to affirm, receive, and nurture strength and leadership from worthy men."[3]

According to Piper, a woman's obligation to submit extends beyond marriage. In *Recovering Biblical Manhood & Womanhood*, he provides a continuum along which Christian women can plot the appropriateness of various occupations along two scales: (1) the degree of authority the woman has over men, and (2) the degree to which the relationship between the woman and her male coworkers is personal. A city planner who indirectly leads men by designing traffic patterns, Piper concludes, exhibits influence that is nonpersonal and is therefore "not necessarily an offense against God's order."[4] However, a woman in military leadership or a woman acting as an official at a sporting event is overstepping her boundaries.

"Biblical submission" according to the CBMW requires that

women yield to their husbands as the primary breadwinners, defer to them when making decisions on behalf of the family, look to men as the spiritual leaders in the home and church, and avoid pursuing careers that place them in a position of authority over men.[5]

"A situation in which a female boss has a male secretary," wrote J. I. Packer, "or a marriage in which the woman (as we say) wears the trousers, will put more strain on the humanity of both parties than if it were the other way. This is part of the reality of the creation, a given fact that nothing will change."[6]

When Dan and I got married back in 2003, we began our marriage with the assumption that I would submit to him because the Bible told me to, that, while I had a voice in our decisions as a couple, Dan held the reins. We just assumed that when push came to shove, we'd stick to the traditional gender roles emphasized by our religious community. Dan would bring home the bacon, and I would fry it. He would lead, and I would follow.

And then life happened.

When you find yourself running two businesses and a household together, tasks tend to get assigned based on efficiency rather than gender. And when you share a common goal of avoiding the nine-to-five lifestyle in order to make a living as creatives, you don't care who brings home the bacon so long as it's enough to pay the Internet bill. And when you realize that faith is not static, that it is a living and evolving thing, you look less for so-called "spiritual leaders" to tell you where to go, and more for spiritual companions with whom to travel the long journey. And when you learn that marriage is a slow dance, not a tango, you worry less about who's taking the lead and instead settle into the subtle changes in each other's movements, the unforced rhythms of each other's body to life's music.[7]

Life happened, and Dan and I quickly realized that we functioned best as a team of equal partners. Sure, we argued from time to time, but we never encountered a situation in which Dan had to invoke some kind of God-ordained gavel strike in order to get his way. It just didn't feel natural to us. It didn't seem necessary.

In fact, it was Dan who began celebrating all our successes, great and small, with a high-five and a lively declaration of "Team Dan and Rachel!"

Upon the completion of a long road trip—"Team Dan and Rachel!"

Upon signing the papers for our first house—"Team Dan and Rachel!"

Upon beating another couple in Wii tennis—"Team Dan and Rachel!"

Upon a particularly fun romp in the hay—"Team Dan and Rachel!"

By the time we changed our minds about gender roles and submission, we'd been living in an egalitarian marriage for years. Team Dan and Rachel was doing just fine.

But this year was different. In deference to Commandment #1, I'd been trying to submit to Dan as his subordinate.

This meant relinquishing control over the Netflix queue, giving him the final say in restaurant choices, asking for permission before I made plans to go out with friends or start a new project, and trying to remember to do all those annoying little things he always pestered me about, like keeping track of business-related receipts and not putting lit candles next to the curtains. In turn, Dan replaced "Team Dan and Rachel!" with a playful, *Family Guy*–inspired dictum—"*I have spoken!*"—which he mostly invoked when telling me to stop working so late and watch *Saturday Night Live* with him instead. (He's a pretty okay boss, actually.)

Our biggest argument in relation to submission occurred at Christmastime. I was swamped with work, we had friends staying at our house for over a week, I still hadn't finished all my Christmas shopping, and yet I got it in my head that I wanted to throw a big, last-minute Christmas party for all my high school friends who were in town for the holidays.

"Absolutely not," Dan said. "You've got too much to do, and it will just stress you out."

"But I want to!" I protested. "It's our only chance to all get together."

"Can't you get together at someone else's house . . . or at a restaurant or something?"

"We've got the best space for it, and I don't want to burden anyone else. I'm sending the Facebook invitations now—"

"Uh, hon. I don't think you can do that."

Under normal circumstances, Dan would have let me self-destruct, as he has in the past when it comes to my tendency to overcommit.

But this year was different. This year, Dan got his way.

I was mad because this was the first time my will had been usurped on something I *really* wanted, so I threw what you might call a fit, before realizing this whole embarrassing episode would end up in a book, so I'd better stop acting like a little kid.

Clearly, I needed to work on the virtue of submission, so I decided to devote the month of June to exploring what it means to submit to one's husband, and to see if a strong-willed, liberated woman like me could truly cultivate a "disposition to yield."

But then, of course, life happened . . .

Dan's Journal

October 9, 2010

It's like I have a trump card. I don't know how I feel about it. For the last decade our relationship has been built on mutual understanding. If disagreements come up, we work through the issues on a level playing field. I've always felt respected by Rachel, so I've never felt the need to have a final, conversation-stopping, decision-making catchphrase. In many ways, our relationship is continuing as usual . . . but just knowing that I have in my possession a "you'd-have-to-if-I-said-so" trump card makes things seem a little out of balance. It's kinda like having a hidden weapon in my possession that only Rachel and I know about. It may not change how other people view me, but I still know it's there. Not sure how I feel about that. I can see why a person would feel powerful having it, but I'm not sure that makes it OK. I don't generally walk around with hidden weapons in real life; I just don't feel that insecure.

As wives, our life's work should be to perfect how we may please our husbands.[8]
—DEBI PEARL, *CREATED TO BE HIS HELP MEET*

In the second Creation account of Genesis, after God formed man from the dust of the earth and placed him in the garden of Eden, God says, "It is not good for the man to be alone. I will make a helper suitable for him" (2:18). The phrase "helper suitable," rendered "help meet" in the King James Version, comes from a combination of the words *ezer* and *kenegdo*.

Ezer appears twenty-one times in the Old Testament—twice in reference to Eve, three times in reference to nations to whom Israel appealed for military support, and sixteen times in reference to God as the helper of Israel. It means "to help," connotes both benevolence and strength, and is a popular name for Jewish boys both in the Bible and in modern times.

Kenegdo literally means "as in front of him," suggesting that the *ezer* of Genesis 2 is Adam's perfect match, the yin to his yang, the water to his fire, the Brad to his Angelina—you get the idea.

Unfortunately, all the color of its original meaning is lost in most translations of *ezer kenegdo*. After the King James Version rendered the two words "help meet," poet John Dryden came along and hyphenated them, describing his wife as his tireless "help-meet." Over time, the expression bled into "helpmeet," an independent term applied exclusively to the role of wives to their husbands, and to this day, the myth that Genesis 2 relegates wives to the status of subordinate assistants persists . . . as is painfully evidenced by Debi

Pearl's *Created to Be His Help Meet*, a book that has sold more than 200,000 copies since its publication in 2004.

"God made us women to be help meets," says Pearl, "and it is in our physical nature to be so. It is our spiritual calling and God's perfect will for us . . . God didn't create Adam and Eve at the same time and then tell them to work out some compromise on how they would each achieve their personal goals in a cooperative endeavor. . . . God gave [Eve] to Adam to be his helper, not his partner." To serve as a helpmeet, she tells women, "is how God created you and it is your purpose for existing. You were created to make [your husband] complete, not to seek personal fulfillment parallel to him."[9]

Flowchart

↓ God ↓

↓ Dan ↓

Rachel

Sprinkled with old-timey illustrations of Victorian women reading, picking flowers, carrying bread baskets, and tending to children, the book reads like an intimate advice column on everything from housekeeping to child care to sex from a fundamentalist perspective. It includes several Q&A-style sections in which Pearl addresses specific domestic scenarios. At one point, she encourages a young mother whose husband routinely beat her and threatened to kill her with a kitchen knife to stop "blabbing about his sins" and win him back by showing him more respect.[10] I threw my copy across the living room a total of seven times.

According to Pearl, "God set up a chain of command" that places women under the direct authority of their husbands. "You are not on the board of directors with an equal vote," she says. "You have no authority to set the agenda. . . . Start thinking and acting as though your husband is the head of the company and you are his secretary."[11]

I'd been exploring biblical womanhood for

nine months now, incorporating into the project the religious practices of a diversity of women, from the Amish to Orthodox Jews to
contemplative nuns, even when those practices didn't particularly
suit my interpretation of the text. So against every good instinct in
my body, I decided to try submission Debi's way.

The first thing I did was make a flowchart as per Pearl's "chain
of command." I found a photo of God from Michelangelo's *The
Creation of Adam* and printed it at the top of a piece of paper, with
an arrow pointing down to a picture of Dan, followed by an arrow
pointing down to a picture of me. I stuck the flowchart on the
refrigerator, ensuring that the few friends we had managed to retain
to this point in the project would be frightened off for good.

Next I wrote up a job description for the executive assistant to
Dan Evans:

> The Executive Assistant to Dan Evans will serve as his help-
> meet in all areas of life, assisting him in both home and busi-
> ness endeavors at his discretion.
>
> Responsibilities include:
>
> - running errands
> - completing paperwork
> - making meals
> - doing chores
> - assisting in home maintenance
> - providing a supportive atmosphere in the home
> - assisting as directed with Dan Evans's business
>   endeavors (Wylio, Chapter 2 Studios)
> - providing food and support to business partners
>   during meetings
>
> In addition, the Executive Assistant to Dan Evans will
> yield to his preferences and wishes in all areas of life, includ-
> ing but not limited to:

- social events
- daily schedule
- entertainment
- errands
- household maintenance
- menus
- sex
- dress
- family decisions

To ensure that the Executive Assistant to Dan Evans meets or exceeds his expectations, the Executive Assistant will submit to him a daily schedule and will be subject to a once-weekly performance review.

I drafted a performance review template, which, along with a job description, Dan stubbornly refused to sign, saying the whole thing had gotten a little too "weird" for him. (Great. I'd spent all afternoon working on this and suddenly—after we'd babysat a computer, subsisted on matzah, observed three-thousand-year-old menstrual restrictions, and feasted with the Amish—Dan thought things had gotten a little too "weird.")

"But I could definitely use some help writing copy for the Wylio site if you want to do that," he offered, seeing a cloud of dejection spread across his poor help meet's face.

Wylio.com is Dan's web start-up. I like to take some credit for its existence because it was my whining about what a pain in the butt it is to incorporate creative commons photos into a blog that inspired Dan and his programming friends James and Matt to create a Web site in which you can find, resize, attribute, and embed free, creative commons licensed photos into your blog in just a few steps. Wylio had been featured on TechCrunch.com back in November, generating thousands of users, but the guys were about to launch a new version to spawn some revenue, and they needed to update the site.

I was a copy editor in a previous life, so taking a red pen to the first drafts of the new web copy proved therapeutic for me and helpful for Dan. Of course, I would have helped him with this task anyway—it had always been Dan's job to keep our businesses in sync with the IRS and my job to keep them in sync with subject-verb agreement.

I felt like I needed to do more to make this month of submission stand out from the others. Debi Pearl provided just such an opportunity with her checklist for "How to Be a Good Wife Today" in *Created To Be His Help Meet.*[11]

The list, which she claims came from a 1950s home economics textbook, includes a list of do's and don'ts befitting the stereotypical 1950s housewife.[12] Pearl praises the list as "more Biblical in perspective than what the churches teach today," so just before Dan came home from his part-time job tech job, I set about preparing for his arrival like a "good wife" should.

"Prepare yourself," the instructions said. "Take 15 minutes to rest so that you'll be refreshed when he arrives. Touch up your makeup, put a ribbon in your hair and be fresh looking. He has just been with a lot of work-weary people. Be a little gay and a little more interesting."[13]

I went to the bathroom to wash my face and put on some makeup. Then I slipped into a brown pencil skirt, white blouse, and canvas pumps, before wasting a full thirty minutes in front of the bathroom mirror in a vain attempt to wrestle my forest of hair into a pretty floral headband I'd picked up at J. C. Penney's back when I was feeling a bit more optimistic about growing out my hair, as per the apostle Paul's instructions. It was a quarter to five when I finally gave up and pulled it all back into a lopsided ponytail. If there was a ribbon in the house, I didn't have time to find it.

"Clear away the clutter," the instructions continued. "Make one last trip through the main part of the house just before your husband arrives, gathering up school books, toys, papers, etc. Then, run a dust cloth over the tables. Your husband will feel he has reached a haven of rest and order, and it will give you a lift, too."[14]

I took "run a dust cloth" rather literally in this case and did a slap-bang dusting job in the living and dining rooms, after which I shoved all the clutter in the house into the guest room down the hall and closed the door.

Haven of rest and order? Check.

"Have dinner ready," said the list. "Most men are hungry when they come home and the prospect of a good meal is part of the warm welcome needed."[15]

Martha Stewart's chicken piccata was on the menu that night, so I pulled my frilly, blue and brown polka-dot apron over my blouse and skirt, broke out four chicken cutlets, and dredged them in a mixture of four, salt, and pepper. I heated some oil and butter and threw the cutlets into the skillet until they cooked through, then set them aside in the oven to stay warm. By the time I'd deglazed the pan with some cooking sherry, sending a greasy plume of steam into the air, I could hear the garage door opening.

Of course he had to come home early today.

"Minimize the noise," the instructions said. "At the time of his arrival, eliminate all noise of washer, dryer, dishwasher or vacuum. Try to encourage the children to be quiet. Be happy to see him. Greet him with a warm smile."[16]

I could hear Dan's heavy footsteps ascending the stairs as I rushed to whip up a sauce of lemon juice, capers, butter, and parsley. In my hurry, I dropped the wooden spoon, sending sticky brown sauce all over the counters, floor, and my white blouse. Dan was nearly through the kitchen doorway when I swallowed down an expletive, pulled off my apron, conjured up a sweet smile, and shouted over the still-sizzling skillet, "Welcome home, sweetie! I'm so glad you're here!"

Dan walked in and looked around. "Is everything okay?"

"Don't greet him with problems or complaints," said the Good Wife instructions. "Make him comfortable. Have him lean back in a comfortable chair or suggest he lie down in the bedroom. Have a cool or warm drink ready for him."[17]

"Why don't you go sit down in the living room and put up your feet?" I offered, with the perky intonations of a Stepford Wife.

Dan went back into the living room and sank somewhat hesitantly into the La-Z-Boy.

"Can I get you some cold water?" I asked.

"Um, okay. You sure everything's all right?"

"Yes . . . It's for the project," I said.

Enough said.

I dashed back to the kitchen to survey the damage induced by my frenzied completion of the chicken piccata. The spoon still lay haplessly in a puddle of sticky brown liquid on the floor, and the sauce had thickened more than I would have liked, but otherwise the situation appeared manageable. I took the cutlets out of the oven, swirled the sauce around a bit, and poured it over the chicken. At that point I realized I'd forgotten to make a vegetable, so I threw a frozen veggie mix into the microwave and toasted some wheat bread.

I think I could hear Martha Stewart sighing all the way from Bedford.

"Arrange his pillow and offer to take off his shoes," the Good Wife instructions said. "Speak in a low, soft, soothing and pleasant voice. Allow him to relax and unwind."[18]

I glided back into the living room, and in a saccharine voice that was not my own, sang, "Dinner's almost ready, sweetie. Can I take off your shoes?"

"Uh, no, I'm fine, thank you . . . Weren't you going to get me some water?"

"Oh, of course! Sorry!"

I ran back into the kitchen, poured a glass of ice water, and brought it back to Dan, who by that time had taken off his own shoes and powered on the Roku box. He seemed relaxed enough to me, so I went about setting the table and lighting a pair of white, long-stemmed candles in the center. Then I turned again to the list of Good Wife Rules.

"Make the evening his," it said. "Never complain if he does not take you out to dinner or to other places of entertainment; instead, try to understand his world of strain and pressure, his need to be home and relax."[19]

"*His* world of strain and pressure," I muttered back in a voice much closer to my own.

"Are you talking to me?" Dan shouted from the living room.

"No, just talking to myself, sweetie. You ready to eat?"

It was like a scene from *Mad Men*. In a matter of minutes, we'd become the model of marital repression.

"You know you don't have to do any of this to make me feel more like a man," Dan said at the dinner table as we dined on Martha's chicken piccata and Wal-Mart-brand mixed vegetables. "In fact, treating me like a baby is a little emasculating."

"I know," I said. "This all feels kinda fake, doesn't it?"

"Yeah, it does."

We ate in silence for a while.

"So what would happen if I ordered you to stop submitting to me?" Dan finally asked, a mischievous grin spreading across his face.

"Well then, I guess I'd have to obey you," I said.

"Then I order you to stop submitting to me," he said. "Or at least stop submitting to me like *this*. It's awkward."

"But what about the Good Wife Rules?"

"Nope. No more."

"But . . ."

"*I have spoken!*"

So that settled that.

Submit to one another out of reverence for Christ.
—EPHESIANS 5:21

Growing up evangelical, I learned to do inductive Bible study before I learned to balance an equation. Inductive Bible study is a method for reading Scripture which, as I remember it, involves three steps: (1) observation, (2) interpretation, (3) application.

One of the most useful tips for inductive Bible reading goes something like this: When you bump into the word *therefore* when reading the Bible, ask yourself, "*What is the 'therefore' there for?*" This usually sends you turning back a few pages to get the full context of the passage and a better sense of what the author is trying to say. The same applies to other conjunctive adverbs, such as "however," "likewise," "also," "finally," and "for example."

So as I was looking at one of the three Bible verses that instruct wives to submit to their husbands—the one from 1 Peter that says, "Wives, *in the same way* submit yourselves to your own husbands" (3:1 UPDATED NIV)—my inductive Bible study skills kicked in, and I dutifully looked back a few verses to see what Peter meant by "in the same way."

To my surprise, the preceding paragraph had nothing to do with the relationship between men and women, but was instead about the relationship between masters and slaves!

"Slaves, in reverent fear of God submit yourselves to your masters," Peter wrote, "not only to those who are good and considerate, but also to those who are harsh . . . Wives, in the same way submit yourselves to your own husbands" (1 Peter 2:18; 3:1 UPDATED NIV).

A little more research revealed that *all three of the passages that instruct wives to submit to their husbands are either preceded or followed by instructions for slaves to submit to their masters.* Right after the apostle Paul encouraged Ephesian wives to submit to their husbands as they would to Christ and Ephesian husbands to love their wives as Christ loved the Church, he instructed Ephesian slaves, "Obey your earthly masters with respect and fear, and with sincerity of heart, just as you would obey Christ" (Ephesians 6:5). The pattern repeats itself again in his letter to the Colossians, where Paul wrote:

> Wives, submit yourselves to your husbands, as is fitting in the Lord. Husbands, love your wives and do not be harsh with them.

Children, obey your parents in everything, for this pleases the Lord. Fathers, do not embitter your children, or they will become discouraged. Slaves, obey your earthly masters in everything; and do it, not only when their eye is on you and to curry their favor, but with sincerity of heart and reverence for the Lord. . . . Masters, provide your slaves with what is right and fair, because you know that you also have a Master in heaven. (3:18–22; 4:1 UPDATED NIV)

The implications of this pattern are astounding. For if Christians are to use these passages to argue that a hierarchal relationship between man and woman is divinely instituted and inherently holy, then, for consistency's sake, they must also argue the same for the relationship between master and slave.

I kept digging, and as it turns out, Peter and Paul were putting a Christian spin on what their readers would have immediately recognized as the popular Greco-Roman "household codes."[20]

As far back as the fourth century BC, philosophers considered the household to be a microcosm, designed to reflect the hierarchal structure of the society, the gods, and ultimately the universe. Aristotle wrote that "the smallest and primary parts of the household are master and slave, husband and wife, father and children." First-century philosophers Philo and Josephus included the household codes in their writings as well, arguing that a man's authority over his household was critical to the success of a society. Many Roman officials believed the household codes to be such an important part of *Pax Romana* that they passed laws ensuring its protection.

Biblical passages about wives submitting to their husbands are not, as many Christians assume, rooted in a culture epitomized by June Cleaver's kitchen, but in a culture epitomized by the Greco-Roman household codes, which gave men unilateral authority over their wives, slaves, and children.

As Sharyn Dowd has observed, the apostles "advocated this system not because God had revealed it as the divine will for Christian homes, but because it was the only stable and respectable system anyone knew about. It was the best the culture had to offer."[21]

However, the household codes found in the epistles differ significantly from the household codes found in the pagan literature of the day. In a sense, they present us with a sort of Christian remix of Greco-Roman morality that attempts to preserve the apostle Paul's earlier teaching that "there is neither Jew nor Gentile, neither slave nor free, nor is there male and female, for you are all one in Christ Jesus" (Galatians 3:28 UPDATED NIV).

Where typical Greco-Roman household codes required nothing of the head of household regarding fair treatment of subordinates, Peter and Paul encouraged men to be kind to their slaves, to be gentle with their children, and, shockingly, to love their wives as they love themselves. Furthermore, the Christian versions of the household codes are the only ones that speak directly to the less powerful members of the household—the slaves, wives, and children—probably because the church at the time consisted of just such powerless people.

To dignify their positions, Peter linked the sufferings of slaves to the suffering of Christ and likened the obedience of women to the obedience of Sarah (1 Peter 2:18–25; 3:1–6). Paul encourages slaves and women to submit the head of the household as "unto the Lord," reminding both slaves and their masters that they share a heavenly Master who shows no partiality in bestowing eternal inheritance (Ephesians 5:22; 6:5).

"When addressing those without power," notes Peter H. Davids, the apostle Peter "does not call for revolution, but upholds the values of the culture insofar as they do not conflict with commitment to Christ. He then reframes their behavior by removing it from the realm of necessity and giving it a dignity, either that of identification with Christ or of identification with the 'holy women' of Jewish antiquity."[22]

In fact, if you look close enough, you can detect the rumblings of subversion beneath the seemingly acquiescent text. It is no accident that Peter introduced his version of the household codes with a riddle—"Live as free people, but do not use your freedom as a cover-up for evil; live as God's slaves" (1 Peter 2:16 UPDATED NIV)—or that Paul began his with the general admonition that Christians are to "*submit to one another* out of reverence for Christ" (Ephesians 5:21; emphasis added). It is hard for us to recognize it now, but Peter and Paul were introducing the first Christian family to an entirely new community, a community that transcends the rigid hierarchy of human institutions, a community in which submission is mutual and all are free.

The question modern readers have to answer is whether the Greco-Roman household codes reflected upon in Ephesians, Colossians, and 1 Peter are in and of themselves holy, or if their appearance in Scripture represents the early church's attempt to blend Christianity and culture in such a way that it would preserve the dignity of adherents while honoring prevailing social and legal norms of the day. The Christian versions of the household codes were clearly progressive for their time, but does that mean they have the last word, that Christians in changing places and times cannot progress further?

It is the question that divided Christians during the Civil War, and it is the question that divides those in favor of the hierarchal-based gender roles and those who believe that the best kind of submission is that which is mutual.

For Christians, the answer must be considered in light of Jesus, who made a habit of turning hierarchy on its head.

When his disciples argued among themselves about who would be greatest in the kingdom, Jesus told them that "anyone who wants to be first must be the very last, and the servant of all" (Mark 9:35 UPDATED NIV).

In speaking to them about authority he said, "You know that the rulers of the Gentiles lord it over them, and their high officials exercise authority over them. Not so with you. Instead, whoever wants to become great among you must be your servant, and whoever wants to be first must be your slave—just as the Son of Man did not come to be served, but to serve, and to give his life as a ransom for many" (Matthew 20:25–28).

This aspect of Jesus' legacy profoundly affected relationships in the early church, to whom Paul wrote: "In your relationships with one another, have the same mindset as Christ Jesus: Who, being in very nature God, did not consider equality with God something to be used to his own advantage; rather, he made himself nothing by taking the very nature of a servant, being made in human likeness. And being found in appearance as a man, he humbled himself by becoming obedient to death—even death on a cross!" (Philippians 2:5–8 UPDATED NIV).

In the biblical narrative, hierarchy enters human relationship as part of the curse, and begins with man's oppression of women—"your desire will be for your husband, and he will rule over you" (Genesis 3:16). But with Christ, hierarchal relationships are exposed for the sham that they are, as the last are made first, the first are made last, the poor are blessed, the meek inherit the earth, and the God of the universe takes the form of a slave.

Women should not have to pry equality from the grip of Christian men. It should be surrendered willingly, with the humility and love of Jesus, or else we miss the once radical teaching that slaves and masters, parents and children, husbands and wives, rich and poor, healthy and sick, should "submit to one another" (Ephesians 5:21).

This sort of mutual submission worked best in our marriage long before we knew what to call it.

That's because I don't respect Dan because he is a man. I respect Dan because when one of his friends moves, he's the first to show up with his Explorer to help. I respect him because he's the kind of guy who treats everyone with the same level of dignity, from his clients to the clerk behind the checkout counter. I respect Dan because he'll come right out and say, "That's not funny" when someone makes a racist or homophobic joke. I respect him because he likes to do things right the first time, even when no one is watching. I respect Dan because he has spent countless Saturday afternoons at my parents' house, planting bushes and installing showerheads and fixing the computer.

I respect him because I've seen him cry on behalf of his friends. I respect Dan because he is smart enough to win just about any argument, but that doesn't mean he always does. I respect him because he gets as excited over someone else's success as he gets over his own. I respect Dan because he taught himself how to play guitar and design Web sites and invest in real estate. I respect Dan because he doesn't take himself too seriously, and he's never afraid to admit when he is wrong. I respect Dan because he has more integrity than any person I've ever known. And I respect Dan because he has never once in our marriage demanded my submission.

I don't respect my husband because he is the man and I am the woman, and it's my "place" to submit to him. I respect Dan because he is a good person, and because he has made me a better person too.

This is grace. And for us, it goes both ways.

TABITHA, THE DISCIPLE

Religion that God our Father accepts as pure
and faultless is this: to look after orphans
and widows in their distress and to keep
oneself from being polluted by the world.
—JAMES 1:27

As in modern times, women in the ancient world tended to outlive their husbands, especially in times of war. While women of high rank occasionally received financial settlements from their husbands' estates, most became the responsibility of a son, a father-in-law, or a brother-in-law. When the financial burden of another woman in the household was too much for her family to bear, or when no such relations existed, a widow would often slip into poverty. Some became wards of the temple complex, working alongside elderly slave women at menial tasks. Others begged. Still others sold themselves or their children into debt slavery, or succumbed to the lifestyle of a prostitute in order to survive.

In a patriarchal culture, a woman without the financial and physical protection of a man was especially vulnerable to violence and exploitation, so the Mosaic Law consistently demands their protection, often grouping widows with other vulnerable members of society—particularly orphans and aliens. "The fatherless, widows, and foreigners," John F. Alexander observed, "each have about forty verses that command justice for them."[23] Israel's neglect of the rights of orphans and widows was a chief concern of the Old Testament prophets, and Jesus himself issued a scathing indictment of first-century religious leaders who "devour widows' houses and for a show make lengthy prayers" (Mark 12:40).

Members of the early church sought to rectify such abuses, so widows flocked to Christianity en masse, so much so that the pagan Celsus criticized Christianity as a pathetic religion of slaves, women, and children.[24] Large portions of the Pastoral Epistles concern themselves with the mounting logistical challenges of caring for so many Christian widows, and the Roman bishop Cornelius noted that by AD 253, the church in Rome supported fifteen hundred of them.

A stalwart force in the first-century effort to restore the dignity of widows was a woman named Tabitha.[25] Likely a widow herself, but with means, Tabitha lived in the port city of Joppa at the time when Peter and Paul were busy spreading the gospel throughout Asia Minor. She was a renowned philanthropist, known throughout the land for "always doing good and helping the poor" (Acts 9:36). She was also a master seamstress, making robes and other clothing for the many widows in her care, presumably imparting on them the skills of the trade.

The biblical story of Tabitha begins with her death.

When first we hear of her in Luke's book of Acts, she has succumbed to an illness, her body washed and prepared for burial. So critical was Tabitha's ministry to the early church that Peter himself was summoned to her bedside, and when he arrived, he found widows from all across Joppa weeping together in Tabitha's home. They showed him all the clothes she had made for them.

Peter sent everyone out of the room and fell on his knees to pray. Apparently, God agreed that Tabitha was indeed indispensable, for Peter turned toward the body and said, "Tabitha, get up" (v. 40).

Tabitha opened her eyes and sat up. Peter took her by

the hand and helped her to her feet. Then he called for the widows, who ran into the room to find Tabitha alive. It is one of just two resurrection stories in the book of Acts.

To Tabitha belongs the worthy distinction of being the only woman in the New Testament identified with the feminine form of the word "disciple"—*mathetria*. The word literally means "pupil," or "apprentice," which may suggest that at some point, Tabitha studied directly under Jesus. Regardless, she must have embodied what Jesus had in mind when he told his followers to make "disciples of every nation" (Matthew 28:19), particularly in her love for those whom her Teacher called "the least of these" (25:45).

July: Justice

Eat More Guinea Pig

She opens her arms to the poor and
extends her hands to the needy.

—PROVERBS 31:20

TO DO THIS MONTH:

- ☐ Switch to fair trade products, especially with coffee and chocolate (Isaiah 58:9–12, Malachi 3:5, James 5:4–5)
- ☐ Start recycling (Genesis 2:15)
- ☐ Read *Half the Sky* by Nicholas Kristof and Sheryl WuDunn, and become a better advocate for the equality and empowerment of women worldwide (Zechariah 7:9–10; James 1:27)
- ☐ Travel to Bolivia with World Vision (Proverbs 31:20; James 1:27)

There is an old Jewish folktale about a man who went out into the world in search of true justice. Somewhere, he believed, a just society must exist, and he would not stop until he found it. His quest lasted many years and took him to many faraway places. He traveled from city to city, village to village, countryside to country-side, seeking justice like a lost treasure, until he had reached the end of the known world.

There, at the edge of the known world, lay a vast, mysterious forest. Determined to continue his quest until justice was found, the man bravely crossed over into the shadows. He searched in the caves of thieves and the huts of witches, where the gruesome inhabitants laughed and scorned him, saying, "Do you really expect to find justice *here?*"

Undeterred, the man wandered deeper and deeper into the woods, until at last he came upon a small cottage. Through the windows, he spied the warm glow of candles.

Perhaps I will find justice here, he thought to himself.

He knocked at the door, but no one answered. He knocked again, but all was silent. Curious, he pushed open the door and stepped inside.

The moment he entered the cottage, the man realized that it was enchanted, for it expanded in size to become much bigger on the inside than it appeared on the outside. His eyes widened as he realized the cavernous expanse was filled with hundreds of shelves, holding thousands upon thousands of oil candles. Some of the candles sat in fine holders of marble and gold, while others sat in holders of clay or tin. Some were filled with oil so that the flames burned as brightly as the stars, while others had little oil left, and were beginning to grow dim.

The man felt a hand on his shoulder.

He turned to find an old man with a long, white beard, wearing a white robe, standing beside him.

"*Shalom aleikhem,* my son," the old man said. "Peace be upon you."

"*Aleikhem shalom,*" the startled traveler responded.

"How can I help you?" the old man asked.

"I have traveled the world searching for justice," he said, "but never have I encountered a place like this. Tell me, what are all these candles for?"

The old man replied, "Each of these candles is a person's soul. As long as a person's candle burns, he or she remains alive. But when a person's candle burns out, the soul is taken away to leave this world."

"Can you show me the candle of my soul?" the man asked.

"Follow me," the old man replied, leading his guest through a labyrinth of rooms and shelves, passing row after row of candles.

After what seemed like a long time, they reached a small shelf that held a candle in a holder of clay.

"That is the candle of your soul," the old man said.

Immediately a wave of fear rushed over the traveler, for the wick of the candle was short and the oil nearly dry. Was his life almost over? Did he have but moments to live?

He then noticed that the candle next to his had a long wick and a tin holder filled with oil. The flame burned brightly, like it could go on forever.

"Whose candle is that?" he asked.

But the old man had disappeared.

The traveler stood there trembling, terrified that his life might be cut short before he found justice. He heard a sputtering sound and saw smoke rising from a higher shelf, signaling the death of someone else somewhere in the world. He looked at his own diminishing candle and then back at the candle next to his, burning so steady and bright. The old man was nowhere to be seen.

So the man picked up the brightly burning candle and lifted it above his own, ready to pour the oil from one holder to another.

Suddenly, he felt a strong grip on his arm.

"Is this the kind of justice you are seeking?" the old man asked.

The traveler closed his eyes in pain and when he opened them, the cottage and the candles and the old man had all vanished. He stood in the dark forest alone. It is said that he could hear the trees whispering his fate.

He had searched for justice in the great wide world but never within himself.

∾

Judaism has no word for "charity."

Instead the Jews speak of *tzedakah*, which means "justice" or "righteousness."

While the word *charity* connotes a single act of giving, *justice* speaks to right living, of aligning oneself with the world in a way that sustains rather than exploits the rest of creation. Justice is not a gift; it's a lifestyle, a commitment to the Jewish concept of *tikkun olam*—"repairing the world."

"What does the LORD require of you?" wrote the prophet Micah. "To act justly and to love mercy and to walk humbly with your God" (Micah 6:8).

"Is not this the kind of fasting I have chosen," God asks through Isaiah, "to loose the chains of injustice and untie the cords of the yoke, to set the oppressed free? . . . Is it not to share your food with the hungry, and to provide the poor wanderer with shelter?" (Isaiah 58:6–7).

"Administer true justice," says Zechariah 7. "Show mercy and compassion to one another. Do not oppress the widow or the fatherless, the alien or the poor" (vv. 9–10).

"Let justice roll down like waters," declares Amos, "and righteousness like an everflowing stream" (5:24 ESV).

Committed to these central Jewish teachings, Jesus spent the majority of his ministry among the poor, sick, and oppressed, and taught that "whatever you did for one of the least of these brothers of mine, you did for me " (Matthew 25:40). The early church followed suit and did such a good job caring for the poor that Julian the Apostate noted with some chagrin that "the godless Galileans [Christians] feed not only their poor but ours also." According to Luke, "there was not a needy person among them, for as many as were possessors of lands or houses sold them . . . and distribution was made to each as any had need" (Acts 4:34–35 RSV).

This is why, when Glenn Beck gets on TV and tells Christians to leave churches that advocate social justice, I slap the screen with the backside of my sandal. Justice is one of the most consistent and clear teachings of Scripture, and traditionally, a crucial function of the Church.[1] A recent study found that Americans who read their Bibles regularly are 35 percent more likely to say it is important to "actively seek social and economic justice" than those who own a Bible but don't bother to open it too often.[2]

So what did all of this mean for my year of biblical womanhood?

I noticed right away that women in Scripture seem particularly concerned with justice. King Lemuel's mother reminded her son to "speak up for those who cannot speak for themselves, for the rights of all who are destitute. Speak up and judge fairly; defend the rights of the poor and needy" (Proverbs 31:8–9). The "woman of valor" of Proverbs 31 "opens her arms to the poor and extends her hands to the needy" (v. 20). Hannah praises a God who "raises the poor from the dust and lifts the needy from the ash heap" (1 Samuel 2:8), and in the Magnificat, Mary vows to serve the God who "has lifted up the humble" and "filled the hungry with good things" (Luke 1:52–53). Women like Tabitha are praised in the Bible, while Amos compares women who "oppress the poor and crush the needy" to cows who will be "taken away with hooks" (4:1–2).

I didn't want to be taken away with meat hooks, or worse yet, compared to a cow, so I dedicated the month of July to practicing justice.

Dan and I already gave to several charities, and we even volunteered from time to time, but these were acts of mercy that had little effect on our day-to-day lives. For the project, I wanted to focus on where the bulk of our money actually went by examining our habits as consumers, particularly what came into the house each week and what left the house each week. This meant taking a hard look at what we ate and what we threw away to see how those habits affected other people and the planet. I also wanted to learn more about the ways women across the world are affected by injustice, so I committed to reading Nicholas Kristof and Sheryl

WuDunn's highly acclaimed book, *Half the Sky*, which describes how empowering women can lift entire communities out of poverty and suffering.

This was all I had planned for the month in my initial outline, but things got a lot more interesting when, in June, I got a call from World Vision inviting me to travel with a team of bloggers to Bolivia for a week.

Bolivia. Like, in South America.

The trip was scheduled for the end of July, and the purpose was to give me a firsthand look at how the organization—one of the largest charities in the world—operates on the ground, and to raise funds for World Vision's child sponsorship program by sharing my experience on the blog.

Opportunities like this one don't come around that often, especially in years in which you are attempting to obey the Bible literally, so in addition to studying up on ethical consumption and reading *Half the Sky*, I found myself prepping for my month of justice by getting vaccinated for yellow fever.

"They're suggesting I get a typhoid shot too," I told Dan over my cell phone from the health clinic. "It's not required for the visa; just a precaution."

"Well, sure, sweetie. Whatever you think."

"It costs ninety-five bucks."

Dan was quiet for a few seconds. Then, "You can *recover* from typhoid, right?"

It was a low point in our personal finance history, but the beginning of my biggest adventure in biblical womanhood yet.

How does God's love abide in anyone who
has the world's goods and sees a brother or
sister in need and yet refuses to help?

—1 JOHN 3:17 NRSV

The cool washcloth over my eyes did little to dull the relentless pulses of pain assaulting my sinuses, head, and shoulders. I'd slept for eleven hours straight, and still no relief. When I tried to sit up, it was as though a magnetic pull forced me back down into the damp, twisted sheets. I was too tired to throw up again, too nauseated to move. My limbs felt heavy. The room spun around. So I lay in the fetal position for hours more, listening to the gentle swoosh of the ceiling fan and praying for death.

No, I didn't get typhoid.

I quit coffee, cold turkey.

There were several reasons for doing so. First, Dan had been pestering me about kicking my caffeine habit for years, and now, with the power invested in him by Commandment #1, he'd become insistent.

"You going to quit caffeine this week?" he kept asking throughout the year.

I managed to put him off for ten months by laughing like he'd just told a good joke, but with Bolivia approaching, I'd been entertaining the notion of quitting anyway. My experience with international travel, particularly in the third world, had taught me that a dependency on two to three cups of coffee each morning can swiftly turn into a liability when you're staying with a family without a microwave or dishwasher, much less a coffeemaker, or when you're on a train from Rishikesh to Delhi and everything you've ingested so far has resulted in explosive diarrhea. I didn't want to experience South America in a fog because of a missed cup of coffee . . . even though South America seemed like just about the best place in the world to find one.

More important, my research into consumerism and trade practices had revealed that little to none of the money I shelled out to the big coffee companies each month actually reached the farmers who grew the beans. While demand for coffee has surged over the past twenty years, the price per pound paid to growers has plummeted. Consumers want cheap coffee, and corporations want to keeping posting record profits, and as a result, many of the 25 million farmers who grow coffee for a living are forced to sell their coffee at prices far below the cost of production. Despite long hours in the fields, they struggle to earn a living wage that can support their families.[3]

The good news is that there are simple ways to ensure that, in the words of activist Deborah James, you "never have to voluntarily put someone in a situation of poverty, exploitation and debt just to enjoy a cup of joe."[4] These days, you can find an array of fair trade coffee products online, at most grocery stores, and even at Starbucks. You just have to look for the black-and-white "fair trade certified" symbol on the package, which ensures that farmers received a guaranteed minimum price for what they produced, that working conditions were safe and ethical, that no child labor was employed, and that workers have a say in the functioning of the farming cooperative.

The bad news, at least for me, is that fair trade coffee is more expensive than what I'd grown accustomed to buying (as it should be, in order for farmers to actually earn a profit), and grocery stores in Dayton aren't always stocked with the fair trade options. In order to stick to my resolution to only drink fair trade coffee, I had to reduce my dependency, so that my coffee consumption wouldn't break the bank and so that, in the event that fair trade options weren't available, I wouldn't be tempted to settle for my old plastic canister brands. My three-cup addiction was unhealthy enough as it was. I hated the idea of remaining addicted to a product that, when mindlessly consumed, keeps millions of people in poverty. I wanted to get back to the point that coffee was something I enjoyed, not something I *needed*, so on the morning of July 3, I declared my independence from caffeine and refused to turn on the coffeepot.

The migraine arrived at about three that afternoon.

I went to bed around seven.

The next morning I woke up at eleven, threw up, and immediately crawled back into bed. My state resembled that which theologian

C. S. Lewis imagined for the willfully damned: "shrunk and shut up in themselves . . . Their fists are clenched, their teeth are clenched, their eyes fast shut."[5]

Dan poked his head in at around four that afternoon to see if I was still alive.

I rose a few hours later to eat, shower, and curse the day I was born.

Then I spent another feverish night curled up in the fetal position, as a bunch of kids down the road set off fireworks like they had some sort of *right* to do so.

The cycle repeated itself for two more days.

Through it all, I discovered yet another advantage to working from home: you can successfully undergo detox without a whole lot of people noticing. Readers assumed I'd taken a long weekend for the holiday. Friends figured their Fourth of July cookouts included some kind of food that for biblical reasons I couldn't consume. My family was used to me being distant and crabby. I suffered alone . . . which is exactly how someone who hasn't washed her hair or put on a bra for three days wants it to be.

Finally, after a week, the headache went away, and I began thinking clearly again, clearly enough to wonder what the heck had convinced my caffeinated self to follow all the Bible's commandments for women as literally as possible for a year. I found a nice array of fair trade coffee shops online as well as a fair trade, naturally decaffeinated, organic coffee brand at BI-LO that will probably cost my future children their college tuition, but which gives me access to good coffee whenever I get a craving.[6] The next task in my month of justice proved a lot less traumatic, even though it involved reexamining a staple product in the Evans household: chocolate.

As it turns out, the majority of the world's cocoa beans come from West Africa, where farmers sell to major chocolate companies like Hershey's, Nestlé, and Mars. For the last decade, media reports have detailed horrific working conditions on these cocoa farms, including what can only be described as child slavery. According to the International Institute of Tropical Agriculture, there are around 285,000 children working on African cocoa farms. Many of these children have been trafficked from neighboring countries, kidnapped from their families and forced to work without pay on the cocoa farms. The BBC reports that the going rate for a young boy in Mali is around thirty dollars.[7] Conditions are hazardous, and child workers are often abused. In fact, the International Labor Rights Fund recently sued the U.S. for failing to enforce laws prohibiting the import of products made with child labor, but the big chocolate companies continue to dodge the numerous deadlines set by Congress to regulate their trade practices.[8] A quick survey of the chocolate on our snack shelf revealed that *all* of it came from chocolate companies associated with child slavery.

I'd love to say I suffered for Jesus on this one, but let me tell you, fair trade chocolate is spectacularly delicious. I asked friends for recommendations, then purchased four chocolate bars from three different fair trade retailers to see which ones Dan and I liked the best. The official taste test, accompanied by a tall glass of milk for Dan and a bottle of rosé for me, began with Green & Black's Dark 70%, the only fair trade bar I could find in Dayton. I broke off two squares, and together we indulged in one minute of cool, bittersweet chocolate ecstasy. I gave the Green & Black's a 4.5 out of 5. Dan gave it a 4.

Next we tried the Divine Milk Chocolate bar, which we didn't like as much, just because we generally preferred dark. Then came the Equal Exchange Organic Dark Chocolate with Almonds, which I officially declared the most wonderful thing I'd ever put in my mouth. I gave it a 5. Dan gave it a 3. We finished with Divine 70% Dark Chocolate with Raspberries, a rich and tart little bite of heaven that we both agreed deserved a 4.

Who knew justice could be so delicious?

While buying and eating fair trade chocolate bars was easy enough, eliminating every trace of big-brand chocolate from our pantry proved a lot more challenging. From the chocolate chunks in our granola bars to baking chips to hot chocolate mix, I found the stuff everywhere, and alternatives were expensive and hard to come by. But knowing what I did about the modern-day slave trade, I couldn't just shrug it off, not anymore.

The coffee-and-chocolate experiment forced me to confront an uncomfortable fact to which I suspect most Americans can relate: I had absolutely no idea where the majority of my food came from. I didn't know how much it should actually cost, how it affected the people who harvested and prepared it, or what sort of toll its production took on the planet. I never thought to question the fact that I could purchase a plump red tomato in the middle of January or ask myself why I was willing to regularly ingest a product we call "cheese food."

So I dedicated the rest of the week, and indeed the rest of the year, to learning more about our habits as consumers. The results were shocking and in some cases disturbing. I'd never realized the degree to which big corporations rely on the mindless habits of consumers to get away with exploitation and neglect. We started to make adjustments here and there, sometimes paying a little extra for items that were fairly traded and, as far as we could tell, ethically produced. It wasn't easy, and it certainly wasn't cheap, but it would be one of the most important long-term changes to come out of the project. In a small but daily way we were doing our part to repair the world.

Dan's Journal
July 15, 2011

This month Rachel has been focusing on charity and justice. This includes learning more about where the things we consume come from and how our actions can affect the lives of those living thousands of miles away. We've started recycling, which is a bit of a feat in Dayton since the city doesn't offer recycling services. The nearest place to recycle glass and plastic is about a half hour away. So far, "recycling" has meant piling pizza boxes, milk cartons, paper, plastic, and glass containers in various places around the kitchen and laundry room with the expectation that, at some point, we'll try to bring it down to Soddy-Daisy, (yes, that's the name of the town), where we can recycle them. While living in New Jersey, I got into the habit of recycling, so it was strange to throw everything away when I moved to Dayton. If we could just throw all the recycling into one container and all the trash into the other, life would be a lot easier. But maybe life isn't supposed to be easy. And how hard is my life, really, when I consider it a bother to sort materials into separate disposal units?

Feminism is the radical notion that women are people.

"It appears that more girls have been killed in the last fifty years, precisely because they were girls, than men were killed in all the wars of the twentieth century," wrote Nicholas Kristof and Sheryl WuDunn in *Half the Sky: Turning Oppression into Opportunity for Women Worldwide.* "In the nineteenth century, the central moral challenge was slavery. In the twentieth century, it was the battle against totalitarianism. We believe that in this century the paramount moral challenge will be the struggle for gender equality in the developing world."[9]

So begins the book that forever enlarged my view of what it means to fight for women's equality. In *Half the Sky*, Kristof and WuDunn, the first married couple to win a Pulitzer Prize in journalism for their international reporting for the *New York Times*, explore the worldwide scourges of sex trafficking, gender-based violence, and maternal mortality and explain in vivid detail how investing in the health and autonomy of women can lift millions out of poverty.

They share the stories of women like Meena Hasina, a young Indian woman who was kidnapped and sold into sex slavery when she was nine years old. When she escaped and contacted the police, the police only laughed at her, for they were regular customers at the brothel in which she was enslaved. There are at least 3 million women and girls like Meena enslaved in the sex trade.

And the story of Dina, a seventeen-year-old Congolese girl who was gang-raped by five men on her way home from working in the fields. The men shoved a large stick through Dina's vagina, creating a debilitating fistula—a common ailment among rural African women who have been raped or who suffered through traumatic childbirth without medical attention. Women ages fifteen to forty-four are more likely to be maimed or die from male violence than from cancer, malaria, traffic accidents, and war combined.

And the story of Prudence Lemokouno, a twenty-four-year-old mother of three from Cameroon who went into labor seventy miles from the nearest hospital without any prenatal care. After three days of labor, her untrained birth attendant sat on Prudence's stomach and bounced up and down to try to get the baby out, rupturing Prudence's uterus. She died a few days later. A woman like Prudence dies in childbirth every minute.

In addition to excruciating stories like these, Kristoff and WuDunn share the stories of women like Sunitha Krishnan, a tiny but spry Hindu woman from Hyderabad, India, who, after being gang-raped as a young woman, devoted her life to fighting sex trafficking. And Catherine Hamlin, a gynecologist who has presided over more than twenty-five thousand fistula surgeries in Ethiopia. And Sakena Yacoobi, who even under the oppressive rule of the Taliban, opened eighty secret schools for girls.

"Women aren't the problem," wrote Kristoff and WuDunn, "but the solution. The plight of girls is no more a tragedy than an opportunity."[10]

Indeed, UNICEF reports that the ripple effects of empowering women can change the future of a society. It raises economic productivity, reduces infant mortality, contributes to overall improved health and nutrition, and increases the chances of education for the next generation.[11] Several studies suggest that when women are given control over the family spending, more of the money gets devoted to education, medical care, and small business endeavors than when men control the purse strings.[12]

Similarly, when women vote and hold political office, public spending on health increases and child mortality rate declines.[13] Many counterterrorist strategists see women's empowerment as key to quelling violence and oppression in the Middle East, and women entering the workforce in East Asia generated economic booms in Malaysia, Thailand, and China.[14]

"In general," say Kristoff and WuDunn, "the best clue to a nation's growth and development potential is the status and role of women."[15] "Investment in girls' education," says Lawrence Summers, former chief economist of the World Bank, "may well be the highest-return investment available in the developing world."[16]

Women aren't the problem. They are the solution.

The impact of the words reverberated through my thoughts and dreams for months, generating a strange mix of anger and hope that calcified into resolve. These are my sisters who are being abused, silenced, neglected, raped, and sold as slaves. These are my sisters who struggle each day to survive. These are my sisters who, if given the chance, can change the world.

Catholic activist Dorothy Day once said that the "greatest challenge of the day is how to bring about a revolution of the heart, a revolution which has to start with each one of us."

I knew somewhere deep in my bones that a revolution was afoot, that the women of this earth were rising up, and that, in some way, great or small, I was going to be a part of it.

"Blessed are you who are poor,
for yours is the kingdom of God.
Blessed are you who hunger now,
for you will be satisfied.
Blessed are you who weep now,
for you will laugh."

(LUKE 6:20–21)

The terrain of Cochabamba, Bolivia, is both beautiful and rugged. In the shadow of its snow-covered mountains lie hundreds of arid, rocky hills, where horses and cows perch as skillfully as mountain goats upon the steep slopes where people too make their homes. The high altitude—around 9,000 feet above sea level—leaves even the most skilled climbers breathless. It takes most children over an hour to walk the winding gravel roads to school, and women who live close enough to a health facility to deliver their babies there face a three-mile walk while in labor. The average income is $450 a year.

It's tough land to farm, so many men leave their families to migrate to Santa Cruz in hopes of harvesting better crops and sending money home. This leaves women and children vulnerable to poverty, malnutrition, dangerous living, and sexual exploitation. Our Bolivian guide told us of children left behind to fend for themselves while their mothers work in the fields, only to fall prey to sexual abuses by relatives and neighbors. Sometimes the fathers return. Sometimes they never do. Sometimes the money suddenly stops coming.

Cinda, a soft-spoken woman with earnest eyes, who like most women in the country wears her long, black hair in two braids down her back, had three little girls and several acres of land to tend when her husband abandoned the family without warning. Although she had the skills she needed to harvest potatoes and beans, her planting time, yield, and variety were severely limited due to a lack of irrigation to her property. It would be difficult for her family to survive with only one adult tending the fields.

Cinda wasn't the only one facing a water problem. She and her neighbors lived beneath the snow-capped mountain called Hanu. To catch the runoff from melted snow, residents had built a dam, but it was inefficient, providing water for only a few dozen families, and stirring up strife between neighbors desperate for its lifesaving waters. Fortunately, Cinda and her family are part of a World Vision ADP (area development program). Her three girls have sponsors, whose contributions are not only used to purchase school supplies and meals, but are also pooled together with other contributions to help solve community problems.

Partnering with local leaders, World Vision helped the community build and maintain a better dam—a beautiful reservoir of deep blue beneath Hanu, capable of providing irrigation to more than 170 families and stocked with fish for extra protein. The dam and irrigation system were designed by Bolivian engineers, built by local farmers, and are so well maintained by Cinda's community that they have become self-sustaining, with no additional funding from World Vision necessary.

When I met Cinda, I was heaving from the steep climb through thin air to the mud hut she and her children called home. I'd arrived with three other bloggers, a translator, and Luciano, the World Vision staff member who oversaw the reservoir project. On our way up the hill, we passed a flock of sheep, a couple of llamas, and a very noisy pig—all of whom now belonged to Cinda. Luciano pointed to the small stream flowing through the property and explained it came from the Hanu dam. Three little girls ran out to greet us, a mix of curiosity and shyness on their faces.

"Before the water, I could only grow one kind of potato," Cinda explained once we'd caught our breath. "Now I have three varieties, and beans too. I sell the extra at the market and use the money to buy sheep."

The addition of livestock has dramatically improved Cinda's standard of living. Her daughters are in school. She puts healthy food on the table each day. She can afford basic health care.

Cinda not only cares for her own property but for her mother's property as well. She is known throughout the area as one of its most successful and generous farmers. Her mother, wrinkled and bent over and browned by the sun, stood behind Cinda and beamed, pride visible in her sunken eyes.

It was all I could do to keep myself from throwing my arms around Cinda and shouting, "*Eshet chayil!* Woman of valor!"

I met so many women of valor in Bolivia that there is not the space to tell their stories. Each morning, our team of eleven—most of us bloggers—would rise early and climb into our fifteen-passenger van to rumble up and down the steep gravel roads that lead to the isolated towns of rural Bolivia. There we would listen mostly, scribbling in our notepads the stories of mothers and fathers, grandparents and children, schoolteachers and aid workers, in hopes that they might inspire our readers to act. We learned about how poor Bolivian women are often forced to work in the potato fields from sunup to sundown, leaving their young children vulnerable to accident and exploitation; how alcoholism and drug abuse plague the teenage population, resulting in school dropouts and domestic abuse; how proper irrigation can turn a deflated community into a thriving one; and how guinea pigs offer more protein than beef and less fat than chicken, making them a highly valuable food source among Bolivia's malnourished and a worthy income-producing venture for those who farm them.

In a town called Viloma, we met Marta. Now in her forties, Marta was once one of World Vision's sponsored children. She grew up in a rural area west of Cochabamba, where most girls dropped out of school, married young, and worked in the fields to support their families. As soon as she hit puberty, Marta's parents tried to convince her to marry a man from Viloma, but Marta loved school and begged to continue. With the help of a teacher, she escaped to the city, where she learned a trade by day and attended school at night.

"I did not oppose getting married and having children," she told us, "but the women here work in the fields from the moment the sun rises to when it sets. They leave their little ones to play in dangerous places, and are exhausted each night. I wanted something different—for my future children and for myself."

Marta became such a skilled seamstress that when she married and moved back to Viloma, the area development program sponsored by World Vision employed her. Now Marta manages ten other seamstresses—all mothers of sponsored children—who make blankets, purses, and satchels for World Vision as well as several local clients. The sewing station is located right next to the local school, so Marta can keep an eye on her three children. Mothers of younger children are allowed to care for their toddlers while they work, and their wages far surpass those they would earn by working in the fields.

When we visited the ADP, Marta's sewing crew had just finished making more than two hundred colorful winter blankets to hand out to every sponsored child in Viloma, enough to fill two rooms, floor to ceiling! As Marta brought us from room to room, I grasped her hand in mine and told her that she reminded me of Tabitha from the Bible, the disciple who made clothing for orphans and widows.

Women aren't the problem; they are the solution.

In a dusty neighborhood nearby, we met Elena. Though Elena's home is located right in the middle of a village outside of Cochabamba, to get there, we had to cross a muddy ravine by walking across a plank. A brood of chickens guarded the other side, clucking nervously at our arrival. We must have been a sight, inching our way across that narrow beam, most of us women with cameras and notepads and giant sunglasses. As soon as we crossed the ravine, we passed through a tall fence made of branches and brush, where we were greeted by the distinct stench of a pig farm, the unmistakable sound of oinks and squeals issuing from two rows of covered pig stalls, and giggles.

A six-year-old girl welcomed us at the gate and led us down the dusty path between the stalls. She served as our official guide through the small, enclosed family farm that, in the space of about fifteen hundred square feet, included more than thirty sows, twenty piglets, several chickens and a rooster, and a brand-new World Vision–sponsored guinea pig module housing dozens of guinea pigs and their babies. When we asked where she lived, she pointed to a heap of blankets and crude kitchen in one corner of the flimsy metal structure that covered the pig stalls.

In spite of the mess around her, the little girl wore a pristine plaid jumper over a light-pink shirt. Her face and hands were clean and her tennis shoes in good shape. No doubt this was the work of her mother, who emerged from the kitchen area to welcome us to her home.

Elena bears all the marks of rural poverty—a weathered face, missing teeth, a curved back—and yet she carries herself with the confidence and ease of a beautiful woman. With full lips, high cheekbones, and kind eyes, Elena is indeed beautiful, and she, too, had worn her best clothes that day, a light-blue top and dusty purple skirt, covered by an embroidered apron. She rested her hands affectionately on the little girl, named Arminda, and told us her story.

Five years before, Elena's husband had suffered a minor stroke. He waited years before going to a doctor, and Elena had no idea what might be wrong with him. The farm fell into disrepair. Food became scarce. Like a quarter of the Bolivian population, the family began to suffer from malnutrition.

It was in the midst of all of this that Elena took Arminda in. Arminda had been abandoned by her own poverty-stricken family at the age of two, left to live on a street corner, where she ate dirty noodles off the ground. When Elena saw the little girl, her heart was moved with compassion. She took Arminda home with her, inquired after her family, and when Arminda's mother said she didn't want the child anymore, filed papers to officially adopt her.

When Arminda and her brothers got World Vision sponsors, the World Vision staff finally convinced Elena's husband to see a doctor. His condition is improving, and with the addition of the guinea pig farm, the family hopes to earn enough money to build a house, a prospect that fills Elena's eyes with hopeful tears. It would only cost around fifteen hundred dollars for Elena to have a real home.

When we marveled at her generosity

for adopting Arminda despite her own difficult circumstances, Elena shrugged like it was nothing, looked down at Arminda, and smiled. In that moment I officially ran out of excuses for not caring for children in need.

Women aren't the problem; they are the solution.

In the rural region of Colomi, we met a brave group of women who, together, changed their community's esteem for children with special needs. When World Vision first began working in Colomi just two years ago, aid workers began by asking the women there what they most wanted to change about their community. The answer surprised the aid workers. The women said that, more than anything, they wanted to learn how to care for children with special needs.

In countries like Bolivia, children with special needs are so stigmatized and misunderstood that their mothers are often blamed for their illnesses.

"They told me that I must have been drinking while I carried the baby," one mother told us, weeping openly. "But I was not drinking. I took care of my child, like any mother would. When he was born, I carried him on my back, even when I was working in the fields."

"Some [special needs] children were being totally neglected," another mother said. "They had to drag themselves across the floor because they could not walk. Some were simply left for dead."

We heard stories of children who had been locked in rooms for weeks without being bathed or cared for, others who had been beaten nearly to death, and still more who had been abandoned because of fear and superstition.

Before World Vision came to Colomi, the mothers tried to organize. They formed a support group, where they exchanged stories and ideas, but they lacked basic information about how to care for their children with special needs and faced nearly constant ridicule from neighbors who said they were wasting their time.

So at these mothers' request, the first major project undertaken by World Vision in Colomi was to establish a special needs center in its most populous community. There, children receive hearing aids, prosthetics, access to lifesaving surgery, and an education. Mothers gather each week to learn more about their children's conditions and to offer support to one another. The facility still needs additional funding (when we were there, they had to lift children in wheelchairs up and down the stairs), but the sound of

laughter echoes continually off the cement walls.

Women aren't the problem; they are the solution.

In Bolivia I understood in a way I hadn't before that women are capable of changing the world. Sometimes, all they need are the right tools. Cinda needed water. Marta need a sewing machine. Elena needed a few dozen guinea pigs. The women of Colomi needed only to be heard.

But I needed things too. I needed to be blessed by these women,

to be challenged by them, to be embraced and made uncomfortable by them.

What I love about the ministry of Jesus is that he identified the poor as blessed and the rich as needy . . . and then he went and ministered to them both. This, I think, is the difference between charity and justice. Justice means moving beyond the dichotomy between those who need and those who supply and confronting the frightening and beautiful reality that we desperately need one another.

That's what I love about the Kingdom: For the poor, there is food. For the rich, there is joy. For all of us, there is grace.

READ MORE ONLINE:

"Greenlife"— http://rachelheldevans.com/greenlife

JUNIA, THE APOSTLE

It's not what you call me, but what I answer to.
—AFRICAN PROVERB

Although her name appears just once in Paul's letter to the church at Rome, Junia the Apostle is perhaps the most silenced woman of the Bible.

"Greet Andronicus and Junia," Paul wrote in Romans 16:7, "my fellow Jews who have been in prison with me. They are outstanding among the apostles, and they were in Christ before I was" (UPDATED NIV).

Junia is one of nine women mentioned by Paul in this correspondence. Others include Phoebe, a deacon; Priscilla, a teacher and church planter who along with her husband was described as "co-workers" in the Church (UPDATED NIV); Mary; Persis; Tryphena; and Tryphosa. But Junia stands out among all of these women because she is the first and only woman in Scripture to be explicitly identified as an apostle.

Apostles in the New Testament were disciples of Jesus devoted to spreading his teachings abroad. In addition to the original twelve apostles, the Bible speaks of apostles who served as traveling missionaries, teaching and leading the early church as it endured persecution and struggled through religious growing pains. Paul, Timothy, Barnabas Silas and Apollos were all apostles, as were Andronicus and Junia. The fourth-century bishop of Constantinople, John Chrysostom, said of Junia, "To be an apostle is something great. But to be outstanding among the apostles—just think what a wonderful song of praise that is! . . . Indeed how great the wisdom of this woman must have been that she was even deemed worthy of the title of apostle."

But as time went on, the mention of a female apostle

in Scripture became inconvenient for the increasingly hierarchal Church, so a medieval theologian found a creative
solution to the problem: he turned Junia into a man.[17]

Andronicus and Junia became Andronicus and
Junias.

This was no small error. The masculine name Junias
does not occur in a single inscription, letterhead, work of
literature, or epitaph in the Greco-Roman world, while the
feminine name Junia is everywhere. None of the Greek
manuscripts suggests that a masculine form of this name
should be used, and for the first thousand years of church
history, Christian theologians ranging from Chrysostom
to Origen to Jerome all identified the apostle Junia as a
woman. But the myth caught on, especially after Martin
Luther used Junias, rather than Junia, in his German translation of the Bible and identified the pair of former prisoners
as male. To this day, one can find English translations of the
Bible that turn the apostle Junia into a man.

How could this happen?

"The answer," says Wheaton College professor Lynn
Cohick, "lies in the [translation] committees' convictions that a female apostle was unlikely, and so the name
Junias—unknown throughout the Greco-Roman world—
was created ex nihilo to match their presuppositions." Or,
as Bernadette Booten put it, "Because a woman could not
have been an apostle, the woman who is here called an
apostle could not have been a woman."

Confronted with the mounting evidence against the
claim that Junia was a man, some contemporary theologians have begun arguing that the phrase "outstanding
among the apostles" should instead read "esteemed by the

apostles," thus allowing Junia to be female so long as she is not actually an apostle.

If Dan Brown needs inspiration for his next religious cover-up story, he need only look to the tale of Junia to see the lengths to which some will go to try and silence a strong woman.

August: Silence

I Am Woman, Hear Me No More

TO DO THIS MONTH:

- ☐ Remain totally silent in church (1 Corinthians 14:34–35)
- ☐ Avoid teaching or speaking (1 Timothy 2:11–14)
- ☐ Take an Internet vacation
- ☐ Spend three days at St. Bernard Abbey in Cullman, Alabama, practicing prayer, silence, and contemplation (1 Thessalonians 5:17)
- ☐ Visit a Quaker congregation

Dan's Journal
August 7, 2011

Today Rachel gets back from Bolivia . . . well actually, tonight. This will conclude the month of charity and she will enter her month of silence.

I don't think this means she is going to be silent all month. I suppose I could take this opportunity to make some crack about her talking too much. But she doesn't. And besides, I miss her talking. I miss her around here; it gets kinda lonely. Her plane, flight 4215 from Charlotte to Chattanooga, is scheduled to arrive at 11:36 p.m. She was away with World Vision this past week, and based on our limited correspondence, seems to have had an excellent time learning about the organization and child sponsorships.

But today is a long day for me. Not just because I'm looking forward to her return, but because tonight after I pick her up, I have to give Rachel some bad news. We just found out this past Thursday that Rachel's mom has breast cancer. I haven't told Rachel yet. I didn't want her to grapple with that at the same time she was writing about her trip, spending time with the Bolivian children, saying goodbye to her fellow travelers, and trying to catch planes in airports as she makes her way home. The good news is the cancer is in an extremely early stage, very small, and was found during a routine mammogram. Robin will need to go in for some treatment and more tests, but according to the doctors this cancer can be dealt with. The news is bad, but it could be much worse. Maybe I'll wait until tomorrow, after Rachel's gotten a chance to sleep. She's going to be exhausted, and I want her to get some rest.

> *A woman should learn in quietness and full submission. I do not permit a woman to teach or to assume authority over a man; she must be quiet.*
> —1 TIMOTHY 2:11–12 UDPATED NIV

Fortunately, my mom gets mammograms more regularly than she goes to the movies. And fortunately, it was a really small lump, so she only needed radiation, not chemotherapy. The whole ordeal would be over in a matter of months.

"There's a woman receiving surgery on the same day as Robin who will more than likely die from breast cancer," the surgeon told my father at their first appointment. "So that's one end of the spectrum. Your wife, on the other hand, is on the complete opposite end of the spectrum. Odds are that we will get this nodule out, do some radiation, and it will never be an issue again."

This was supposed to make us feel better, and indeed we welcomed it as good news, but the mention of the other woman haunted me, and throughout my mother's treatment and recovery, I never forgot that there was another family living through a very different story.

Of course, friends and family rallied. Church ladies brought casseroles. Fellow teachers graded papers. When Ahava heard the news, she sent me a short message:

> I went down to the Western Wall today and said all of the Psalms for your mother's complete healing. I wrote her name on a piece of paper and placed in the wall with my request. *Refuah shlema.* Complete healing!

The gesture meant more than I could express in my letter of thanks.

And yet the Almighty Project rolled on. My hair, now an inch or two past my shoulders, had grown heavy and limp in the summer humidity. Dan found a giant, desk-sized calendar in the trash at Bryan and brought it home, so I could cross off the days—just fifty-four . . . fifty-three . . . fifty-two . . . fifty-one more to go! I dreamed of tossing out my head coverings, leaving the dishes in the sink, and reading something other than Bible commentaries for a while, maybe *The Hunger Games.*

But first I had to tackle the virtue I'd been dreading for months: silence.

The Bible has been used to silence women for centuries, largely on account of two passages from the New Testament.

In 1 Timothy 2:11–14, the apostle Paul wrote, "A woman should learn in quietness and full submission. I do not permit a woman to teach or to assume authority over a man; she must be quiet. For Adam was formed first, then Eve. And Adam was not the one deceived; it was the woman who was deceived and became a sinner" (UPDATED NIV).

And in 1 Corinthians 14:34–35, he says, "Women should remain silent in the churches. They are not allowed to speak, but must be in submission, as the Law says. If they want to inquire about something, they should ask their own husbands at home; for it is disgraceful for a woman to speak in the church."

For the first seven months of the project, I got around the 1 Corinthians 14 prohibition by using what I like to call the "prophesy loophole." Since the Bible includes multiple stories of female prophets who spoke in public, and since the book of Acts says the Holy Spirit would enable "both men and women" to prophesy (2:17–18), and since Paul himself, just a few verses earlier, in 1 Corinthians 11:4, instructed women who *prophesy in church* to cover their heads, I allowed myself to speak up in church now and then, with the understanding that I was "prophesying," not "teaching" . . . which of course didn't make anyone uncomfortable whatsoever.

However, back in March I'd broken my eighth commandment— "Thou shalt not teach in church"—rather overtly when I "prophesied" on a Sunday morning at a church in Virginia. The good people at RISE Church in Harrisonburg had invited me to speak to their year-old congregation and offered to pay for my travel. The dates lined up perfectly with my trip to Amish country, and I really liked the church, so I was eager to make it work. I told the assistant pastor, Brent, that I could speak to the members of the church, so long as it wasn't on a Sunday morning in their sanctuary, as that would definitely qualify as "teaching in church." Seeing as how RISE's senior pastor is a smart and spunky young woman named Amanda, Brent seemed a little perplexed by the whole scheme, but agreed to try and set up a Sunday night meeting at another venue in town.

The poor guy spent weeks searching for just such a venue, but apparently Harrisonburg is *the* place to be in late March, so everything was either booked or beyond the church's budget. Of course I felt terrible because you know how much I hate bothering people, so I caved and said I would speak at their Sunday morning service, as long as it was clear that I was "prophesying," not "teaching." I wore my head covering, and God didn't strike me dead, so I suppose I got away with it. It seemed rather silly to go to all that trouble when I'd be speaking to the same group of people no matter what. The Church was never meant to be confined to a building, after all.

I'm not the only one to struggle with the interpretation of 1 Timothy 2 and 1 Corinthians 11. Even the spokesmen for the biblical womanhood movement who claim to take the silence passages literally engage in some dizzying mental gymnastics when applying them.

When asked if it is wrong, in light of 1 Timothy 2, for men to listen to popular female teachers like Beth Moore, founder of the

Council on Biblical Manhood & Womanhood (CBMW), John Piper said, "No, unless you begin to become dependent on her as your shepherd-teacher. This is the way I feel about women speaking occasionally in Sunday school . . . The Bible is clear that women shouldn't teach and have authority over men. In context, I think this means that women shouldn't be the authoritative teachers of the church."[1]

(In other words, a Christian man can learn from a Christian woman, as long as he doesn't learn *too* much.)

Even more confusing is the fact that Piper cites the first half of 1 Timothy 2:12 (a woman should not "have authority over a man") as universally applicable by discouraging women from becoming pastors, but disregards the second half ("she must be silent") by encouraging women like Moore to continue speaking.

Cofounder of the CBMW, Wayne Grudem offers equally confounding advice for women by extracting from 1 Timothy 2:12 an eighty-three-item list detailing exactly what women can and cannot do in the church.[2] A woman can be a choir director, but not preside over a baptism or communion service, he says. She can write a book about theology that is read at Christian colleges and seminaries, but she cannot teach theology at Christian colleges or seminaries herself. She can teach vacation Bible school to children, but she cannot lead a Bible study with adults.

I've watched congregations devote years and years to heated arguments about whether a female missionary should be allowed to share about her ministry on a Sunday morning, whether students older than ten should have female Sunday school teachers, whether girls should be encouraged to attend seminary, whether women should be permitted to collect the offering or write the church newsletter or make an announcement . . . all while thirty thousand children die every day from preventable disease. If that's not an adventure in missing the point, I don't know what is.

So for the project I decided to take two approaches to silence. First, I would focus on the sort of silence that has been enforced by the Church for so many years. I'd been careful not to schedule any speaking gigs for the month of August—no chapel addresses, no classroom lectures, no conference appearances, no Sunday sermons. I also refused interviews and article requests and enforced a week of online silence to completely disengage from my blog and social networking. For the month, I would remain completely silent in church. I could not pray or read Scripture out loud, nor join in the conversation following the Bible study.

But I also wanted to explore what you might call the upside of silence, the sort of silence that has been practiced by contemplatives for centuries to quiet the spirit and turn the soul toward God. My experience with contemplative prayer back in October had been quietly germinating in my soul, and I wanted to water that impulse and feed it and expose it to more sunlight. So I scheduled a three-day visit to St. Bernard Abbey, a Benedictine monastery in, of all places, Cullman, Alabama. I planned to stay in the monastery itself, eating meals with the monks, joining them in ritualized prayer, and seeing what they might teach me about disciplined silence. Then, to conclude the month, I'd visit a Quaker congregation, where I'd been told services were held in complete silence as congregants await the word of the Inner Light.

So that was the plan. But first, I wanted to talk to a woman who, in spite of centuries of opposition, has managed to shatter the stained-glass ceiling. I wanted to talk to a female pastor.

Because I am a woman, I must make unusual efforts to succeed. If I fail, no one will say, "She doesn't have what it takes." They will say, "Women don't have what it takes."

—CLARE BOOTHE LUCE

When Jackie Roese delivered her first sermon at Irving Bible Church near Dallas, Texas, in 2008, she had to have a bodyguard for protection.

"It probably wasn't necessary, but things had gotten so crazy, so controversial, we weren't taking any chances," she told me.

For daring to speak before the church's thirty-five hundred attendees, the forty-six-year-old mother of three was called a "cancer in the Church," a "dangerous sign," and a "threat to Christianity."

Tom Nelson of nearby Denton Bible Church reacted to the news of Jackie's impending sermon by calling a meeting with area pastors to unequivocally condemn Irving Bible Church's actions. "I believe this issue is the carrier of a virus by which liberalism will enter the evangelical church," he told the *Dallas Morning News*. Mark Bailey, president of Dallas Theological Seminary, removed himself from a team of regular guest preachers in protest. Denny Burk, a professor of biblical studies at Boyce College, called Jackie's presence behind the pulpit "a matter of grave moral concern."[3]

"I think the strangest thing I heard was that a woman preaching on a Sunday morning would inevitably lead to the acceptance of bestiality," Jackie said with a laugh. "Part of me wanted to end the sermon with, 'Okay, so how many of you want to have sex with a monkey now'?"

With a head of wild curls, commanding voice, and contagious laugh, Jackie's not the kind of woman you can safely ignore. You would never guess from her confidence that she grew up in a dysfunctional home with an abusive and sex-obsessed father who called her a "whore" when she was just in elementary school, repeatedly telling her that women were "only good for one thing, and most of the time, they're not even good at that."

Over the phone, Jackie's voice sounds just like Julia Roberts's.

"The congregation itself was, for the most part, incredibly supportive," she told me. "I think it was because they were so used to me. I had been teaching for so many years, it only seemed natural for them to hear from me on a Sunday morning."

As the teaching pastor to women, Jackie oversaw more than a thousand women's Bible studies, developed curriculum, trained other women to teach, and worked with the church's pastoral board to cast vision for the congregation.

After four years on the job, Jackie said, "I decided to launch a series of forums in which prominent female leaders and theologians discussed important issues in the Church. We talked about everything from women's roles in the Church to human trafficking to complex theological topics, and before long, the series had sucked in the rest of the church. Men were asking if it was okay to attend our women's events!"

In the midst of all of this, Jackie earned her doctorate degree in preaching at Gordon Conwell Theological Seminary, where she twice received the merit award for top scholar in her class.

In 2008, the elders at Irving Bible Church produced a twenty-four-page position paper on the role of women on the church, which argued that the biblical passages restricting from teaching "were culturally and historically specific, not universal principles for all times and places" and that the Bible presents "an ethic in progress leading to full freedom for women to exercise their giftedness in the local church."[4]

This cleared the way for Jackie to begin teaching from the pulpit from time to time. But when the elders invited her to do so, she was reluctant.

"It cracks me up when people try to present me as this aggressive, manipulative woman who had her eye on the pulpit from the start," Jackie said. "When the elders asked me to preach, I tried to pass the job to someone else! But they insisted, so you could say I was just being submissive to authority."

Still, Jackie was aware of the significance of her presence behind the pulpit. "Before I went out to give the sermon, I was hanging out backstage with my daughter," Jackie said. "I told her, 'Sweetie, I'm doing this for Jesus, but I'm also doing this for you.'"

The action came with some cost. A few disgruntled families left the church, and to this day, there are members of the congregation that have to be "warned" ahead of time before Jackie preaches a sermon, so they can make other arrangements for church that morning. Even some of Jackie's closest friends left the church because they could not tolerate a woman preacher.

But Jackie says that, to this day, people will approach her after a sermon and apologize for ever doubting her. Many say that she slowly won them over by consistently hitting her sermons out of the park.

"Women don't have a lot of margin for error when it comes to preaching, do they?" I asked Jackie. "You've *always* got to be as good as the men in order to be accepted."

"No, we have to be *better*," Jackie said. "We have to be *better* in order to receive the same level of respect as the men."

Fortunately, change is afoot. The number of female senior pastors in Protestant churches has doubled in the past decade, rising from around 5 percent to 10 percent.[5] More women are enrolling in seminary now than ever before, and by 2006 women made up 51 percent of divinity school students.[6]

While most mainline Protestant denominations (American Baptist, United Methodist, Episcopal, Evangelical Lutheran Church, Presbyterian Church USA) now welcome women in leadership, other denominations continue to forbid it. The Baptist Faith and Message, which is espoused by the largest Christian denomination in America, states that, "while both men and women are gifted for service in the church, the office of pastor is limited to men as qualified by Scripture."[7]

"I see myself as a woman who is traveling through a thick jungle with a machete," Jackie told me. "I can see where other women have forged a path for me, but there are still a lot of vines in the way. My goal is to cut down some of those vines, so that the next generation will have a clearer path."

I had no plans to deliver any sermons to three-thousand-member congregations—at least not at the time—but after talking with Jackie I knew that, in no small way, she had cleared a path for me.

> *I think Paul would roll over in his grave if he*
> *knew we were turning his letters into torah.*
> —F. F. BRUCE[8]

We forget sometimes that the Epistles are just that . . . epistles. They are letters, broken pieces of correspondence between early Christians, dating back thousands of years.

In our rush to extract sound bites for our nature-themed desk calendars, we tend to skip past the initial greetings that designate the recipients of the message—"to the church of God in Corinth," "to the churches in Galatia," "to God's holy people in Ephesus," "to Timothy," "to Titus," "to Philemon our dear friend and fellow worker—also to Apphia our sister and Archippus our fellow soldier—and to the church that meets in your home"—and scan over the details that should remind us that we are essentially listening in on someone else's conversation—"I have made a fool of myself," "I don't remember if I baptized anyone else," "When you come, bring the cloak that I left with Carpus at Troas, and my scrolls, especially the parchments" (1 Corinthians 1:2; Galatians 1:2; Ephesians 1:1; 1 Timothy 1:2; Titus 1:4; Philemon 1–2; 2 Corinthians 12:11; 1 Corinthians 1:16; 2 Timothy 4:13 UPDATED NIV).

We also tend to ignore the embarrassing bits, like when Paul tells Titus, "Cretans are always liars, evil brutes, lazy gluttons" (Titus 1:12 UPDATED NIV).

I've never once heard a sermon preached on this passage, and yet, if these words are truly the inerrant and unchanging words of God intended as universal *commands* for all people in all places at all times, then the Christian community needs to do a better job of mobilizing against the Cretan people, perhaps constructing some "God Hates Cretans" signs, or warning Christian travelers not to get off the ship when they stop at Crete on their Mediterranean cruises, or boycotting movies starring Jennifer Aniston, whose father, I am told, is a lazy, evil, gluttonous Cretan.

My point is, we dishonor the original intent and purpose of the Epistles when we assume they were written in a vacuum for the purpose of filling our calendars and bumper stickers.

Like the rest of the Bible, the Epistles were written *for* us, but they were not written *to* us. With the letters of Peter, Paul, James, John, and the other apostles, we are given the priceless gift of seeing how early followers of Jesus applied his teachings to their unique circumstances. While these letters are packed with important and timeless theological truths—"If anyone is in Christ, the new creation has come," "Conduct yourselves in a manner worthy of the gospel" (2 Corinthians 5:17; Philippians 1:27 UPDATED NIV), "Have this attitude in yourselves which was also in Christ Jesus" (Philippians 2:5 NASB)—they also include lengthy discussion concerning how first-century house churches should operate, how unprecedented influxes of poor widows should be handled, how slaves should behave toward their masters, whether Christian converts should be circumcised, whether Christians should eat meat sacrificed to idols, how to endure persecution, how not to offend the surrounding culture, and how to follow Christ with conviction while avoiding unwanted attention from the suspicious Roman officials.[9]

The apostles never meant for their letters to be interpreted and applied as law in the same way that the Torah had been, so careful readers must do the hard work of sorting through which instructions might continue to illuminate and guide the modern church, and which are more specific to the context.

Just as I've never heard a sermon against the Cretans, I've also never heard a sermon on 1 Timothy 2:8, in which Paul tells Timothy, "I want men everywhere to pray, lifting holy hands without anger or disputing" that included a universal dictum that all men everywhere must raise their hands whenever they pray (UPDATED NIV). But I've heard more than I can count on 1 Timothy 2:11, just three verses later, which says, "A woman should learn in quietness and full submission" that have included universal dictums that all women everywhere must submit to male authority in the church.

So what was the context of these words? Were they really meant to be applied universally to all women everywhere?

In keeping with the trend of early Christianity, the first-century churches at Ephesus and Corinth attracted a lot of women, particularly widows. As a result, large portions of the pastoral epistles tackle the mounting logistical challenges of caring for so many unmarried women.

Of particular concern to Paul was a group of young widows who had infiltrated the church and developed a reputation for dressing promiscuously, sleeping around, gossiping, spreading unorthodox ideas, interrupting church services with questions, mooching off the church's widow fund, and generally making common floozies of themselves (1 Timothy 5). Scholars believe these women may have been influenced by the popular Roman fertility cults of Artemis that encouraged women to flaunt their sexuality and freedom to a degree that scandalized even the Roman establishment, hardly known for its prudish morals.

It seems that enough of these women had joined the church to tarnish its reputation, repelling potential converts and giving the Roman authorities yet another reason to be suspicious of the church, which was the last thing the early Christians needed.

"Give proper recognition to those widows who are really in

need," Paul tells the elders at Ephesus. But "younger widows," he says, are "to marry, to have children, to manage their homes and to *give the enemy no opportunity for slander*" (1 Timothy 5:14; emphasis added).

He didn't want the church, so full of unmarried women, to be seen as just another Roman cult. He also didn't want pagans unfamiliar with the teachings of Christ and the Jewish culture interrupting services with questions or bossing around other converts. Is it any wonder, then, that he expected some women in Corinth to prophesy, but challenged others to "remain silent," or that he advised the women at Ephesus not to seize authority over men but to "learn in quietness and full submission"?

"We are thus led to the conclusion that when Paul asks women to be silent . . . he is not talking about ordinary Christian women; rather, he has a specific group of women in mind," wrote theologian Scot McKnight. "His concern is with some untrained, morally loose, young widows, who, because they are theologically unformed, are teaching unorthodox ideas."[10]

So what about women today? Can we really compare Jackie to the promiscuous, first-century Roman widows mooching off the church and spreading idle tales from door to door? Obviously, Paul didn't have a problem with women teaching in general. In his letters, he honored Priscilla, a teacher to the apostle Apollos, and praised Timothy's mother and grandmother for teaching Timothy all he knew about faith. In fact, these days, women in the pulpit are more highly educated than their male counterparts. While over three-quarters of female pastors (77 percent) hold seminary degrees, less than two-thirds of male pastors (63 percent) can say the same.[11] It continues to amaze me that some evangelicals believe that Fred Phelps of Westboro Baptist Church, who was ordained at seventeen without a seminary degree, is more qualified by virtue of being a man to speak to the Church than someone like Jackie, who received top honors at her seminary, or Catherine Hamlin, who devoted her life to caring for fistula patients in Africa, or Sarah

Coakley, who is one of Christianity's most influential theologians and philosophers, currently working on a four-volume systematic theology.

It is a tragic and agonizing irony that instructions once delivered for the purpose of avoiding needless offense are now invoked in ways that needlessly offend, that words once meant to help draw people to the gospel now repel them. Research shows that the overall number of women attending church has dropped by 11 percent in the last twenty years.[12] When female executives, entrepreneurs, academics, and creatives are told that they have to check their gifts at the church door, many turn away for good. And while our sisters around the world continue to suffer from trafficking, exploitation, violence, neglect, maternal mortality, and discrimination, those of us who are perhaps most equipped to respond with prophetic words and actions—women of faith—are being systematically silenced in our own faith communities.

McKnight wisely asks: "Do you think Paul would have put women 'behind the pulpit' if it would have been advantageous 'for the sake of the gospel'?"[13]

The answer to that question should be a lot simpler than it has become.

There are times when good words are to be
left unsaid out of esteem for silence.
—Holy Rule of St. Benedict

5:40 a.m.—Rise
6:00 a.m.—Matins & Lauds (Morning Prayer)
7:15 a.m.—Breakfast, in silence
11:55 a.m.—Sext (Midday Prayer)
12:10 p.m.—Lunch
5:00 p.m.—Mass

5:30 pm.—Vespers (Evening Prayer)
6:00 p.m.—Supper (Night Prayer)
7:00 p.m.—Compline

This was not my normal schedule, particularly the 5:40 a.m. part, but for the three days I spent practicing silence at St. Bernard Abbey, it served as a sort of corrective guide, holy bumpers meant to keep my bowling ball of an inner voice from veering into the gutters.

Cullman, Alabama, is not the first place you'd expect to find a monastery. I drove past three farm supply stores and twenty-one Baptist churches on my way into town via Highway 278 West, and that was after I started counting. Summer tends to overstay its welcome down South, but a morning shower had made the afternoon air unseasonably clean and cool, so I rolled down my window, cranked up my Patty Griffin CD, and breathed in the earthy smell of Alabama.

Finally I arrived at St. Bernard, an austere Benedictine monastery hidden inside 180 acres of wooded land.

Built in 1891 by a group of German monks whose community dated back to the 700s, the monastery is now home to around twenty

monks, a Catholic prep school, a hospitality center, and the famous Ave Maria Grotto—a garden of folk art–style miniatures designed by Brother Joseph, who lived at St. Bernard in the 1920s and 1930s.

A palpable silence welcomed me the moment I slipped through the back door of the monastery and stepped into the long, cavernous hallway between the monks' residence and the church. It was about three in the afternoon, so all the monks were out working, and the place seemed so quiet and still, I feared a single breath might knock something over.

There were plenty of things to knock over, too: porcelain statues of the Virgin, glass tables lined with votive candles, fine vases filled with faux flowers, and a bunch of other Catholicy-looking things that triggered my longstanding fear of accidentally desecrating something I didn't know was considered holy in a Catholic church. I found my room assignment on the bulletin board in the entryway, and as I crept toward Room 113, my duffel bag and laptop case over my arm, I realized that I'd already made a big mistake.

Clop. Clop. Clop. Clop. The sound of my heels against the linoleum floor reverberated off the walls like shots from a gun.

(Ladies, if you ever find yourself temporarily living in a convent, do remember to bring flats. I might as well have brought a bullhorn with which to shout, "Hey monks! I'm here!")

St. Benedict was big on hospitality, and wrote that "all who present themselves are to be welcomed as Christ" (even those with loud heels I presume), so the monks at St. Bernard have a nice arrangement for guests. My room was simple, but comfortable, with two narrow beds, a bed stand, a desk, a lamp, a plush chair, and an adjoining bathroom. A giant crucifix hung on the wall so that I could see it from just about every angle in the room. It made me kind of nervous to glance in the bathroom mirror and see Jesus watching me brush my teeth. Though the room was located in the monastery, it was outside the cloister area upstairs, so I wouldn't be bumping into any holy men in their underwear in the middle of the night. I noticed from the guest list that a couple—Greg and Susan—was staying next door.

"Monastery guests take their meals with the monks at the guest table in the refectory," the guest book said. "Breakfast is eaten in silence, lunch is an informal buffet, and the supper meal is a formal monastic meal with public reading while the community eats in silence . . . Monastery guests are welcomed to pray the Hours of the Divine Office and celebrate mass with the monks in the Abbey Church."

The next event on the schedule was Mass, which didn't happen for another two hours, so I was confronted with my first expanse of solitude with which to mediate and pray. Instead I used the time to check to see if the place had Wi-Fi (it didn't), call Dan, fret over my shoes, and wander around the grounds a bit before arriving at the Abbey Church early and *clop-clop-clop*ping my way down the nave.

The place was completely empty, and I began to wonder if anyone actually lived in this monastery. I sat down in the back pew and, as any good sacred space should inspire one to do, I looked up. Afternoon light poured in through the clerestory and lit up the sandstone columns, walls, and parabolic arches, so that they glowed with a golden haze. The ceiling was made of stained pine, giving the massive, seven-hundred-person-capacity sanctuary a surprisingly intimate feel. Ten imposing limestone statues, about twelve feet tall, were carved into each of the supporting columns of the church. I tried to identify them, but the only one I recognized right away was

John the Baptist, with his long scraggly beard, giant staff, and over-all dubious appearance.

At the front of the church, an ornate, gold-trimmed cross hung over the stone altar, as if floating in space. On one side was painted the crucified Christ in blacks, browns, and reds. Later, when I joined the monks for prayer in the choir, I noticed that on the other side was painted the victorious Christ, in blues and purples and golds. A forty-four-rank pipe organ took up the east end of the building in front of me, and a stained glass window the west end behind me. Stationed along the sides of the church were little alcoves, each one different from the last, with places to light candles, kneel before icons, or simply sit in a wooden pew beside a stained glass window. I felt my spirit settling down a bit as it slowly dawned on me that my only assignment for the next forty-eight hours was to *be* in this sacred space.

People began to trickle in for mass. Monday, I take it, is not a big day for going to church, because only about fifteen people showed up, mostly teachers and students from the prep school and old people. We all sat in separate pews, spaced out like pieces at the end of a chess game. Finally, just before the service began, I caught my first glimpse of the monks with whom I'd be eating and praying for the next two days. They wore black robes and walked down the nave with their heads bowed. When they started to chant, their deep, harmonized voices echoed off the walls. It was as if the sanctuary suddenly woke up.

I fumbled my way through mass, keeping my eye on the bald guy in front of me for cues for when to kneel, bow, cross myself, and sit still. Afterwards, the monks gathered in the choir for Vespers, and I sat alone in the sanctuary, listening to them chant through the Psalms until the light began to fade and shadows crept through the nave.

I wasn't sure what to do with myself when Vespers concluded, but thankfully, a thin, middle-aged monk broke the line of monks filing out of the sanctuary, approached me, and whispered, "Are you a guest?"

"Yes," I said, extending my hand. "I'm Rachel."

"I'm Brother Brendan, the guestmaster," he answered, turning also to a middle-aged couple that I suddenly realized had been sitting behind me. *Must be Greg and Susan, my neighbors.*

The time between Vespers and supper is a sacred one for Benedictines, usually observed in complete silence. So the three of us followed Brother Brendan out of the church, down my favorite echo chamber of a hallway, and to the refectory for dinner, without saying a word to one another. I took to walking on my tiptoes to minimize the clopping, and resolved to wear my tennis shoes to the next service regardless of how stupid they looked with my long, black skirt. On the way, Brother Brenden paused in front of my room, where for some reason I'd left the door wide open.

"Oh," I whispered, blushing. "I didn't mean to do that."

I closed the door, feeling all awkward and scandalous. Susan, a tall, graying woman with a lace head covering pinned to her hair, took the opportunity to smile warmly at me, issuing a gentle *Nice to meet you* with her eyes that set me at ease.

The dining hall was small but well equipped with a buffet not unlike what you might see in a small college cafeteria. A few tables had been set aside for guests, so Greg, Susan, and I, along with a splattering of other folks who weren't wearing black robes, sat there with Brother Brendan. It was a little strange going through the buffet line and eating without saying a word to the people around me, but I confess I rather enjoyed escaping what would have been thirty minutes of awkward small talk. Instead, an older monk read aloud selections from Thomas à Kempis, and a biography on Dietrich Bonhoeffer.

After dinner we joined the monks back in the church for Compline, the final office in the Liturgy of the Hours, and many people's favorite. The Liturgy of the Hours is a collection of daily prayers, gathered mostly from the Psalms but including other traditional hymns, prayers, and chants, recited together by the monks at fixed points in each day.

The main sanctuary was enshrouded in darkness now. We faced one another in the illuminated choir section and proceeded to chant our way through the lectionary and Psalter, at one moment sitting, another standing, another bowing, another kneeling, another leaning forward in prayer. I felt a little like I was back in middle school, trying to keep up with the cheerleaders as they performed the Macarena, and the plaintive, monotone back-and-forth between the officiant and the choir proved a bit distracting. At one point I dropped my lectionary, and from the sound of it hitting the floor, you would have thought an earthquake had hit. I was so worried about not making any noise, I almost forgot to listen to the poetry issuing from our lips:

> He who dwells in the shelter of the Most High abides under the shadow of the Almighty. He shall say to the Lord, "You are my refuge and my stronghold, my God in whom I put my trust . . ."
>
> Into your hands, O Lord, I commend my spirit. For you have redeemed me, O Lord, O God of truth. Keep us, O Lord, as the apple of your eye. Hide us under the shadow of your wings . . .
>
> The Lord Almighty grant us a peaceful night and a perfect end . . .
>
> Glory to the Father, and to the Son, and to the Holy Spirit, as it was in the beginning, is now, and ever shall be—world without end. Amen.

After Compline, the monks observe the Grand Silence, which means no talking until after breakfast the next morning, so I retreated to my room, where I began reading through *Revelations of Divine Love* by Julian of Norwich:

> I saw that [God] is to us everything that is good and comfortable for us: He is our clothing that for love wrappeth us, claspeth us, and all encloseth us for tender love, that He may never leave us; being to us all-thing that is good . . .[14]

Wrapped in that love as if in a blanket, I finally stopped worrying so much about disturbing the silence of the monastery and instead allowed myself to nestle into it.

That night I dreamed I'd left my door opened again and that the Virgin Mary herself walked by, surrounded by a hazy white glow. In my dream she turned and smiled, and I noticed she wore a bright red pair of high heels that, miraculously, didn't make a sound.

The Prophet Jeremiah is the last person you want to hear from at six o'clock in the morning, let me tell you.

"Cursed be the day I was born" I found myself intoning flatly the next morning before the sun rose at Lauds. "May the day my mother bore me not be blessed. Cursed be the man who brought my father the news, who made him very glad, saying, 'A child is born to you—a son.' May the man be like the towns the Lord overthrew without pity. May he hear wailing in the morning, a battle cry at noon. For he did not kill me in the womb, with my mother as my grave, her womb enlarged forever. Why did I ever come out of the womb to see trouble and sorrow, to end my days in shame?"

All of this we sang in expressionless monotone, followed by Psalm 49, where David pipes in with "For all can see that the wise die, that the foolish and the senseless also perish, leaving their wealth to others. Their tombs will remain their houses forever, their dwellings for endless generations."

Just the sort of thing you want to think about before you've even had a cup of coffee.

Silent breakfast, on the other hand, seemed to me a marvelous idea, one that should be instituted into every God-fearing home on behalf of those of us who are decidedly *not* morning people. I sat next to Susan in the dining hall, lathering my bagel with creamed cheese in perfect, contented silence—absolute heaven for the introverted night owl who would rather spend her mornings with complex carbohydrates than with people.

Poor Susan, who I suspect might be a morning person, looked ready to burst. We'd been to three prayer services and eaten two meals together without so much as a "So, what brings you to a Benedictine monastery in the Middle of Nowhere, Alabama?"

Finally, as the monks began to file out of the dining hall on their way to work, we were able to strike up a conversation.

Turns out Greg works for a communications company that sells important equipment to the military, and was in the area for a business meeting in Birmingham. When Susan was researching places to stay, she found St. Benedict's and said, "I just knew it was the place for us." She said she planned to visit Irondale, a city about sixty miles south of Cullman, the next day to get a tour of EWTN, the Catholic television network.

"Mother Angelica is a saint living in our times," Susan said with a sigh. "Don't you think she's a saint living in our times?"

"Sure . . . I mean, definitely."

(I wasn't entirely sure who Mother Angelica was, to be honest.)

Susan seemed a little shocked to learn that I wasn't a Catholic, but I assured her that I wasn't the type of evangelical who thought that she and all the rest of the Catholics would burn in hell for eternity. It didn't occur to me until later that her concern might have been over *my* eternal destiny.

While Greg and Susan went to check out the gift shop, I decided to explore the Abbey Forrest. Located on the south side of the

campus, the forest had a Narnia-like entrance, complete with two mossy stone pillars flanking the overgrown pathway that led through a canopy of oaks, hickories, sweet gums, and loblolly pines. I followed the path for about a quarter of a mile and came upon a clearing where a shrine to Mary had been built into a knoll. Dew still clung to the grass, so I stood there for a while, looking at the statue before which gifts of candles and rosaries had been laid, listening to the birds, and wondering what sort of prayer I ought to pray.

Back on the main campus, I found a shaded bench advertising "Cullman Lumber" under a sprawling oak next to the monastery's little lake. A cool morning breeze—*was it really still morning?*—blew over the water, which rippled peacefully in response. I started to pull my devotional books out of my bag, but then stopped. I wanted to quiet my mind for a while, to simply listen to my inner voice.

Unfortunately, my inner voice can be a royal pain in the rear.

An obstreperous child, impatient with questions and eager for attention, my inner voice likes to focus on the future, not the present, and already she had some rather strong opinions about lunch.

"Quiet, quiet, quiet," I kept telling myself. "Embrace the silence. Focus on God."

But nothing seemed to work. My mind kept drifting from one thing to another, and before I knew it, I was outlining an article in my head.

Finally, I remembered something my agent told me before I left.

"When you're on a spiritual retreat," she said, "don't try too hard

to make something mystical happen. Just go and *be*. If you enter with too many expectations, you'll be disappointed."

So, in obedience to my spiritual guru, who doubles as my literary agent, I quit trying and just sat there in the sunlight, turning my face toward the breeze, and allowing my thoughts to travel wherever they pleased. It was then that I noticed a little water turtle poking its head out of the murky water of the lake. I liked how he paddled around with his neck stretched out and his eyes wide, like something out of Jurassic Park. He must have seen a water bug swimming around down there because he plopped back into the murky depths, and I waited for him to return. Sure enough, after about three minutes, he reappeared a few feet away, this time revealing the top of his muddy brown shell. I watched that little turtle go about his day among the cattails for what must have been an hour . . . and darned if it wasn't the best hour I'd spent in a long time.

A cold front must have been moving through because the breeze turned into a steady, chilly wind, and goose bumps appeared on my arms—a certifiable miracle for August in Alabama. I closed my eyes, breathed in deeply, and listened to the trees "clap their hands," as the psalmist liked to say.

A favorite psalm came to mind:

O LORD, my heart is not proud, nor my eyes haughty;
Nor do I involve myself in great matters,
Or in things too difficult for me.
Surely I have composed and quieted my soul;
Like a weaned child rests against his mother,
My soul is like a weaned child within me.

(PSALM 131:1–2 NASB)

My soul is like a child, and God is like a mother. What a strange and beautiful idea.

I sat with these words a while longer before gathering my things and heading back to the abbey to prepare for midday prayers, which are called Sext by the Benedictines. I laughed to myself when I thought about spending my afternoon "sexting" with the monks.

So what did God say to me in the silence that morning? I'm not sure, but I think God said something like, *Don't try so hard, little child,* and, *Hey, check out this cool turtle I made.*

"*Silence is God's first language; everything*
else is a poor translation."[15]

Quakers are pretty much the opposite of Catholics. Or at least that's what I thought when I first walked through the meetinghouse door to join the West Knoxville Society of Friends for First Day worship.

I found myself in a simple, unadorned room with three walls of windows opened to the surrounding woods. Folding chairs formed a square around the room. There was no pulpit and no piano, just a group of about twenty people—some young, some old—sitting in perfect silence, many with their eyes closed in meditation.

"Have you ever been to a Quaker service before?" a white-haired lady named Judith whispered as I found a seat.

"No, I haven't," I said, suddenly aware of the fact that I was significantly overdressed compared to the rest of the congregation, most of whom wore jeans and T-shirts. At least this time I'd remembered to wear flat shoes.

"We do things a little differently," Judith whispered before jumping out of her seat.

She returned a few seconds later with a stash of pamphlets detailing the traditions of the Friends.

The Religious Society of Friends, known popularly as the Quakers, is a loosely knit religious group that strongly emphasizes the apostle Peter's concept of the "priesthood of all believers." Established in the seventeenth century by George Fox, the Friends are known for their commitment to nonviolence and social justice, plain dress, plain speak, simple services, and refusal to swear oaths. Historically, they have played an important role in abolishing slavery and working for prison reform in the U.S.

"Our chairs face each other because we all minister to each other," the pamphlet said. "There are no prearranged prayers, readings, sermons, hymns or musical orchestration because we wait for God's leading and power in our lives."

It was funny reading this just days after my trip to St. Bernard, where I'd spent three days kneeling and chanting and crossing myself with holy water.

In contrast, the Quakers have no religious dogma, no creeds, no priests, no pastors, no liturgy, no religious imagery, no *outward* sacraments, no ritual, and no set worship service. Instead, they spend most of their meetings in complete silence, meditating and awaiting internal illumination from the Inner Light.

Funny how my quest for silence brought me to such seemingly unlike places.

"Occasionally, during Meeting for Worship, someone is moved to speak out of the silence," the program said. "Although Friends value spoken messages which come from the heart and are promoted by the Spirit of God, we also value the silence and find that expectant worship may bring profound leadings. Friends have found that some leadings are for sharing immediately, some for sharing on another occasion, and some for our personal reflection."

Having grown up evangelical, where folks feel "moved to speak" pretty much all the time, I assumed the service would be something like a Sunday night sharing time or open mic night. But after thirty minutes of total silence, I realized these people were serious.

My inner voice was having none of it.

I'm never going to get out of that parking space. Wait. Did I leave my lights on? I bet I did. Great. And no one can come in and say that there's a turquoise Plymouth Acclaim in the parking lot with its lights on because that would interrupt the silence. Maybe I should go check . . .

Look at all the bare feet. Should I take my shoes off? Judith has her shoes on, but that guy who looks like a hippie has his off. Actually, most of these folks look like hippies. Why was I expecting Amish?

No communion, huh? That seems a little fishy to me. And no water baptism? Not sure I could jibe with that. I like a good dunkin' when it comes to baptism.

Oh gosh. I think someone just farted.

Okay, I need to focus on being quiet.

Quiet, Rachel, quiet.

The Inner Light couldn't get a word in edgewise.

Finally, a middle-aged gentlemen stood up and started to speak. In a thick, East Tennessee accent, he said, "At the football game Friday night, I couldn't help but notice how many different kinds of people were there. There were elderly, being pushed in wheelchairs and helped along. There were mothers and fathers. There were tiny children, too young to walk. Everyone was talking and laughing and enjoying one another so much that I don't think any of us were watching the action on the field. It was beautiful, and I thought to myself, *What a great game.*"

That was it.

He immediately sat down, and we sat in silence for another fifteen minutes or so before another older woman stood up and shared the words of poet and Quaker John Greenleaf Whittier:

> *Drop Thy still dews of quietness,*
> *Till all our strivings cease;*
> *Take from our souls the strain and stress,*
> *And let our ordered lives confess*
> *The beauty of Thy peace.*[16]

Only two people spoke in the span of an hour, and yet somehow, their words lodged themselves inside of me in a way that no sermon had before.

I mentioned this to Judith after the service, and she smiled as if I'd just learned a secret.

"Oh yes. A few words, when carefully chosen, are so much more powerful than a lecture or a sermon," she said. "We Quakers like to say these are 'weighty words.'"

Weighty words. That sounded exactly right, actually.

At the beginning of the month, I confess that I feared my silent retreat would stifle me, that it would divert me from my newfound passion for advocating on behalf of women who preach and teach. But in the quietness of St. Bernard's Abbey and among the West Knoxville Society of Friends, I encountered Something much bigger than myself, Something that assured me everything would be okay if I could just quiet myself and stop trying so hard.

There is a big difference, after all, between being silenced and silencing oneself. And it is precisely because women like Teresa of Avila and Julian of Norwich and Catherine of Siena knew how to silence themselves before God that they gained such significant influence over the Church in times when women had little voice.

In silence, I had found a reservoir of strength that, if I could just learn to draw from it, could make my words weightier. In silence, it seemed, I had finally found my voice.

HULDAH, THE PROPHET

Whoever welcomes a prophet as a prophet
will receive a prophet's reward, and whoever
welcomes a righteous person as a righteous person
will receive a righteous person's reward.

—JESUS, IN MATTHEW 10:41 (UPDATED NIV)

Josiah became king of Israel when he was just eight years old. Described as Israel's last good king, he reigned for thirty-one years during a final period of peace before the Babylonian exile. About halfway through his reign, Josiah learned that a long-lost collection of Scriptures—which may have been Deuteronomy—had been discovered in the temple. Upon hearing the words read aloud, Josiah tore his robes in repentance and summoned a prophet, for he saw how far Israel had strayed from God's ways.

Contemporaries of Josiah included the famed prophets Jeremiah, Zephaniah, Nahum, and Habakkuk—all of whom have books of the Bible named after them. But Josiah did not choose to ask for help from any of those men. Instead he chose Huldah, a woman and prophet who lived in Jerusalem.

"Huldah is not chosen because no men were available," wrote Scot McKnight. "She is chosen because she is truly exceptional among the prophets."[17]

Huldah first confirmed the scroll's authenticity and then told Josiah that the disobedience of Israel would indeed lead to its destruction, but that Josiah himself would die in peace. Thus, Huldah not only interpreted but also authorized the document that would become a core part of Jewish and Christian Scripture. Her prophecy was fulfilled thirty-five years later (2 Kings 22).

The Bible identifies ten such female prophets in the Old and New Testaments: Miriam, Deborah, Huldah, Noadiah, Isaiah's wife, Anna, and the four daughters of Philip. In addition, women like Rachel, Hannah, Abigail, Elisabeth, and Mary are described as having prophetic visions about the future of their children, the destiny of nations, and the coming Messiah.

When the Holy Spirit descended upon the first Christians at Pentecost, Peter drew from the words of the prophet Joel to describe what had happened:

> *Your sons and daughters will prophesy,*
> *your young men will see visions,*
> *your old men will dream dreams.*
> *Even on my servants, both men and women,*
> *I will pour out my Spirit in those days,*
> *and they will prophesy.*
>
> (ACTS 2:17–18)

The breaking in of the new creation after Christ's resurrection unleashed a cacophony of new prophetic voices, and apparently, prophesying among women was such a common activity in the early church that Paul had to remind women to cover their heads when they did it. While some may try to downplay biblical examples of female disciples, deacons, leaders, and apostles, no one can deny the Bible's long tradition of prophetic feminine vision.

And right now, we need that prophetic vision more than ever.

Right now thirty thousand children die every day from preventable disease.[18]

Right now a woman dies in childbirth every minute.[19]

Right now women ages fifteen to forty-four are more likely to be maimed or to die from male violence than from cancer, malaria, traffic accidents, and war combined.[20]

People who see the leadership of women like Huldah and Junia as special exceptions for times of great need are oblivious to the world in which we live. Those who think the urgency of Pentecost has passed are deluding themselves. They "have eyes to see but do not see and ears to hear but do not hear" (Ezekiel 12:2).

So my advice to women is this: If a man ever tries to use the Bible as a weapon against you to keep you from speaking the truth, just throw on a head covering and tell him you're prophesying instead.

To those who will not accept us as preachers, we will have to become prophets.

September: Grace

Days of Awe

*"On the first day of the seventh month you
are to have a day of rest, a sacred assembly
commemorated with trumpet blasts."*

—LEVITICUS 23:24

TO DO THIS MONTH:

- ☐ Make challah from scratch using Ahava's recipe (Numbers 15:17–21)
- ☐ Observe Rosh Hashanah by sounding the *shofar* and serving the traditional foods (Leviticus 23:23–24; Numbers 29:1–6)
- ☐ Make a list of New Year's resolutions
- ☐ Mark the end of the year with a *Tashlich* ceremony
- ☐ Get a haircut!

"I need to find a *shofar* somewhere," I shouted to Dan from the kitchen.

"A what?"

"A *shofar*! I need to find a *shofar* to blow."

"Come again?"

"I said, I need a *shofar*! I need to find a *shofar* to blow for Rosh Hashanah!"

Dan hit the pause button on *Stephen Hawking's Universe*, and walked into the kitchen with a perplexed look on his face.

"You know; a ram's horn," I said. "I need to find a ram's horn to blow for Rosh Hashanah."

"Oh, I thought you were saying *chauffeur*," Dan replied with a chuckle. "You had me worried there for a second."

What a year it had been for Dan! One minute his wife is camping out in the front yard with nothing but a walkie-talkie for protection; the next she's announcing that she's adopting a computer baby; the next she's living in a monastery; the next she's searching for an ancient instrument with which to mark the beginning of the New Year . . . *in September.*

We were just weeks away from finishing the project, and by this point I'd abandoned any pretense of having it together. I let my big, scary hair run wild. I ignored the extra eleven pounds I'd gained since the start of the project and reverted to my peasant skirts for comfort. I locked myself in my office for hours at a time to write, struggling to finish the book by deadline. I neglected the blog. I ran around town, collecting ingredients and supplies for my final few tasks, unconcerned with the crazed, frantic appearance that prompted one friend to ask, "Should you maybe consider taking a break for a month or two, maybe pick this up after Christmas?"

A break this close to the end was beyond the realm of possibility. I had that end-of-the-semester feeling, the kind that inspires you to pull three all-nighters in a row if that's what it takes to just be finished, to turn in that last paper, get in your car, and drive the heck home.

Needless to say, our sex life suffered.

As did our social life.

As did just about every other life we might have once had.

On top of all of this, back in August a reporter for *Slate.com* had called me up for an interview and published a nice, long online article about my year of biblical womanhood. The article generated something like one thousand comments, a front-page feature, no small amount of controversy, and the interest of several major new outlets across the U.S., the UK, Australia, and even Israel.[1] Before I knew it, my in-box was bulging with interview requests from the *Guardian*, the *Toronto Star*, the *Times* of London, *Huffington Post*, the BBC, a newspaper in Tel Aviv, Oprah's blog, and—this is the one that made me scream like a little girl—NPR.

That's right. Ira Glass wanted to know about my year of biblical womanhood! Well, actually, the producer of the weekend edition of *All Things Considered* with Guy Raz wanted to know about my year of biblical womanhood . . . but close enough.

I drove to the radio station on the University of Tennessee–Chattanooga campus for the interview, trembling all the way and praying I'd manage to speak in complete sentences. Let me tell you, nothing will make you forget just how fat and dysfunctional and asexual you've become more than hearing your own voice between a segment on North American oil reserves and a plea for listener donations on National Public Radio.

As it turns out, not everyone likes the idea of a girl following the Bible literally for a year. Online, a shared hatred of the project developed between two unlikely groups: atheists who assumed I was a naive religious nut doing this as an act of piety to glorify the patriarchal elements of Scripture, and evangelicals who assumed I was a raging liberal feminist doing this as an act of rebellion to make the Bible and those who love it look stupid.

"An affront to all who hold dear," one person called it.

"An embarrassment," said another.

"A pathetic waste of space and time on the planet."

"A mockery of God and Scripture."

"Yet another example of the dangers of religion and the idiocy of those who subscribe to it."

You would think all this negative attention would have deflated me, or at least diluted some of the mania with which I was tackling the final days of the project, but I noticed that this time around, the online hate didn't penetrate me the way it had before, back when I first announced the project. It wasn't that I'd cut myself off from my feelings or convictions; it was just that, through the practices of contemplative prayer and meditation, I'd finally developed a strategy for controlling them. When I felt my spirit begin to grow volatile, rocked by the colliding waves of criticism and praise, I'd take a moment to close my eyes and meditate on a psalm or a word or a prayer until I found equilibrium. Time and again I returned to the prayer of St. Teresa of Avila that I discovered back when the project first started:

> *Let nothing upset you,*
> *Let nothing startle you.*
> *All things pass;*
> *God does not change.*
> *Patience wins all it seeks.*
> *Whoever has God lacks nothing.*
> *God alone is enough.*

That, or a piece of Divine 70% Dark Chocolate with Raspberries, usually did the trick.

I didn't have much time to engage in online banter anyway, as I was busy preparing for my final biblical holiday—Rosh Hashanah.

Rosh Hashanah is the Jewish new year, and a sacred time of evaluation and reflection among the devout. While many around the world welcome the new year with drunken parties and gross excess, Rosh Hashanah provides the opportunity for an annual *cheshbon hanefesh*, or "inventory of the soul." It is described in Leviticus 23 as a period in which the children of Israel must sound the *shofar*, a ram's horn that recalls the giving of the Torah at Mount Sinai and summons the faithful to "wake from their lethargy" and humble themselves before their Creator.

"One year we had a neighbor who blew his shofar faithfully every evening during the month leading up to Rosh Hashanah," Ahava told me over a Skype call. "Unfortunately we had a newborn who liked to nap during that time, so I admit I started to get a little annoyed with the whole thing."

Rosh Hashanah begins a ten-day period of repentance that culminates with Yom Kippur, the Day of Atonement. These Days of Awe, as they are often called, hold mystical significance in the Jewish community, for it is believed that they represent a period of judgment in which all the people of the world fall under the scrutiny of the Almighty.

"In the month leading up to Rosh Hashanah, we say prayers of repentance and the shofar is blown every day," Ahava explained. "We prepare ourselves spiritually with an accounting of our soul. It's easy to ask daily for normal forgiveness, but this time of year we take into account the things that we might have neglected, especially those petty things that can build up over time. We seek forgiveness from those we may have wronged, even our closest family members, children, spouses, and parents."

This year, Rosh Hashanah corresponded exactly with the final three days of my year of biblical womanhood, so it seemed fitting that I should conclude the project with a time of evaluation and introspection, and that I should mark the end of the project with the foods and traditions that mark the "biblical" new year.

Fortunately, after I posted a rather desperate Facebook status asking if anyone knew where a girl could get herself a *shofar*, my dad called and said, "Rachel, I've got a shofar in my office, remember? I use it as a teaching aid in my Bible classes."

Let the Days of Awe begin!

"Present a loaf from the first of your ground meal
and present it as an offering from the threshing floor.
Throughout the generations to come you are to give this
offering to the Lord from the first of your ground meal."
—NUMBERS 15:20–21 UDPATED NIV

When I asked Ahava if there was anything else "biblical" I needed to try before the end of the year, she wrote back, "Have you made bread yet? That's an important command for women: making bread and separating the tithe for the priests. I usually bake round challahs through the holidays to symbolize the cycle of life. If you need a recipe, let me know."

Challah—pronounced a bit like "holla," but from the back of your throat—is a traditional braided bread eaten on Sabbath and Jewish holidays. The double loaf recalls how, when the Israelites wandered the desert, manna fell from heaven every day except the Sabbath and on holidays, so God provided a double portion the day before. According to tradition, three Sabbath meals and two holiday meals should begin with challah bread.

Numbers 15 stipulates that a portion of the dough must be separated out and presented as an offering for the Lord. "Even though there is no Temple or priests to receive it," Ahava explained, "we still separate the portion, (the size of an egg from the whole batch), and it is holy. But what to do with it? Burning it to make it unfit for any other purpose and to keep us from wanting to eat it ourselves is what we do. This portion is called challah, and is where the bread gets its name, not the other way around."

For centuries, Jewish women have observed this custom, tearing a portion from the risen dough, burning it in the oven, and saying a blessing. I agreed with Ahava. I definitely had to try this before I concluded my year of biblical womanhood.

The thing was, I'd never made bread from scratch before, and the process intimidated me. The notion that eggs, yeast, flour, and water could magically materialize into bread fit into the same category of my mind in which plastic, silicon, and metal magically materialize into a computer. That such a miracle could occur in my own kitchen seemed outrageous and required quite a bit of faith.

I asked Ahava for her recipe, and she sent it to me with a note that said, "When we were dating, my husband made this bread, which was yards better than any challah I'd ever made or tasted. But he refused to give me the recipe until we were married. Now I make the bread all the time, and am free to give the recipe out. You don't even have to marry me to get it!"

The recipe made enough for six loaves, which meant it called for 5 pounds of flour, 7 egg yolks, 4 1/2 cups of water, 1 1/2 cups of sugar, 7 teaspoons of yeast, and 4 tablespoons of salt. That seemed like a lot, but I figured it would be easier to make six loaves of challah than to do the math required to divide the recipe in half.

Before I started, I used the blog to solicit advice from seasoned bakers. Advice poured in:

- "The main thing to remember is that sugar acts as a catalyst and salt as a blocker (anti-catalyst). The ratio of sugar/salt/yeast is the most important thing, so be especially careful when measuring those ingredients."—Kenton
- "That sounds like a HUGE recipe! How many loaves is it supposed to make? If it were me, I'd cut it down by at least

half, if not 3/4. I'm thinking of the 'I Love Lucy' episode where the bread kept coming out of the oven. Also, if your oven has a Proof feature on it, it creates the perfect temperature for bread to rise properly."—Patricia

+ "Make sure your water is warm enough to get the yeast going, but not too hot that it will kill the yeast. It shouldn't scald your hand. I also had to learn patience when I first made Challah—it takes a while for the dough to rise and double."—Sherry

+ "Tip from seasoned bread baker: Make sure your yeast isn't expired. (There should be a date on the package.) Depends how much bread baking goes on in your neck of the woods, but if their yeast stock isn't turning over regularly by purchases, the stores sometimes aren't good about noticing that their yeast is expired. And you want lively yeast . . ."—Becky

+ "Just put my challah loaves in the oven! Remember that loaves for Rosh HaShanah are round to symbolize the continuity of life . . . just like how we both finish the Torah reading and begin with Genesis again. Shana tovah!"—Lindsay

You don't exactly "whip up" six loaves of bread, so I set aside the two days before the start of Rosh Hashanah to make my challah. I decided to work on the dining room table because the faux butcher-block surface provided the most space. So on a Tuesday afternoon, I dusted the table with flour, put on my frilly apron, pulled back my hair, and got to work.

Dan grew up watching his mother make bread and had a sort of manly respect for the scientific processes involved, so he helped me measure out all the ingredients, careful to be precise, like my readers said: 4 1/2 cups of warm (but not scalding) water, 1 1/2 cups of sugar, and 7 teaspoons of yeast.

Then we combined the water and sugar in the biggest bowl we owned, added the yeast, and watched. Little bubbles appeared in the pale brown mixture, which I'd been told meant it was working.

After five minutes, we added the egg yolks, oil, sugar, and salt.

"Slowly begin adding flour," Ahava's directions said. "After a while, it will be impossible to stir."

Dan tilted the bag of flour over the bowl while I stirred. The mixture slowly transformed into a gooey dough . . . and lots of it. I stirred until my arm hurt, gave Dan a turn, and then we dumped the recalcitrant mixture onto the table.

"Turn the dough out onto a floured surface and begin kneading in the rest of the flour," Ahava's directions continued. "It all has to go in according to Jewish law. If you find the dough is too dry, add more water."

I had to Google "kneading" to see how it was done. Within a few seconds, I found a YouTube video in which a chirpy thirty-something in an apron demonstrated the proper method—press, stretch, fold, rotate; press, stretch, fold, rotate—but she did this so quickly, I kept falling behind, and I couldn't replay the video because my hands were coated in sticky dough.

Kneading nine pounds of dough is like getting thrown into a wrestling ring with the Pillsbury Doughboy. I struggled and sighed and cursed, while Dan coached me in my technique.

According to the YouTube lady, you can tell that you're done kneading if you press the dough with two fingers and the indentations stay after you move your fingers away.

Well, we kept kneading and testing and kneading and testing, but that mound of dough just kept springing right back under our fingertips.

Even Dan got frustrated.

"It shouldn't be taking this long," he said. "Maybe we did something wrong."

We must have kneaded for thirty minutes, taking turns, before we gave up and assumed we'd passed the finished point long ago and probably destroyed our bread.

"Put dough ball into LARGE oiled bowl or pot, cover with plastic wrap, and let rise overnight in a warm place, for at least six hours,"

Ahava had written. "The longer it rises, the better the flavor. Punch it down a few times if you need to."

We didn't have a mixing bowl the size that Ahava showed me in our Skype conversation, so I'd gone to Wal-Mart and gotten a 18-quart plastic bin in which to let the bread rise.

Everyone and their mother had an opinion about where to store the bread overnight so that it rose properly, but I'd decided on an unconventional method: we heaved the blob of dough into the bin, covered it with a towel, put it in the guest bathroom with a space heater, and closed the door.

Now all we had to do was wait . . .

One of them, an expert in the law tested [Jesus]
with this question: Teacher, which is the greatest
commandment in the Law? Jesus replied: "'Love
the Lord your God with all your heart and with all
your soul and with all your mind.' This is the first
and greatest commandment. And the second is like
it: 'Love your neighbor as yourself.' All the Law and
the Prophets hang on these two commandments."
—MATTHEW 22:35–40

Because I started the project with a list of ten commandments, I decided to end it with a list of ten resolutions.

The question everyone was asking as I approached the conclusion of my year of biblical womanhood was what, if anything, I planned to hold over from the project and incorporate into my regular life. While I'd be happily ditching the head coverings and "Yes, Masters," I'd learned a lot over the past 363 days, some of which had changed my life. The New Year seemed as good a time as any to make resolutions for the future, so, while I waited for the bread to rise, I got out my journal and wrote down my "10 New Year's Resolutions":

1. **Try a new recipe every week.** I like to cook. I like it because it helps me get out of my head and channel my creative energies into something tangible, something I can taste, touch, smell, and share with other people. A new recipe, complete with mysterious ingredients and religious symbolism, is like a little adventure I can embark on every week. Success makes for good food; failure makes for good stories.

2. **Eat more ethically.** It's worth paying extra to know we did our due diligence to ensure that the food we eat does not perpetuate the exploitation of other people. I'd like to continue learning about the origin and production of the products we buy so that I can make more informed decisions as a consumer, doing my part to "repair the world."

3. **Identify and praise women of valor.** Ahava inspired me to "take back" Proverbs 31 as a way of honoring other women of faith for their accomplishments and bravery. I want to learn more about influential women like Dorothy Day, Catherine Hamlin, Julian of Norwich, Catherine of Siena, and Sojourner Truth so I can draw inspiration from their lives and share their stories with others. I also want to be quick to cheer my sisters on, for big victories or small, by declaring, *"Eshet chayil!* Woman of Valor!"

4. **Embrace the prospect of motherhood.** The project reminded me that I can do anything I set my mind to, and that includes parenting. I'm still scared, and I'm still unsure of what motherhood will look like for me, but I'm not going to wait until I've overcome all of my fears to start a family.

5. **Nurture the contemplative impulse.** It may be nothing more than a bunch of neurons firing in just the right places of my brain, but something powerful and life-giving happens when I take the time to calm and quiet my soul. In the year to come, I want to nurture that impulse by practicing

contemplative prayer, returning to St. Bernard, studying the mystics, and maybe even praying the daily office from time to time. I want to gain better mastery over my volatile spirit, so I can understand for myself what St. Teresa meant when she said "patience wins all it seeks."

6. **Make room for ritual and remembrance.** From celebrating the Passover Seder, to walking through the stations of the cross, to lighting candles in honor of the victims of the text of terror, engaging in rituals throughout the year helped connect me to the past in ways that illuminate the present, making the everyday sacred. I want to make more room in my faith for rituals like these, perhaps by observing the church calendar, celebrating Jewish holidays, or helping to create new rituals that honor the particular struggles and triumphs of women of faith.

7. **Champion women leaders in the Church.** Whatever small influence I may have over the Christian community, I will use to advocate on behalf of my talented sisters who long to use their gifts to benefit the Church and the world. I will share my platform with women writers. I will lend my support to women leaders. I will cheer on women scholars and teachers. And I will speak out against those who try to silence them with patriarchal readings of Scripture that idolize the culture and context in which the Bible was written over the equality and freedom granted to each of us in Christ.

8. **Partner with World Vision to work for the education and empowerment of women around the world.** In addition to devoting more of my own resources to assisting my struggling sisters around the world, I will partner with World Vision to launch several annual advocacy and fund-raising initiatives on the blog that focus on women's education and job training.

9. **Honor Dan.** It may not always be at the city gates, but

Dan deserves my thanks and praise. He is patient. He is kind. He treats me with respect and is the biggest champion of my success. This project would have been miserable in the company of a lesser man, but he made it a joy. The gift of a true partner is one I should never take for granted. I need to thank him more often.

10. **Keep loving, studying, and struggling with the Bible—** because no matter how hard I fight it, it will always call me back.

That last one surprised me a little. I figured I'd be so sick of the Bible after this project was over that I'd have to take a break and start reading the Bhagavad Gita for a while. But somewhere between the rooftop and the red tent, I'd learned to love the Bible again—for what it is, not what I want it to be.

The Bible isn't an answer book. It isn't a self-help manual. It isn't a flat, perspicuous list of rules and regulations that we can interpret objectively and apply unilaterally to our lives.

The Bible is a sacred collection of letters and laws, poetry and proverbs, philosophy and prophecies, written and assembled over thousands of years in cultures and contexts very different from our own, that tells the complex, ever-unfolding story of God's interaction with humanity.

When we turn the *Bible* into an adjective and stick it in front of another loaded word (like *manhood, womanhood, politics, economics, marriage,* and even *equality*), we tend to ignore or downplay the parts of the Bible that don't fit our tastes. In an attempt to simplify, we try to force the Bible's cacophony of voices into a single tone, to turn a complicated and at times troubling holy text into a list of bullet points we can put in a manifesto or creed. More often than not, we end up more committed to what we *want* the Bible to say than what it actually says.

So after twelve months of "biblical womanhood," I'd arrived at the rather unconventional conclusion that that there is no such thing.

The Bible does not present us with a single model for womanhood, and the notion that it contains a sort of one-size-fits-all formula for how to be a woman of faith is a myth.

Among the women praised in Scripture are warriors, widows, slaves, sister wives, apostles, teachers, concubines, queens, foreigners, prostitutes, prophets, mothers, and martyrs. What makes these women's stories leap from the page is not the fact that they all conform to some kind of universal ideal, but that, regardless of the culture or context in which they found themselves, they lived their lives with valor. They lived their lives with faith. As much as we may long for the simplicity of a single definition of "biblical womanhood," there is no one right way to be a woman, no mold into which we must each cram ourselves—not if Deborah, Ruth, Rachel, Tamar, Vashti, Esther, Priscilla, Mary Magdalene, and Tabitha have anything to say about it.

Far too many church leaders have glossed over these stories and attempted to define womanhood by a list of rigid roles. But roles are not fixed. They are not static. Roles come and go; they shift and they change. They are relative to our culture and subject to changing circumstances. It's not our roles that define us, but our character.

A calling, on the other hand, when rooted deep in the soil of one's soul, transcends roles. And I believe that my calling, as a Christian, is the same as that of any other follower of Jesus. My calling is to love the Lord with all my heart, soul, mind, and strength, and to love my neighbor as myself. Jesus himself said that the rest of Scripture can be rendered down into these two commands. If love was Jesus' definition of "biblical," then perhaps it should be mine.

Philosopher Peter Rollins has said, "By acknowledging that all our readings [of Scripture] are located in a cultural context and have certain prejudices, we understand that engaging with the Bible can never mean that we simply extract meaning from it, but also that we read meaning into it. In being faithful to the text we must move away from the naïve attempt to read it from some neutral, heavenly height and we must attempt to read it as one who has been born of

God and thus born of love: for that is the prejudice of God. Here the ideal of scripture reading as a type of scientific objectivity is replaced by an approach that creatively interprets with love."[3]

For those who count the Bible as sacred, interpretation is not a matter of *whether* to pick and choose, but *how* to pick and choose. We are all selective. We all wrestle with how to interpret and apply the Bible to our lives. We all go to the text looking for something, and we all have a tendency to find it. So the question we have to ask ourselves is this: Are we reading with the prejudice of love or are we reading with the prejudices of judgment and power, self-interest and greed?

If you are looking for Bible verses with which to support slavery, you will find them. If you are looking for verses with which to abolish slavery, you will find them. If you are looking for verses with which to oppress women, you will find them. If you are looking for verses with which to liberate and honor women, you will find them. If you are looking for reasons to wage war, you will find them. If you are looking reasons to promote peace, you will find them. If you are looking for an outdated and irrelevant ancient text, you will find it. If you are looking for truth, believe me, you will find it.

This is why there are times when the most instructive question to bring to the text is not, *what does it say?* but *what am I looking for?* I suspect Jesus knew this when he said, "ask and it will be given to you; seek and you will find; knock and the door will be opened to you."

If you want to do violence in this world, you will always find the weapons. If you want to heal, you will always find the balm.

So what was I looking for when I started this project?

I think, at the surface, I was looking for a good story. And I certainly found one.

But further down, in the deeper recesses of my heart and mind, I think I was looking for permission—permission to lead, permission to speak, permission to find my identity in something other than my roles, permission to be myself, permission to be a woman.

What a surprise to reach the end of the year with the quiet and liberating certainty that I never had to ask for it. It had already been given.

*"What shall I compare the kingdom of
God to? It is like yeast that a woman took
and mixed into about sixty pounds of flour
until it worked all through the dough."*
—LUKE 13:20–21 UPDATED NIV

I tossed and turned the night before Rosh Hashanah, worried that
I'd awake to find a massive glob of dough oozing out from under the
bathroom door. But when I stumbled out of bed at 5 a.m. to check
on the progress of my challah, I found it had risen impressively, yet
within the bounds of my 18-quart container. Success!

"The dough has risen!" I shouted at Dan when he walked into
the dining room a few hours later, rubbing his eyes and looking for
cereal. "It has risen indeed!"

"Sweet. Go, Team Dan and Rachel," he replied, still only half-awake.

As the blue light of morning lit the windows, I turned to Ahava's
instructions.

"Turn dough out onto lightly floured surface, separate the challah with a bracha (a blessing), and burn the portion," they said.

This was the important part.

I dumped the dough out onto the table, removed a small piece
with a carving knife, cupped the warm mound of dough in my
hands, and whispered, "Blessed are you, Lord God, King of the universe, who has blessed us with his commandments and commanded
us regarding the separation of challah."

At this point, most Jews burn the challah portion as a sacrifice,
but I decided instead to save it for the *tashlich* ceremony I'd planned
for the final day of Rosh Hashanah. In a *tashlich*, the repentant
gather before a river or stream and cast bread crumbs and pebbles
into the water to be swept away by the current. This symbolic casting away of sins is meant to remind them of the forgiveness of God,
who "will cast all their sins into the depths of the sea" (Micah 7:20

NASB). This seemed like a more fitting sacrifice for me, so I wrapped the portion in aluminum foil and set it aside.

"Cut the dough into the desired number of loaves," the directions continued. "Then cut the loaf section into pieces and braid. For Rosh Hashanah, consider rolling the challah into a circular shape to symbolize the cycle of the year."

Ahava sent me a link to the Challah Blog, which included directions and pictures for braiding challah into the shape of a Croatian Star—perfect for Rosh Hashanah![4] Dan helped me separate the dough into six relatively even sections. We rolled each one into a long, snakelike shape, which we then cut into quarters. The quarters were rolled out, laced over one another in a star pattern, then coiled. They looked like doughy little pinwheels.

I found this part of the process to be great fun, much like messing around with Play-Doh as a kid. Dan left after I'd finished braiding three of the six loaves, confident that I could handle things from here on out.

"Place braided loaves on flat pans lined with parchment paper," the directions continued, "cover with plastic wrap or a towel and place in a warm spot for 40–60 minutes until the loaves have approximately doubled in size."

The warm bathroom worked before, so I placed the braided loaves, two to a pan, on the floor, on top of the sink, and in the bathtub, and closed the door. Sure enough, they doubled in size.

As per Ahava's directions, I preheated the oven, made an egg wash, and brushed each loaf before sprinkling them with sesame seeds.

You know that scene in *Castaway* where Tom Hanks finally gets a fire started, and as it roars on the beach that night, he stands before it with his chest puffed out, his arms raised triumphantly, and in a deep, godlike voice shouts to the heavens, "Look what I have created!" Well, that's exactly what I did when I pulled my first two challah loaves out of the oven to find them all soft and golden and brown. I, Rachel Grace Held Evans, had just created bread . . . basically ex nihilo.

The house smelled heavenly as, over the course of the morning, I baked four more loaves of challah. When Dan came home, he took a bite, said the challah tasted a little dense, and blamed himself for letting me knead it too long. But I didn't care. The challah looked pretty and it was edible—tasty, even—an outcome that far exceeded my expectations.

Rosh Hashanah officially began at sunset, so at seven, just before the light went all blue again, I went out on the back deck to welcome the High Holy Days with the sounding of my dad's *shofar*.

To blow a *shofar*, you've got to form an embouchure, like you're blowing into a trumpet, and you've got to blow really, really hard. The idea is to call forth the faithful, to remind them of the mighty deeds of God. It was the *shofar* that was heard when the Ten Commandments were given, the *shofar* that brought down the city of Jericho, the *shofar* that for centuries has marked the beginning of a new year.

"Listening to the primitive wail of the ancient musical instrument, not only reminds worshippers of Judaism's beginnings in a long ago, far-away desert," wrote Rabbi Dosik, "but also touches the deepest and most basic places in the human soul—those places where each human being searches for and finds primordial beginnings and the mysteries of existence."[5]

Unfortunately, what issued from my dad's twelve-inch, lacquered, authentic ram's horn that evening sounded more like a cross between a party horn and an elephant's sneeze—the party horn being exceptionally loud and the elephant being especially congested.

Perhaps the residents of Jericho fled voluntarily.

Dan came out to see what on earth was happening on his back porch, and I tried again.

Another shrill honk echoed through the neighborhood, where a bunch of unsuspecting white Protestants sat at their dinner tables, wholly unaware that they were supposed to be celebrating the new year. It sounded even worse the second time because, with Dan watching, I started to giggle.

"I think you need a bigger *shofar*," Dan said, "or more air."

Then he gave it a try, with the same result.

Undeterred, I fumbled my way through the four distinct sounds to be produced during Rosh Hashanah: *teki'ah*, one long blast; *shevarim*, three short blasts; *teru'ah*, nine staccato blasts; and *teki'ah gedolah*, a final sustained blast. After I finished, and Dan uncovered his ears, I heard in the distance what sounded like an echo, a second plaintive wail issued as if in response. Was I not alone? Could it be that here, in East Tennessee, a Jew was greeting the New Year in this ancient, primordial expression of hope?

As it turns out, the *shofar* has the same effect as an ambulance and had excited some of the neighborhood dogs. Dan encouraged me to come back inside before we started getting phone calls.

The next night, we threw a little party to celebrate Rosh Hashanah and the end of my year of biblical womanhood. Tony, Dayna, and the girls came, and my parents, and Kristine, and some neighbors. Chris and Tiffany called to say that Early was sick and offered their congratulations. I sounded the *shofar* at each person's arrival, scaring poor Aury half to death.

At sunset we gathered around the table, and I lit the holiday candles with a prayer:

> "*Blessed are you, Lord, our God, sovereign of the universe*
> *Who has sanctified us with His commandments*
> *And commanded us to light candles of the holiday.*"

Then I broke the challah and recited the blessing:

> "*Blessed are you, Lord, our God, sovereign of the universe*
> *Who brings forth bread from the earth.*"

Next I poured glasses of cranberry pomegranate juice (because we were out of wine, and I didn't have the heart to serve the leftover Mogen David we still had sitting in our refrigerator), and said the *kiddush*, accompanied by a special blessing for Rosh Hashanah:

"Blessed are you, Lord, our God, sovereign of the universe,
Who creates fruit of the vine,
Who made all things exist through His word.
You gave us, Lord our God, with love, this day of
remembrance,
A day of shofar blowing,
A holy convocation,
A memorial of the exodus from Egypt
Blessed are You, Lord our God, King over all the world,
Who sanctifies the Day of Remembrance."

As I explained to everyone the significance of the food on the table, I was surprised to feel tears gathering in my eyes. The round challah represented the cycle of life, but it also reminded me of my dear friend Ahava and the prayer she left in the Western Wall. The traditional apples and honey, meant to signify a sweet new year, reminded me of St. Bernard's, for the honey was made by the bee-keepers at the monastery. A pomegranate, broken in two so that seeds spilled out, symbolized good deeds for the year to come; the black-eyed pea dip represented good luck. A bowl of pretzels recalled the snacks that Mary served in Amish country, and the fair trade chocolate bars, my hope for a more just world. The only thing missing was some roasted guinea pig.

After we ate, I concluded with a final prayer for Rosh Hashanah:

"Blessed are you, Lord, our God, sovereign of the universe
Who has kept us alive, sustained us, and enabled us to
reach this season."

Dan's Journal
September 30, 2011

Recently my mom said she was proud that I'm able to support Rachel in her successful career. She said that was something that "many men couldn't do."

The comment revealed a strange absurdity about this "year of biblical womanhood." For the past 365 days, I've embraced the role as the hierarchical leader of our relationship, yet at the same time, by doing so, I'm playing a supporting role in Rachel's career. I didn't know how to respond to the compliment until it hit me: Our roles change depending on context.

At its core, our relationship isn't a hierarchy; it's a partnership. What kind of person doesn't want success for their partner? A weak, insecure, person. What kind of man doesn't want success for his wife? A weak, insecure man. I'm not supporting Rachel like a passive piling supports a dock. I'm supporting her like the Saturn V supported Apollo 11. I want her to succeed in her pursuits, and will do everything in my power to make it happen. She wants the same for me. When I'm working on a film project, who's taking the supporting role and feeding the crew? Rachel. When I took a year to buy, renovate and sell an investment property, who supported me throughout the project? Rachel. Our life decisions are made in partnership. We're the ones leading our lives.

To be "a leader" is meaningless without context. A leader of what? Too many of us have succumbed to the idea that "leaders" are a specific type of people or that "leadership" is a character quality to be obtained like political capital—the more the better. But I view leadership differently. Leadership isn't a goal. Leadership is a role. Wisdom and strength are what we should pursue. Not leadership. Wisdom is discerning when to lead. Strength comes from practicing wisdom. Leadership is a role that changes hands depending on context. In that light, it is important to learn how to lead not because you want to be "a leader" but because when your wisdom and strength have placed you in a position of leadership, you don't want to screw it up.

On that note, I'm really proud of Rachel for taking on this project. It was a good life experience for both of us. Kinda like the time that my best friend Doug and I pushed a stalled car half a mile on the Tappan Zee Bridge in New York in the middle of the night, amidst heavy traffic, until the cops arrived to help. I wouldn't want to do it again, but it makes for a good story to tell grandchildren someday.

I'm glad we did it, and I'm glad it's over.

Some rabbis say that, at birth, we are each tied to God with a string, and that every time we sin, the string breaks. To those who repent of their sins, especially in the days of Rosh Hashanah, God sends the angel Gabriel to make knots in the string, so that the humble and contrite are once again tied to God. Because each one of us fails, because we all lose our way on the path to righteousness from time to time, our strings are full of knots. But, the rabbis like to say, a string with many knots is shorter than one without knots. So the person with many sins but a humble heart is closer to God.

At the end of my year of biblical womanhood, my string was full of knots. Like any other year, this one had been full of grudges and judgments, hypocrisy and fear, careless words and forgotten truths. And like any other year, it had yielded surprising moments of forgiveness and grace, insights and friendships. Anne Shirley liked to say that "tomorrow is fresh, with no mistakes in it."[6] And at Rosh Hashanah, the Jews believe, the world gets a fresh start. So, on the final day of the project and the first day of a brand-new year, I made my way to Laurel-Snow wilderness west of town to watch my sins wash away.

A vast 2,259-acre forest marked by the deep gorges of the Cumberland Plateau, Laurel-Snow was known for years as Pocket Wilderness. If you want to know how long a person's lived in Rhea County, ask him how well he knows Pocket. For those of us who grew up in this town, the trails and creeks and old mining caves that make up its rugged and verdant landscape are an indelible part of our shared history. I know a lot of people who skipped their first rock across Richland Creek, smoked their first joint at Buzzard Point, and had their first kiss under Laurel Falls. We've gotten caught out there in countless thunderstorms. We've sprained our ankles on silver maple roots. We've gone skinny-dipping in the swimming holes. We know Pocket like we know our mother's scent . . . so don't trust anyone who calls it the Laurel-Snow State Natural Area to tell you how to get around.

Dan and I went together, partly because we needed the four-wheel drive on his Explorer to get up the winding gravel road that leads to the entrance of the forest, but mostly because this was a big day for both of us, and we couldn't think of a better way to spend it than in each other's company.

To my delight, September 30 turned out to be my favorite day of each year: the first day of the season in which you can get away with wearing a sweater. The sun shone brightly in a cloudless fall sky, but a chilly wind whipped through the cove, making all the trees shiver and sigh. Everything felt so alive, so connected. It was as if the earth itself knew that a new year had begun, and it was whispering with excitement.

We started down the sun-dappled path along the creek, and as any good space should inspire people to do, we looked up. Light poured through the leaves, bright with the first flush of color. Squirrels and birds leapt from limb to limb. The ridge to our right towered over us, making us seem suddenly small in comparison. We passed giant boulders, the old mine shaft, a tree across the path. The creek got louder and louder as we walked along. We were getting closer to the spot I had in mind.

I wore a sweatshirt and a brimmed, cadet-style hat and carried a handmade wool satchel I'd bought from Marta, the Tabitha of Bolivia. In the satchel was the portion of challah I'd set aside for my sacrifice, which I'd gone ahead and braided and baked so that it looked like a mini loaf of bread, the shofar, and my well-worn copy of the Book of Common Prayer.

"How about here?" Dan asked as we passed the swimming hole.

"It needs to be by rushing water," I said. "I've got a spot in mind."

"What about this?" he said a few minutes later as we came upon a narrower section of the creek where white water crashed over the mossy rocks.

"Nope. I know just where I want to go," I said.

Finally, I saw it: a wide expanse of water where a path of dry, flat rocks crossed right over the creek and formed a sort of ridge between slow-moving water at the top and the cascading water at the bottom.

Just as I'd remembered it.

"This is it!" I said, and we maneuvered our way down the steep bank.

Dan helped me find the perfect spot—a sunbathed rock right between two little waterfalls—and then went exploring up the creek to give me some privacy for my *Tashlich* ceremony.

The *Tashlich* (literally, "casting") is a tradition dating back to the Middle Ages in which the sins of the repentant are ceremonially cast into the deep, ever-flowing currents of God's grace. It is a time of both penitence and celebration as a year's worth of shortcomings and failures are acknowledged, accepted, and then washed away so that life can begin again, fresh, with no mistakes in it.

I began my *Tashlich* ceremony by sounding the *shofar*, which promptly sent a flock of birds fleeing for their lives. Then I sat down and worked my way through the Litany of Penitence in the Book of Common Prayer, which begins, "Most holy and merciful Father: I confess to you and to the whole communion of saints in heaven and on earth, that I have sinned by my own fault, in thought, word, and deed; by what I have done, and what I have left undone. I have not loved you with my whole heart, and mind, and strength. I have not loved my neighbors as myself. I have not forgiven others as I have been forgiven."

Then I took out the challah and began tearing it into little pieces. With each crumb, I acknowledged a sin I'd committed during the year.

Some of these sins were specific to the project: I'd grown petulant and impatient over simple household tasks, I'd judged other women for choosing lifestyles that differed from my own; I'd complained; I'd indulged; I'd thrown books across the room; I'd put a lot of pennies in that jar; I'd failed to appreciate how much Dan sacrificed for the project and how much crap my friends and family put up with to help me get through; I'd been vain about my appearance and obsessed with trivial things while women around the world suffered from atrocities I could help prevent; I'd held grudges against those who criticized my work; I'd looked down on those who interpreted the Bible differently than I; I'd gotten angry at God and demanded answers rather than simply asking questions with patience and with faith; I still hadn't taken out my recycling.

Others were sins that I've struggled with all my life: I'd obsessed over what people thought of me; I'd assumed that money would fix everything; I'd failed to listen well; I'd steamrolled; I'd confused my wants with needs; I'd prioritized work over relationships; I'd gossiped; I'd worried; I'd feared; I'd doubted the goodness in others and in myself; I'd done injury to the world through my carelessness, my neglect, my unkind words, and my self-centeredness.

I held each crumb between my fingers until I had fully forgiven myself for the sin that it represented. Then I cast them, one by one, with abandon, into the rushing water below. Some I held on to longer than others. Some I watched get washed down the river and swirled about in the eddies. By the time I finished, the fish had lots of challah to eat, and somehow, I'd grown lighter.

"Who is a God like you?" the traditional *Tashlich* prayer asks, "who pardons sin and forgives the transgression . . . You do not stay angry forever but delight to show mercy. You will again have compassion on us; you will tread our sins underfoot and hurl all our iniquities into the depths of the sea" (Micah 7:18–19).

To conclude, I closed my eyes, breathed in the damp, cool air, and focused with a centering prayer. I chose *grace* as my sacred word, but under the warm sunlight, the water rushing beside me and the trees clapping their hands around me, it became something other than a word, something that expanded my consciousness, so that for a brief moment I thought I could feel my roots commingling with the roots of everything else in the world. I opened my eyes and let the blue sky, the yellow leaves, and the gray water become my prayer.

God had long ago forgiven me, but with this prayer, I had

forgiven myself for all I had done and all I'd left undone. I was starting fresh.

I sounded the *shofar* to let Dan know I was finished. (He'd been collecting discarded soda cans and trash from the crannies in the rocks to throw away bless his heart.) We climbed our way back up the bank and headed down the trail.

"Let's say what we are thankful for," I suggested as we stomped through the forest, holding hands. "Like the things we are thankful for from the project."

"You mean that it's over?" Dan asked with a grin.

"No, I mean things like, 'I'm thankful that the turkey turned out so great on Thanksgiving, and I'm thankful that we had nice weather for my time in the tent.'"

"Oh, I see what you mean. Well, I'm thankful for that French toast BLT you learned to make."

"I'm thankful for Ahava," I said.

"I'm thankful that we could put Chip in the mail and send him back," Dan said.

"I'm thankful for the opportunity to go to Bolivia."

"I'm thankful for safe travels."

"I'm thankful for silence."

"I'm thankful for 'Dan is Awesome' signs."

"I'm thankful for you."

We went back and forth like this for fifteen minutes, until I wasn't sure where my thanks ended and his began. When we reached the end of the trail, we exchanged a high five and a "Team Dan and Rachel!" Then we got into the truck and took the winding gravel road back home.

Three days later, I'm in the hydraulic chair at Market Street Hair and Nails, explaining to a roomful of foil-wearing women the difference between the English word *helpmeet* and the Hebrew phrase *ezer kenegdo.* At first, only Tiffany, my perky blond stylist, seems to care much about my year of biblical womanhood, but by the time I get to the part about camping out in the front yard during my period, the whole place has gone silent, save the roar of a hair dryer two chairs over.

"He kept a hatchet under the bed?" Tiffany asks to a chorus of giggles. "Oh, my word. What on earth did he plan to do with that?"

With each snip of the scissors, I feel lighter and chattier, and Tiffany skillfully shapes what remains of my hair into a cute, chin-length bob. I don't have enough to donate to locks of love, but that's okay. Ridding the world of my unruly "glory" seems charitable enough.

By the time I get to Rosh Hashanah, Tiffany has pulled off my cape, dusted off my shoulders, and spun me around to face a brand-new me talking back at myself in the mirror.

Or is it just the old me again?

Or someone entirely different?

A chorus of "Oooooh!" and "You look good, girl!" fills the room.

And for the first time in 368 days, I look the way I feel—like a true woman of valor.

Acknowledgments

THIS IS THE SORT OF PROJECT THAT TAKES A VILLAGE, AND I could not have undertaken it without the help, encouragement, wisdom, and talent of some extraordinary men and women of valor.

I am blessed to have an agent, Rachelle Gardner, who often understands my ideas before I do, even crazy ideas like this one. Thank you, Kristen Parrish, for sticking your neck out for this project and bringing so much color and life to it with your enthusiasm and creativity. Thank you, Jim Chaffee, for telling me like it is, yet making me feel like a champion. Thanks to Kristi Henson, Jason Jones, and Jennifer Womble for making this project a priority, right from the beginning.

I am grateful beyond words for my readers at rachelheldevans. com, who inspired me to write this book and whose comments, criticisms, stories, and questions made it what it is. Our little online community feels like home to me in so many ways. Your honesty and grace are rare gifts that I hope never to take for granted.

Thank you, Ahava, for being my go-to girl on everything Jewish. You brought this book to life and have forever changed how I read the Bible. I never expected a source to become such a good friend. *Eshet chayil!* Thank you, Hillary McFarland, for what you do and who you are. Thank you, Mary Kassian, for being so funny and honest and delightful, even when we disagree. Thank you, Jackie Roese, for being brave for the rest of us.

I am grateful for hosts: Flora Mainord, Janet Oberholtzer, Dave and Maki Evans and Chloe, Mary King, Levi and Lydia Stoltzfus, Andrea Rodriguez and World Vision Bolivia, Brother Brendan and St. Bernard Abbey, the West Knoxville Society of Friends.

I am grateful for teachers: Scot McKnight, John Stackhouse, Ellen Davis, Peter Enns, Carolyn Custis James, Rabbi Wayne Dosick, Carol Newsom, Sharon Ringe, and of course, Martha Stewart.

I am grateful for knitters, and seamstresses, and cooks: Jan Vanderwall, Darlene Bruehl, Robin Meloncon, Kelli Grandy, Courtney Shenkle, Lauren Ange, Cheryl Fields, Jane Ardelene, and Betty Palmer.

I am grateful for friends: Monika Barger, Tony and Dayna Falzone (Addy, Aury, and Dany), Brian and Carrie Ward (Avery and Adi), Chris and Tiffany Hoose (Early and Willa).

Thank you, Mom, for being the kind of woman who refuses to fit into a box—for loving football, despising potlucks, traveling the world, reading biographies, surviving cancer, escaping legalism, being everyone's favorite fourth-grade teacher at Dayton City School, and teaching your girls to have compassion for "the least of these." Thanks to Dad for being the kind of man who celebrates and affirms such women. Thanks to Amanda for being a little sister I look up to, and to Tim for having the good sense to marry such a kind, wise, and Christlike person.

Thanks most of all to Dan—for your patience, your wisdom, your sense of humor, your support, your spontaneous bursts of "Team Dan and Rachel!" What an uncommon joy it is to be part of a happy marriage, for better or worse, richer or poorer, computerized baby or Levitical purity laws. May you ever be praised at the city gate!

Notes

Introduction

1. Elisabeth Elliot, *Let Me Be a Woman* (Carol Stream, IL: Tyndale House, 1976), 54.
2. *Theopedia*, s.v., "Complementarianism," http://theopedia.com/ Complementarianism.
3 "Core Beliefs: The Danvers Statement on Biblical Manhood and Womanhood," The Council on Biblical Manhood & Womanhood, http://www.cbmw.org/Danvers.
4. A. Roberts and A. Donaldson, eds, *The Ante-Nicene Fathers*, v. 4 (4), trans. S. Thelwall (Ages Software), 1997.

October

1. Warren St. John, *Rammer Jammer Yellow Hammer: A Journey into the Heart of Fan Mania* (New York: Crown, 2004), 1.
2. From the New American Standard Bible; emphasis is added.
3. Tina Fey, *Bossypants* (New York: Reagan Arthur, 2011), 39.

November

1. Martha Stewart, with Sarah Carey, *Martha Stewart's Cooking School: Lessons and Recipes for the Home Cook* (New York: Clarkson Potter, 2008), vi.

2. Martha Stewart, *Martha Stewart's Homekeeping Handbook: The Essential Guide to Caring for Everything in Your Home* (New York: Clarkson Potter, 2006), 9.

3. Using Paul's instructions in Titus 2 to argue that a woman's work is restricted to the domestic sphere is quite a stretch. By the same logic, his instructions in 1 Timothy 3:4–5 that a male leader in the church should "manage his own household" (NASB) would have to mean that a man also cannot work outside of the home.

4. John Piper and Wayne Grudem, *Recovering Biblical Manhood & Womanhood*, 2nd ed. (Wheaton, IL: Crossway, 1991), 366, 375.

5. Debi Pearl, *Created to Be His Help Meet* (Pleasantville, TN: No Greater Joy Ministries, 2004), 210.

6. Jennie Chancey and Stacy McDonald, *Passionate Housewives Desperate for God* (San Antonio: Vision Forum, 2007), 145.

7. Martha Stewart, *Martha Stewart's Cooking School: Lessons and Recipes for the Home Cook*, 38.

8. Martha Stewart, *Martha Stewart's Homekeeping Handbook: The Essential Guide to Caring for Everything in Your Home* (New York: Clarkson Potter, 2006), 31.

9. Brother Lawrence, *The Practice of the Presence of God, and The Spiritual Maxims* (New York: Cosimo, 2006), 16.

10. Ibid., 61.

11. Martha Stewart, *Martha Stewart's Cooking School: Lessons and Recipes for the Home Cook*, 149.

12. Ibid., 437-445. All pie-related quotes in this chapter are from this selection.

December

1. Sad to say, virginity tests are still a reality for women in many parts of the world today. See http://www.amnesty.org/en/for-media/press-releases/egyptian-women-protesters-forced-take-%E2%80%98virginity-tests%E2%80%99-2011-03-23.

2. http://www.visionforumministries.org/home/about/biblical_patriarchy.aspx.

3. http://www.bibletopics.com/biblestdy/92b.html.

4. To learn more about the biblical patriarchy movement, see Kathryn Joyce, *Inside the Christian Patriarchy Movement* (Boston: Beacon Press, 2009).

5. Names have been changed to protect privacy.

6. Nicola Slee, *Praying Like a Woman* (Oxford: SPCK2006), 36–37.

7. Madeleine L'Engle, *Walking on Water: Reflections on Faith and Art* (New York: North Point Press, 1995), 18.

8. Ibid., 22–23.

January

1. Bruce Waltke, *The Book of Proverbs: Chapters 15–31*(Grand Rapids:Wm. B. Eerdmans Publishing Co., 2005), 517. The quote from Erika Moore comes from an unpublished paper titled "The Domestic Warrior" submitted for OT 813, Proverbs, to Brucke Waltke, Westminister Theological Seminary, 1994 (p. 18).

2. Ellen F. Davis, *Proverbs, Ecclesiastes, and the Song of Songs* (Louisville: Westminster John Knox Press, 2000), 154.

3. Jan Saunders, *Sewing for Dummies* (Foster City, CA: IDG Books Worldwide, 1999), 14.

4. According to Wikipedia, schmaltz is "rendered chicken, goose, or pork fat used for frying or as a spread on bread, especially in German and Ashkenazi Jewish cuisine" (http://en.wikipedia.org/wiki/Schmaltz). This sounds like something Southerners should never be informed about.

February

1. Collin Hanson, "Pastor Provocateur," *Christianity Today* 51, no. 9, September 30, 2007, 4, http://www.christianitytoday.com/ct/2007/september/30.44.html.

2. Piper and Grudem, *Recovering Biblical Manhood & Womanhood*, 369.

3. Martha Peace, *The Excellent Wife: A Biblical Perspective* Bemidji, MN: Focus Publishing, 1995), 121.

4. Lawrence K. Altman, "Study Finds That Teenage Virginity Pledges Are Rarely Kept," *New York Times*, March 10, 2004, http://www.nytimes.com/2004/03/10/us/study-finds-that-teenage-virginity-pledges-are-rarely-kept.html.

5. Pearl, *Created to Be His Help Meet*, 165.
6. Editor, "Mark Driscoll, The Biblical Admonition to Women to Perform Oral Sex," Christian Research Network, July 2, 2009, http://christianresearchnetwork.com/2009/07/02/mark-driscoll-the-biblical-admonition-to-women-to-perform-oral-sex/.
7. Pearl, *Created to Be His Help Meet*, 171
8. William Ramsay, Westminster Guide to the Books of the Bible. (Westminster John Knox Press, 1994), 177.
9. Mark Driscoll, *Confessions of a Reformission Rev: Hard Lessons from An Emerging Missional Church*, (Grand Rapids: Zondervan, 2006), 95–96.
10. If you aren't familiar with "Ars Poetica" by Archibald MacLeish, dig out your Introduction to Literature textbook from freshman year and check the first few pages.

March

1. Orthodox Jews typically cite Numbers 5:18 as Torah-based support for the requirement that married women cover their hair. In this passage, a woman suspected of adultery is subjected to the "loosening" of her hair, an act of humiliation. According to Philo of Alexandria, "this is the origin of the daughters of Israel not going out in public with uncovered hair."
2. http://cora.dashjr.org/trad/modesty.html
3. Sarah's name has been changed to protect her privacy.

April

1. Rabbi Wayne Dosick, *Living Judaism: The Complete Guide to Jewish Belief, Tradition, and Practice* (New York: Harper One, 1995), 269.
2. In deference to Deuteronomy 12:3, many observant Jews use "G-d" to avoid writing out God's name, lest it be erased or defaced at a later time.
3. Lynne Meredith Schreiber, "Why Orthodox Jews May Have the Hottest Sex Lives, February 2, 2006, http://www.yourtango.com/200623/forbidden-desires.

May

1. "What AP is: 7 Baby B's," the Ask Dr. Sears website, http://www. askdrsears.com/topics/attachment-parenting/what-ap-7-baby-bs.
2. Piper and Grudem, *Recovering Biblical Manhood & Womanhood*, 343.
3. Walter J. Chantry, "Tract: The High Calling of Motherhood," Sermons by Walter J. Chantry website, http://www.chantry-sermons.com/motherhood.htm.
4. Carolyn Custis James, *Half the Church: Recapturing God's Global Vision for Women* (Grand Rapids: Zondervan, 2010), 103.
5. For more of Hillary's story, see Hillary McFarland, *Quivering Daughters* (Dallas: Darklight Press, 2010).
6. "Michelle Duggar Receives 'Mother of the Year Award' at Historic Baby Conference," Doug's Blog: A Daily Log & Online Journal from Doug Phillips, Vision Forum, July 12, 2010, http://www. visionforum.com/news/blogs/doug/2010/07/8547/.
7. Kathleen Norris, *The Cloister Walk*, 24.

June

1. The website of the Council on Biblical Manhood & Womanhood, "Core Beliefs," http://www.cbmw.org/Danvers; see the box titled "Key Texts" in the margin at the right of the Danvers Statement.
2. Piper and Grudem, *Recovering Biblical Manhood & Womanhood*, 72.
3. Ibid., 6, 47.
4. Ibid., 51.
5. http://www.cbmw.org.
6. Piper and Grudem, *Recovering Biblical Manhood & Womanhood*, 52.
7. My friend Sarah wrote a beautiful essay about egalitarian marriage as a slow dance: Sarah Bessey, "In which [love looks like] a real marriage," January 4, 2012, http://www.emergingmummy. com/2012/01/in-which-love-looks-like-real-marriage.html.
8. Pearl, *Created to Be His Help Meet*, 151
9. Ibid., 96–97.
10. Ibid., 133.
11. Ibid., 133

12. *Created to Be His Help Meet*, 155.
13. For a study on the origins of this list, see the Snopes article about it: "How to Be a Good Wife," http://www.snopes.com/language/document/goodwife.asp.
14. Ibid., #2.
15. Ibid., #3.
16. Ibid., #1.
17. Ibid., #5.
18. Ibid., #6, #7.
19. Ibid., #7.
20. Ibid., #9.
21. See W. R. F. BROWNING, *A Dictionary of the Bible* (1997) at *Encyclopedia.com*, s.v., "household codes," http://www.encyclopedia.com/doc/1O94-householdcodes.html. Accessed March 1, 2012.
22. Carol A. Newsom and Sharon H. Ringe, *Women's Bible Commentary: Expanded Edition* (Louisville, KY: Westminster John Knox Press, 1998) 463.
23. Peter H. Davids, "A Silent Witness in Marriage" in *Discovering Biblical Equality*, eds. Ronald W. Pierce and Rebecca Merrill Groothuis (Downers Grove, IL: IVP Academic, 2005), 238.
24. Ronald Sider, *Rich Christians in an Age of Hunger: Moving from Affluence to Generosity* (Nashville: Thomas Nelson, 2005) 56.
25. Diana Severance, *Feminine Threads: Women in the Tapestry of Christian History*, 50.
26. Tabitha's Greek name was Dorcas, so she is often recognized by that name.

July

1. For a comprehensive, readable, and challenging look at what the Bible says about justice, see Ronald Sider, *Rich Christians in an Age of Hunger: Moving From Affluence to Generosity* (Nashville: Thomas Nelson, 2005).
2. Aaron B. Franzen, "Survey: Frequent Bible Reading Can Turn You Liberal," *Christianity Today*, October 12, 2011, http://www.christianitytoday.com/ct/2011/october/

survey-bible-reading-liberal.html.

3. For activities during this month of justice, I relied heavily on Julie Clawson's excellent book, *Everyday Justice: The Global Impact of Our Daily Choices* (Downers Grove, IL: IVP Books, 2009).

4. Starbucks Campaign Background Info, Tamara Straus, "Fair Trade Coffee: An Overview of the Issue," November 30, 2000, Organic Consumer Association website, http://www.organicconsumers.org/starbucks/coffback.htm.

5. C. S. Lewis, *The Great Divorce*, 139.

6. You can find all kinds of delicious fair trade coffees at equalexchange.com, amazon.com, and even your local grocery store. You can also purchase fair trade tea, sugar, spices, vanilla, rice, fruit, and nuts. To learn more about buying more justly, see Clawson, *Everyday Justice*.

7. Humphrey Hawksley, "Mali's children in chocolate slavery," BBC News, April 12, 2001, http://news.bbc.co.uk/2/hi/africa/1272522.stm. See also "Tracing the bitter truth of chocolate and child labour," March 24, 2010, http://news.bbc.co.uk/panorama/hi/front_page/newsid_8583000/8583499.stm.

8. Learn more about chocolate and child slavery at http://vision.ucsd.edu/~kbranson/stopchocolateslavery/ or the website of the International Justice Mission: http://www.ijm.org/.

9. Nicholas Kristof and Sheryl WuDunn, *Half the Sky: Turning Oppression into Opportunity for Women Worldwide* (Toronto: Vintage 2010), xvii.

10. Ibid., xviii.

11. Ibid., xx.

12. Ibid., 192, 194.

13. Ibid., 198.

14. Ibid., 209.

15. Ibid., 160.

16. Ibid., xx.

17. For the full story, see Eldon J. Epp, *Junia: The First Woman Apostle* (Minneapolis: Fortress, 2005).

August

1. http://www.christianpost.com/news/
   is-it-wrong-for-men-to-listen-to-female-speakers-55118/.

2. Wayne Grudem, "Which Church Roles Should Be Open to
   Women," http://www.beliefnet.com/Faiths/Christianity/2006/11/
   Which-Church-Roles-Should-Be-Open-To-Women.aspx?p=1.

3. Denny Burk, "First Female Preacher at Irving Bible Church,"
   Denny Burk: A Commentary on Politics, Theology, and
   Culture, August 25, 2008, http://www.dennyburk.com/
   first-female-preacher-at-irving-bible-church/.

4. Jeff Robinson and Brent Nelson, "Irving Bible Church Puts
   First Woman in the Pulpit," *The Council on Biblical Manhood &
   Womanhood* (blog), August 28, 2008, http://www.cbmw.org/Blog/
   Posts/Irving-Bible-Church-Puts-First-Woman-in-the-Pulpit.

5. The Barna Group, "Number of Female Senior Pastors in Protestant
   Churches Doubles in Past Decade," 2009, http://www.barna.org/
   barna-update/article/17-leadership/304-number-of-female-senior-
   pastors-in-protestant-churches-doubles-in-past-decade.

6. Neela Banerjee, "Clergywomen Find Hard Path to Bigger
   Pulpit," *New York Times*, August 26, 2006, http://www.nytimes.
   com/2006/08/26/us/26clergy.html?th&emc=th.

7. Bob Allen, "Pastor says Jesus wouldn't remove church with woman
   pastor," Associated Baptist Press, December 7, 2011, http://www.
   abpnews.com/content/view/6988/53/.

8. Scot McKnight, *The Blue Parakeet: Rethinking How You Read the
   Bible* (Grand Rapids: Zondervan, 2008), 207.

9. Titus 1:5-9, 1 Timothy 5:3-16, 1 Peter 2:18-25, Romans
   2:25-28Galatians 5:2-7, I Corinthians 10, 1 Peter 3:8-22,1 Peter
   4:1-19.

10. Scot McKnight, *The Blue Parakeet: Rethinking How You Read the
    Bible* (Grand Rapids: Zondervan, 2008), 202.

11. Barna Group, "Number of Female Senior Pastors in Protestant
    Churches Doubles in Past Decade."

12. http://www.barna.org/faith-spirituality/508-20-years-of-
    surveys-show-key-differences-in-the-faith-of-americas-men-and-
    women.

13. Scot Mcknight, *The Blue Parakeet: Rethinking How You Read the Bible* (Grand Rapids: Zondervan, 2008), 205.

14. Julian of Norwich, *Revelations of Divine Love*, transl. Grace Warrack (Grand Rapids: Christian Classics Ethereal Library, 1901), 11, http://www.ccel.org/ccel/julian/revelations.pdf.

15. Thomas Keating, *Invitation to Love: The Way of Christian Contemplation* (1992; New York: Continuum, 2006), 90.

16. John Greenleaf Whittier, "The Brewing of Soma," http://www.poemhunter.com/poem/the-brewing-of-soma/.

17. Scot McKnight, The Blue Parakeet: Rethinking How You Read the Bible (Grand Rapids: Zondervan, 2008), 174.

18. http://www.doh.gov.za/show.php?id=500.

19. Nicholas Kristof and Sheryl WuDunn, Half the Sky: Turning Oppression Into Opportunity for Women Worldwide (Toronto: Vintage, 2010), 98.

20. Ibid., 61.

September

1. Ruth Graham, "A Year of Biblical Womanhood: An evangelical blogger is spending 12 months following the Bible's instructions for women—and she's doing it for egalitarian reasons," *Slate*, September 1, 2011, http://www.slate.com/articles/double_x/doublex/2011/09/a_year_of_biblical_womanhood.html.

2. Peter Rollins, *How (Not) to Speak of God* (London: Paraclete Press, 2006) 60.

3. Peter Rollins, *How (Not) to Speak of God*, 60.

4. http://www.thechallahblog.com/2011/07/challah-shape-croatian-star.html.

5. Rabbi Wayne D. Dosick, Living Judaism: The Complete Guide to Jewish Belief, Tradition, and Practice (New York: Harper One, 1995), 133.

6. From *Anne of Green Gables*.

About the Author

Rachel Held Evans is a popular blogger and the author of *Evolving in Monkey Town: How a Girl Who Knew All the Answers Learned to Ask the Questions*. Join the conversation at http://rachelheldevans.com.